Children's Literature

Volume 7

Volume 7

Annual of
The Modern Language Association
Group on Children's Literature and
The Children's Literature
Association

Published by Parousia Press for
Children's Literature An International Journal, Inc.

Children's Literature

Editor-in-Chief:
  FRANCELIA BUTLER
Editor:
  LEONARD R. MENDELSOHN
Assistant Editor:
  T. C. FODOR
Book Review Editors:
  MARGARET P. ESMONDE
  MERADITH TILBURY MCMUNN

BOARD OF DIRECTORS, The Children's Literature Foundation, publishers of Children's Literature An International Journal, Inc.—Francelia Butler, Rachel Fordyce, John C. Wandell
ADVISORY BOARD: Marilyn Apseloff, Bennett Brockman, Chairman; Edward G. Fisher, Martin Gardner, Narayan Kutty, Alison Lurie, William T. Moynihan, Peter F. Neumeyer, Glenn E. Sadler, William E. Sheidley
CONSULTING EDITORS: Jan Bakker, Rachel Fordyce, Anne Jordan
CONSULTANT FOR THE CHILDREN'S LITERATURE ASSOCIATION: Alethea Helbig
SPECIAL CONSULTANT: Charity Chang
MANAGING EDITOR: Peter S. Anderson
EDITORIAL ASSISTANTS: Ruth Maksvytis Howe, Howard Mayer

Editorial Correspondence should be addressed to:
  The Editors, *Children's Literature An International Journal*
  Department of English
  University of Connecticut
  Storrs, Connecticut 06268

Manuscripts submitted should conform to the *MLA Handbook.* An original and one copy are requested. Manuscripts should be accompanied by a self-addressed envelope and postage.

Checks for subscriptions or single orders should be mailed to Children's Literature An International Journal, Inc., P.O. Box 370, Windham Center, Conn. 06280.

Cover design by James Marshall

Contents

Reviews

Children's Literature

Volume 7

EDITOR'S HIGH CHAIR

CHILDREN'S LITERATURE AS ACTIVE MEDITATION

When adults tell a child a story, they may be doing themselves as big a favor as they are doing the child.

Telling a story is a loving act and loving acts are generally repaid in one way or another.

But there is another reward and it lies in the nature of story itself. Reading a story is a form of meditation on life, and children's stories are particularly refreshing forms of meditation. Bruno Bettelheim has already described the consolation to be found in the old folktales, but much contemporary children's literature from the best writers still is based on the old folk plots in which all knots are tied at the end: people find companions, justice reigns, quests are successfully completed, and love of one kind or another overcomes all difficulties.

Such reading is not only aesthetically satisfying but it is wholesome to weary and troubled human beings of all ages. Adults need it at least as much as children, for, according to James Hillman of the Jung Institute, Zurich, adults are "adulterated" people who can only be restored by being "re-storyed."

Semester after semester at the University of Connecticut I have seen over 300 young adults, most of them 21 or 22 years old, come into the auditorium where the class in children's literature is held. They come voluntarily with a bounce in their step, a look of expectation on their faces: they are going to hear children's rhymes, children's stories, children's plays. Later they will become actively involved in the material, skipping to the rhymes, changing the stories into games, performing the plays.

When they become parents or teachers or librarians themselves, they will continue this practice because they delight in it. The material has become a kind of mantra and the active involvement is like a meditational exercise.

To be more specific, many children's rhymes can be skipped to, or parents, with the help of a child, can make up their own rhymes and skip to them. The major themes of the traditional rhymes that children skip to are protest, loneliness, love, and nonsense to express the inexpressible and this is true in every country in the world. Any new rhymes are likely to follow the same themes, as I discovered at the University of Connecticut, when a football player made up this one and skipped to it:

> My girl has left me / My grades are down
> Shall I stick it out / Or just leave town?

In the invisible world of the turning rope, he performed a ritual to ease his hang-ups. What's more, he got some good exercise. Rope skipping is recommended strongly in physical health programs and there are even adult skip ropes with computers in the handles now being sold in department stores.

One thing all children and adults whom I know love to do is to change a story into a game. It can be any kind of game, and any kind of story can be used for the purpose. Suppose it is an old story like Cinderella. One can make a board game in which Cinderella's progress from the ash heap to the palace is played out until she gets together with a prince of a man back home. Or it can be a ringtoss game around a "glass" slipper. There are hundreds of possibilities. Some of the original ideas for converting stories into games I wish I could have kept and patented. They would make a game company envious. Here is something any adult—with the help of a child—can do at home without spending money. To make such a game is a challenge to the imagination because it means transferring an idea from one medium to another, and when it is made, it is fun to play.

To make plays or puppet shows out of a story is an activity with which many teachers are familiar, but it is also something that can be done in neighborhoods. For the puppet show, wires can be attached to small figures that can be manipulated through the top of a large cardboard box, with the front cut out for the stage.

A children's book, then, is a wonderful investment because it can not only be read, but it can be made into a play or a game, and portions of it can be skipped to or sung. A springtime message about life is to be found in much children's literature—that life is circular, that everything revolves and returns. Some adult literature is a complex spin-off of this theme, but often with disturbing loose ends and unsolved problems.

This annual was founded in 1972. The first three issues and the present one were published by Edward G. Fisher of Parousia Press, who saw the need for an in-depth study of the world of the child as reflected in literature and had the vision and generosity to support the endeavor. Beginning with volume eight, the annual will be published by Yale University Press. The fact that a great Ivy League press is taking on children's literature marks a major milestone for a despised field.

Francelia Butler

Articles

THE LITTLE HOUSE BOOKS:
ROSE-COLORED CLASSICS

Rosa Ann Moore

As a middle-aged English teacher, awash among freshman compositions, splintered by faculty duties, graduate study, and domesticity, I once looked forward with hope to retirement at age sixty-five when I, like Laura Ingalls Wilder, would have the chance at last to sit down, take a breath, and turn out my long-delayed creative masterpiece which would bring to the gate of the poultry farm where I grew up in Virginia hordes of readers singing my praises.

But now I do not think that they will sing to me.

For I have spent the summer among the papers and places of Laura Ingalls Wilder, and with people whose lives crossed hers, and I have learned that the story of her books is much different from what I once thought, or from what is commonly believed by most of her readers. My first work examining her revisions put me in some awe of the remarkably critical and subtle editing which had taken place. [1] I clung to the illusion of Mrs. Wilder's naive artistry even after Donald Zochert, in the writing of his biography *Laura* (Henry Regnery, 1976), came across material which indicated what the facts were. I am indebted to him for the initial suggestion that there was evidence which might eventually be released and settle the question that had puzzled me: could the difference between the manuscripts and the finally published books be accounted for by Laura's own artistic control, or by the masterful editing of someone else? I am grateful to readers of my article whose similar questions and intentions to study Mrs. Wilder themselves indicated that the time to build whatever bibliographical foundations could be based on that evidence, if it might be had, was now.

In the summer of 1976 I put this situation to the heir of Rose Wilder Lane and executor of her estate, Roger Lea MacBride. In late winter, after rest and recuperation from the campaign in which he was the Libertarian candidate for President of the United States, Mr. MacBride granted me permission to study those papers in his possession which were pertinent to my query and to prepare a catalog of them for publication. This work is well under way; when it is complete he plans to deposit the papers in the manus-

Laura Ingalls Wilder

Rose Wilder Lane

Photographs courtesy of Laura Ingalls Wilder Home and Museum,
Mansfield, Missouri.

cripts division of the Alderman Library of the University of Virginia where they will be accessible to others who wish to study them.

Mr. MacBride extended every courtesy to me and gave me a free hand to do with the papers as I thought fit. During the Summer, 1976, supported by a research grant from the University of Chattanooga Foundation, I spent three weeks in Charlottesville, working in his office at sorting, assembling, ordering, and describing the jumbled contents of a brown corrugated file box—packets assembled in rubber bands, stuffed into envelopes, filed in crumbly folders. The experience was both personally and professionally exciting and, I believe important. It is to some of my findings and their implications for the creation of the Little House books that I should like to introduce you now.

I arranged the papers first in what I believe to be a fairly accurate chronological order and then in topical order, and placed them in file folders numbered I through XXXV. These cover a range from personal letters between members of the family to manuscripts and childhood recollections from Aunt Martha (Laura's Ma's sister). But the letters between Laura (and occasionally, her husband Almanzo Wilder) and their daughter Rose Wilder Lane, a real estate woman, journalist, and novelist, are the most significant to us, for they develop two interwrapped and inseparable strands that have a crucial bearing on the writing of the Little House books. One of these strands is the consciousness of the pressing need for money, the other the slow evolution of the idea that Laura will write. Writing as the most congenial source of income gradually separates itself from the other possibilities they consider, and the need for money is the goad which moves Rose, while Laura goes a-fishing in the stream of time, to clean the fishes—chop off their heads and tails—and serve them up.

The two strands are bound together in Folder I. These Portions of letters and torn scraps of paper, dating from some time prior to 1915, were folded together in a pink business envelope and headed by Laura "Ideas for work." They are a hodge-podge of papers proposing all kinds of money-making projects for Laura to undertake. Rose's strategies for getting a foothold on newspapers (I.4) [2] are succeeded by her scheme for organizing a syndicate to collect eggs in Mansfield and send them on the early morning train to the hotels of Springfield. (I.11)

But the suggestions which both apparently took most seriously

all along have to do with writing. Rose approves Laura's idea for
"a Sunday story about the old mill," and mentions detail "that
will appeal most to the Sunday editors." (I.3) A typed undated
post-script to a missing letter from Rose tells Laura of having just
written a two thousand word article on a milk dairy; if Laura will
collect data on the largest certified dairy in Missouri, she can begin
a similar one. (I.7) The next letter to "Muvver dear" explains the
idea further: "I thought if you could get some local names to hang
it upon you might resell my stuff bodily for say, the first story for
the Ruralist, or perhaps to the Kansas City Star." (I.8) Rose is full
of ideas about Mansfield which would provide appealing copy.
Tell about the time, she urges Laura, when two prisoners escaped
by lifting up the whole jail and carrying it away. "A peaceful little
mountain village," she calls Mansfield, "where the leading business
men on a summer day play marbles in the shade of the depot . . .
the sort of a little story that will appear harmless enough to the
editor, and make Mansfield sore as the dickens. It will sell fine . . ."
(I.8)

Folder III, from 1919, no longer suggests projects but concen-
trates on an article which Laura has already written contrasting
modern girls with their old-fashioned sisters. Rose now is serving
as Laura's editor, propping up her sagging confidence and criti-
cizing what Laura has written. "Don't be absurd about my doing
the work on your article," she says. "I didn't re-write it a bit more
than I rewrite Mary Heaton Vorse's articles, or Inez Haynes Irwin's
stories." The remaining four pages are a handbook for writers: "In
the first place, I don't feel reality in the opening scene." "In your
transition, don't *say* that you have been remembering—simply
remember. Transitions are the hardest things to write—" "I think
on page 9, while good stuff intrinscially (sic), it has little bearing
on the theme—strays afield a little." "Tell about them in detail."
"Keep throughout to the narrative style . . . Cut out every scrap
of editorializing."

A very small assortment of papers, dated from 1924 to 1929,
comprise the contents of Folder IV. The issue here is an article
Laura has written describing her country kitchen in Mansfield, and
which Carl Brandt, Rose's agent, eventually sold to Curtis magazines. The themes are the same that were occupying Laura's and
Rose's minds five and more years earlier. Rose encloses a carbon
copy of her revision of the article, with this advice: "carefully study

the changes that were made, until you see clearly why each one was done, and how it has changed the article . . . for selling purposes." (IV.3) In a later undated letter, but apparently enclosing a check for the same article, Rose is again reassuring and encouraging Laura: "I'm sorry that—as you say—knowing it was my work that sold takes some of the joy out of it. It wasn't really *my* work . . . All I did on your story was an ordinary re-write job . . . You don't know how to write stuff for Country Gentleman. You never will know, until you stop and listen to what I tell you." Rose is clearly the guide and mentor, and the tone of this letter is very much that which one assumes in reasoning with a strong-willed child. "I'm trying to train you as a writer for the big market," she continues on page three, "Next time you can do the editing yourself. Above all, you must *listen* to me." After news of her own activities, Rose returns in the last paragraph to writing: "By the way, what I have been telling you about writing relates to *principles*." In pencil after her signature she adds, "This letter is to be *re*-read—*Please*." (IV.6)

Rose's function as Laura's editor expands to include the parallel function of agent. "You want to follow up your first article with another one very quickly," she advises, "in order not to lose the advertising value of the first one, but to add to it." (III.1) From the first undated letter in Folder I, Rose takes the attitude that the time to write can be bought with money. The most vivid expression of this view occurs in an undated letter written some time after 1924: "You mustn't go walking to town in the rain, when there is a perfectly good taxi to be had . . . Dearest, for years upon years I have been telling, 'Stop *saving* money, and *make* money.' . . . Well, now I went out and made you some money, first. To show you that it could be done . . . But God damn it all, you've GOT to go on and make more, now. Can't you see, that if you had spent a dollar for a taxi, gone warm and dry to town and back, and spent that extra time studying how to do your next article, you would have made money by it? I never saw any human being so determined to be hideously and insanely extravagant . . . You'd rather do the washing . . . ."

For years, maybe ten, maybe fifteen, Laura's and Rose's differing apprehensions of time have blocked their getting done the work that both hope eventually to accomplish. While for Laura time is the stream one fishes in, for Rose time is the line one drops into the water. Time, for Rose, is linear. It has duration, and it has an end. Time is a commodity which can and must be bought. The message is: Pay money to buy time from the cowpeas, the laundry, walks in the rain, so that more money can be made, so that a name can be made.

While Rose has been preparing lines and baiting hooks, Laura has been contemplating the stream. From what we have in Folder I, pre-1915, we can infer from Rose's allusion to it that Laura must have mentioned the idea of some kind of autobiography. Rose writes: "you must write just exactly what you think of Mansfield in your 'life story' when you come to it—just think you are writing a diary that no one anywhere will ever see, and put down all the things that you think, regardless." (I.8) In the next letter, Rose pursues the theme: "I bet the letter you wrote for grandma and Mary about your getting started to writing could be put verbatim into that 'story of my life' thing. If I were you I'd have them save it and send it back, and I'd look at it with that viewpoint and see if I'm not right. I bet it's better than you could do trying to write it for the story." (I.9)

By 1919, Laura has said something about children's stories, and sends several (not among these papers) to Rose, who replies: "I have not had time to go over the children's stories. I glanced through them, and think them good. But they are not so important as the articles, for there is no opportunity to make a name with children's stories." (III.1) Rose is wise enough while closing the door not to lock it and adds: "I will get to them as soon as possible and see what can be done about marketing them, however." (III.1)

From 1924 to 1931, few papers remain, partly because Rose was living at home in Mansfield during much of that time. The material which I have filed in Folders VI, VII, VIII, IX, and X, however, shows us the evolution of the "life story" idea.

Folder VI contains a manuscript and related correspondence between Rose and the Children's editor at the publishing house of Alfred A. Knopf. The untitled draft (VI.2) is twenty-two pages, typed on yellow paper, with some lines mm'd out, some additions in ink, most in pencil, all in Rose's hand. This little narrative corresponds to the first one hundred and sixteen pages of *Little House in the Big Woods*. "When Grandma was a little girl she lived in a little gray house made of logs," it begins. The order of events is the same as in *Big Woods,* and the four interpolated stories that Pa tells in those pages are included here. "Grandma" is identified as

"Laura" in paragraph five, and called Laura from then on.

The fifteen or so communications in which Rose and Marion Fiery of Knopf iron out the details are in themselves a private drama of diplomacy, loyalty, and personal crisis. Miss Fiery in her first letter, dated 12 February 1931, inquires whether Mrs. Wilder would be willing to make "some editorial changes" providing "more details . . . such as the making of the bullets, what they eat and wear, etc." for "the more vivid . . . appeal . . . to children's imaginations." (VI.3) She questions the use of "Ma" and "Pa" as "pro-- bably more authentic" but too "colloquial," and suggests that the title, "When Grandma Was a Little Girl," "does not seem to me to convey the true character of the book. Something a little stronger is needed." She remarks that "It is not long enough in its present state" (about 7000 to 9000 words) "to make the kind of book which I have in mind . . . I should recommend a length of about 23,000 words." (VI.3)

On May 27, 1931, three months later, Rose drafts a reply to Marion Fiery. Mrs. Wilder is sending revised manuscript, she reports, and goes on innocently, "I don't know just where or how I come into this, do you? But somehow I do, because my mother naturally consults me about everything concerning her writing." (VI.5)

The story of how *Little House in the Woods* was nearly contracted for by Knopf and finally published by Harper and Row is told in the letters and is beyond my present concerns. But one of Rose's last letters to Marion Fiery, October 3, 1931, introduces a new theme: "George Bye is handling another book of my mothers, PIONEER GIRL. It is slightly older autobiography, picking up where LITTLE HOUSE IN THE WOODS (sic) ends, and going on with my mother's life to the age of eighteen and her marriage. It is full of fascinating material . . . It is told in the first person, but it occurs to me that you might like it enormously for slightly older juvenile readers, if it were written in the third person." (VI.12)

The manuscript of *Pioneer Girl*, which George Bye was not able to sell, occupies Folder X. In two hundred and three pages it tells the story of all the books, placing *Big Woods* after *Little House on the Prairie,* omitting *Farmer Boy* and *The Long Winter,* but including the Burr Oak interlude. Folders VII, VIII, and IX contain evolving versions of *Pioneer Girl.* A good deal of material is deleted from VIII; because some of the deletions turn up in *Big Woods,* we can probably place the *Pioneer Girl* manuscript at some point before 1931.

By mid-1931, a publishable version of *Little House in the Big Woods*, which appeared in '32, was ready, and the grand design laid down. Not until after George Bye is unsuccessful in marketing *Pioneer Girl* do Laura and Rose begin the tedious task of carving out, one by one, the remaining books which we know.

On the basis of much less evidence than this, in a letter of May 20, 1975, Donald Zochert assessed the situation and put it to me this way: "I raise to you the proposition that the Little House books are Rose Wilder Lane's greatest achievement." Thinking ahead to my retirement, I wanted to reject that proposition. After having studied all the letters, I believe there is yet ground for resisting quite so stark a judgment. Because Rose was in Mansfield during the writing of *Big Woods*, we cannot say from the evidence of correspondence between her and Laura precisely what share each of them contributed to its creation. But we can perhaps make some inferences from the letters in Folders XVII and XIX, 1937 and 1938 when *By the Shores of Silver Lake* was being written. In these we see Laura holding her ground against Rose about theme, characterization, and fact, while Rose wins the battles on plot and style. Further, the evidence of Rose's own fiction demonstrates the improbability of her having been able to create the Little House books alone.

Indeed, the key, I think, lies somewhere in the tension between them. Recall the attitudes towards time with which we began: Laura, the stream or pool; Rose, the line. Freud's definition of the relationship between the id and ego accounts remarkably well for the functioning of these two minds: "There is nothing in the id that corresponds to the idea of time," he said—and the id we may equate with Laura; "there is no recognition of the passage of time . . . Impressions . . . which have been sunk into the id by repression, are virtually immortal; after the passage of decades they behave as though they had just occurred."[3] Rose's function in the relationship corresponds to that of the ego: "What distinguishes the ego from the id quite especially," Freud went on, "is a tendency to synthesis in its contents, to a combination and unification in its mental processes which are totally lacking in the id . . . The ego develops from perceiving the instincts to controlling them."[4]

Now look at *Little House in the Big Woods*[5]: "Once upon a time," it begins. The reference is to all time past, to the pool of time. "Once upon a time, sixty years ago . . . " Side-by-side, in the same sentence, time is pin-pointed: This story took place at a specific moment in the past.

Proceed to paragraph two: "As far as a man could go to the north in a day, or a week, or a whole month, there was nothing but woods." Even distance is measured in relation to passing time.

Follow the tenses of verbs throughout the book. On page 9: "When smoke stopped coming through the cracks, Laura would bring more hickory chips and Ma would put them on the fire . . . " This construction, using the modal auxiliary *would* to indicate characteristic activity in the past, recalled from the pool of time, alternates with the specific simple past tense, page 10: "One morning Pa went away before daylight . . . and that night he came home with a wagonload of fish." The alternating pattern established in the first pages persists through about page eighty-five, nearly all of the ground covered by the manuscript "When Grandma Was a Little Girl."

After page eighty-six, the simple past tense prevails; Rose's perception of time, the linear, the specific is ascendant. But consider page 238, the last paragraphs of the book:

". . . (Laura) thought to herself, 'This is now.'

She was glad that the cosy house, and Pa and Ma and the firelight and the music, were now. They could not be forgotten, she thought, because now is now. It can never be a long time ago.

In the context of the simple past, which makes for better storytelling because it is specific, Laura's comprehensive view of all time as simultaneously present is set forth explicitly. The tension between her and Rose is successfully harmonized in the writing of *Little House in the Big Woods*; that end is to make their beginning on the saga.

Laura's last word in life is consistent with the practice and thinking of her lifetime. On July 30, 1952, she wrote the last letter (XXII.20) Rose ever received from her; it was found in her desk in a plain white envelope with Rose's name written across the front.

"Rose dearest," she begins, as she has begun every letter to Rose, "When you read this I will be gone and you will have inherited all I have."

After four short paragraphs assigning various pieces of property, she concludes:

"My love will be with you always." She signs her name "Mama Bess," and in parentheses under this "Laura Ingalls Wilder."

All that Laura had, had already, always been Rose's. "My love will be with you always"—in the pool of time to which she returns there is no diminution, no end. The familiar, affectionate "Mama Bess" was the signature on all her letters. But the formality of the full name is a step away from Rose to individual integrity, as much as to say, I am I; my name is who I am. For Laura's Mary with the outpouring of feeling and memory, Rose's Martha labored at the shaping, finishing, and art. Yet, however Rose-colored these classics are, they are the life, the spirit of Laura, and she claimed this at the end, even from the daughter upon whom she was in many ways financially, emotionally, and artistically dependent.

One perceives with a dash of realism that to create as she seems to have done, sixty-five is too late to begin. One must at middle age already have made a start, for it has truly been said,

In my beginning is my end . . .

The end is where we start from.

NOTES

1. "Laura Ingalls Wilder's Orange Notebooks and the Art of the Little House Books," *Children's Literature*, IV (Winter 1975), pp. 105-119.
2. The Roman numeral indicates the number of the Folder in which the letter is filed; the Arabic numeral indicates the position of the letter in the Folder.
3. "Dissection of the Psychical Personality," *New Introductory Lectures on Psycho-Analysis* . . . XXII of The Standard Edition of the *Complete Psychological Works of Sigmund Freud,* translated under the editorship of James Strachey (London: Hogarth Press, 1968), p. 74.
4. ibid. p. 76.
5. (New York: Harper and Row, 1953), p. 1.

NANCY, TOM AND ASSORTED FRIENDS IN THE STRATEMEYER SYNDICATE THEN AND NOW

Ken Donelson

Around the time when my daughter Sherri was nine or ten, she received a nearly complete set of *Nancy Drew* books from my sister. To say that I was pleased with my sister's gift would be an outrageous lie. As an English teacher still unsure of my role in life, I had all the self-righteous feelings I might have been expected to feel. "I am," I told myself, "an English teacher, guardian of the language, the last bastion against worldwide illiteracy, the champion of great literature, and my innocent daughter will be corrupted by the literary inanities of series books, worst of all by a series I had been taught to abhor." But I loved my sister and it was her gift and since Sherri was pleased, I took the American way out—I did nothing.

Later, when I left the childhood stage of teaching and entered the world of reality and began to look at what kids like to read and were reading despite my increasingly faltering admonitions, I became more and more intrigued by the ubiquitous Nancy Drew books and the fascination kids—especially young girls—felt about Nancy. As I puzzled through the Sears-Roebuck catalogue-of-dreams Nancy personified to her readers, my lingering toleration dimmed and my respect for author Carolyn Keene grew slowly and even grudgingly.

Much later after digging into series books, I found that there was no Carolyn Keene but only Edward Stratemeyer, his Literary Syndicate and his daughter Harriet Adams. I'll confess that I felt a mild let-down somewhat like the disappointment a few of my college students feel when they learn that Carolyn Keene is no more, indeed never was. But for me that let-down was replaced with awe as I dug into the machinations of the Stratemeyer syndicate.

Probably no American writer has had such an impact as Edward Stratemeyer on so many young readers. About his professional life we know much, though some details elude us even today; but about his personal life we know very little.

He was born on October 4, 1862, the son of a German immigrant who migrated to California during the Gold Rush era and then returned to New Jersey to help settle the estate of his dead brother.

In 1886 Stratemeyer was working at his step-brother's tobacco store in Elizabeth, New Jersey. Sometime during that year, Stratemeyer wrote an 18,000 word serial on brown wrapping paper, *Victor Horton's Idea,* and sent it off to *Golden Days,* a Philadelphia weekly boy's magazine. His father or step-brother may have originally questioned his foolish waste of time, but the $75.00 check Stratemeyer soon received alleviated their worries, and his father urged him to continue writing. He followed with *Captain Bob's Secret, or, The Treasures of Bass Island,* again for *Golden Days.*

From about 1890 until 1896 he ran a stationery store in Newark and during that time contributed to Frank Munsey's *Golden Argosy.* In 1893, Stratemeyer was offered the editorship of *Good News,* a boys' weekly published by Street and Smith, one of America's leading publishers. His devout faith in hard work, his writing and his personal life paid off, as his stories for *Good News* eventually built the circulation to more than 200,000. In 1895 he edited *Young Sports of America* (after the twenty-second issue retitled *Young People of America*) and in 1896 *Bright Days.* His work at Street and Smith brought him acquaintance with the reading public, particularly young people, and with staff writers like Frederick Dey (author of *Nick Carter*), Upton Sinclair (who wrote the *True Blue* series under the pen name Ensign Clark Fitch), William T. Adams (the pen name of Oliver Optic), H. R. Gordon (the pen name of Edward S. Ellis), and Horatio Alger. Stratemeyer wrote several dime novels for the *Log Cabin Library,* the first being Crazy Bob, The Terror of Creede, under the pseudonyms Jim Bowie, Nat Woods, and Jim Daly. He also wrote women's serials for the *New York Weekly* using the pen name Julia Edwards.

When Optic and Alger died, publishers asked Stratemeyer to edit the last three Optic novels, and he completed or wrote at least eleven and possibly eighteen Alger books from notes or outlines. Just how many he completed under Alger's name is still uncertain. His first hardback book published under his own name was *Richard Dare's Venture, or, Striking Out For Himself* in 1894, the first in his *Bound to Succeed* series. *Reuben Stone's Discovery, or, The Young Miller of Torrent Bend* appeared a year later. Other Stratemeyer books in 1897 had similar Alger-like titles, *Schooldays of Fred Harley, or, Rivals For All Honors; The Young Auctioneers, or, The Polishing of a Rolling Stone; Shorthand Tom, or, The Exploits of a Bright Boy; Gun and Sled, or, The Young Hunters of*

Snow-top Island; and *Leo the Circus Boy, or, Life Under the Great White Canvas.* By the end of 1897, Stratemeyer has six series and sixteen hardcover books in print.

Stratemeyer's big breakthrough came in 1898. He sent a book about two boys on a battleship to Boston publishers Lothrop & Shepard, one of the most prominent publishers of juvenile fiction. Only a few days later, Admiral Dewey's victory at Manila made headlines, and Lothrop's reader remembered Stratemeyer's manuscript. He wrote to Stratemeyer asking if it would be possible to place the boys at the scene of Dewey's triumph and return the rewritten book within a few weeks. Stratemeyer did, and *Under Dewey at Manila, or, The War Fortunes of a Castaway* hit the streets in time to capitalize on the recent victory. The book went through many printings that year and for several years to follow, and it greatly increased Stratemeyer's popularity and reputation with boys *and* publishers.

Not one to miss an opportunity, Stratemeyer used the major characters from *Under Dewey at Manila* in his next books—*A Young Volunteer in Cuba, or, Fighting For the Single Star; Fighting in Cuban Waters, or, Under Schley on the Brooklyn; Under Otis in the Philippines, or, A Young Officer in the Tropics; The Campaign of the Jungle, or, Under Lawton Through Luzon;* and *Under MacArthur, or, Last Battles in the Philippines,* all published from 1898 to 1901 under the umbrella series-title *Old Glory.* Using the same characters in contemporary battles in the Orient, Stratemeyer created the *Soldiers of Fortune* series with titles like *On to Pekin, or, Old Glory in China; Under the Mikado's Flag, or, Young Soldiers of Fortune; At the Fall of Port Arthur, or, A Young American in the Japanese Navy;* and *With Togo For Japan, or, Three Young Americans on Land and Sea,* all published from 1900 through 1906.

By this time Stratemeyer obviously had recognized his literary destiny although he probably had no inkling of his future productivity as a writer. He turned to full-time writing, sometimes completing a book in two or three days. As early as 1899, major publishers of juvenile books like Grosset & Dunlap and Cupples & Leon were wooing him and requesting that new books be sent to them.

Many of his early series dealt with war and patriotism: the *Old Glory* series, six books, 1898-1901; the *Minute Boys* series, two books, 1898-1904; the *Soldiers of Fortune* series, four books,

1900-1906; the *Mexican War* series, three books, 1900-1902; and the *Colonial* series, six books, 1901-1906. Or they dealt with the Alger theme of getting ahead in life through hard work: the *Working Upward* series, four books, all 1897; the *Bound to Succeed* series, three books, all 1899; the *Ship and Shore* series, three books, 1899-1900; the *Stratemeyer Popular* series, twelve books, 1900-1909; and the *American Boys' Biographical* series, two books, both 1901. He tried a series of six books, 1902-1907, about adventures in Central and South America, the *Pan-American* series, but they were not very successful. Stratemeyer soon learned what every writer of popular literature must learn, that faddish material sells well for the moment but rapidly becomes dated. Stratemeyer also learned that his more serious works may have been applauded by adults but were largely unread by young people no longer entranced by Alger, much less by Alger's imitators.

So Stratemeyer turned to stories of school life and sports, and the two series he produced were incredibly successful at the time and remained in print and popular for years. The *Lakeport* series, six books, 1904-1912 and the *Dave Porter* series, fifteen books, 1905-1919 served as prototypes of later Stratemeyer Syndicate series like *Dave Dashaway, Don Sturdy, College Sports, Fred Fenton, Dave Fearless, Tom Fairfield,* and *Jack Ranger.*

It's fashionable and easy now to revile and ridicule Stratemeyer's series books, but they had a far kinder contemporary press. A reviewer of *Under Otis in the Philippines* wrote:

> Mr. Stratemeyer is in a class by himself when it comes to writing about American heroes, their brilliant doings on land and sea. *(Boston Times)*

And a *Congregationalist* reviewer wrote of *Under Dewey at Manila,*

> Edward Stratemeyer weaves the incidents of the naval conflict at Manila into a narrative of experiences and adventure which is wholesome in spirit and full of excitement, and which the boys will like.

Reviewers of *Between Boer and Briton, or, Two Boys' Adventures in South Africa* were most kind.

> A stirring story of the South African War. *(Indianapolis Journal)*

> The author is one of the most accomplished writers for the young. *(San Francisco Chronicle)*

And reviewers of the *Dave Porter* series said:

> The story is told with great fidelity to real life. *(Brooklyn Eagle)*

> Mr. Stratemeyer has seldom introduced a more popular hero than Dave Porter. He is a typical boy, manly, brave, always ready for a good time if it can be obtained in an honorable way. *(Milwaukee Wisconsin)*

In 1899, Stratemeyer published the first three volumes of a series no longer read but still widely recognizable, *The Rover Boys Series For Young Americans: The Rover Boys at School, or, The Cadets of Putnam Hall; The Rover Boys on the Ocean, or, A Chase For Fortune;* and *The Rover Boys in the Jungle, or, Stirring Adventures in Africa.* The early books in the series were published under the pseudonym of Arthur M. Winfield but after only a few volumes, Stratemeyer listed his name in parentheses below the pen name. The series was set in Putnam Hall, a military academy with three heroes, serious-and-older Dick, fun-loving Tom, and straight-man Sam along with two villains, Dan Baxter and Mumps. In later series, Stratemeyer brought readers up to date by summarizing previous volumes in the series somewhere in the second chapter, but in *The Rover Boys* he wrote introductions to the volumes. Two of those introductions, to the first and the last of the series, may serve as examples of Stratemeyer's style and illustrate the nature of the series:

> MY DEAR BOYS: 'The Rover Boys at School' has been written that those of you who have never put in a term or more at an American military academy for boys may gain some insight into the workings of such an institution.
>
> While Putnam Hall is not the real name of the particular place of learning I had in mind while penning this tale for your amusement and instruction, there is really such a school, and dear Captain Putnam is a living person, as are also the lively, wide-awake, fun-loving Rover brothers, Dick, Tom, and Sam, and their schoolfellows, Larry, Fred, and Frank. The same can be said, to a certain degree, of the bully Dan Baxter, and his toady, the sneak commonly known as 'Mumps.'
>
> The present story is complete in itself, but it is written as the first of a series, to be followed by 'The Rover Boys in the Jungle,' in both of which volumes we will again meet many of our former characters.
>
> Trusting that this tale will find as much favor in your hands

as have my previous stories, I remain,
                    Affectionately and sincerely yours,
                    Arthur M. Winfield
                    March 1, 1889.
(The Rover Boys at School, or, The Cadets of Putnam Hall)[1]

MY DEAR BOYS: This book is a complete story in itself but forms the tenth volume in the line issued under the general title, 'The Second Rover Boys Series for Young Americans.'

In the opening volume of the First Series, 'The Rover Boys at School,' I introduced my readers to Dick, Tom and Sam Rover and their friends and relatives. That volume and those which followed related the adventures of the three Rover boys at Putnam Hall Military Academy, Brill College, and elsewhere.

Leaving college, the three young men established themselves in business in New York City and became married to their girl sweethearts. Dick Rover became the father of a son and a daughter, as did likewise his brother Sam, while Tom was blessed with a pair of lively twin boys. The four youths were first sent to boarding school, as related in the first volume of the Second Series, entitled 'The Rover Boys at Colby Hall,' where the lads made a host of friends. During their outings they went with one of the older Rovers to establish oil wells in Texas and Oklahoma and also went out on Sunset Trail, where we last met them. Their school days had come to an end, and two of the boys were preparing to join their fathers in business when a most disastrous affair occurred. Then the lads went on an ocean trip in an endeavor to aid the family fortunes, and what stirring times their outing led to I leave for the pages which follow to narrate.

Of the twenty-nine volumes issued in this line of 'Rover Boys' stories the publishers have already sold *over three and one-half million copies!* To me this is as astonishing as it is pleasing, and I here wish to thank all the young people, as well as the parents who have stood by me in my efforts to entertain them.
                    Affectionately and sincerely yours,
                    Edward Stratemeyer
(The Rover Boys Winning A Fortune, or, Strenuous Days Ashore And Afloat)[2]

The Rover Boys' adventures filled thirty books, the first twenty *(The First Rover Boys Series)* with Dick and Tom and Sam, the last ten *(The Second Rover Boys Series)* with the sons of the original

Rovers. The books were extraordinarily popular in the United States, and they were also shipped to England, Canada, and Australia and translated into German and Czechoslovakian. The series sold somewhere between 5,000,000 and 6,000,000 copies before the Rover boys disappeared with the publication of the last volume in 1926. The only other series of its time that surpassed it in sales and popularity was the *Bobbsey Twins* (1904-present) with total sales of more than 50,000,000 copies; where the Rover boys did not endure, the *Bobbsey Twins* series goes on and on and on.

Somewhere around 1906 Stratemeyer discovered a most successful way of gaining even wider readership; he convinced Cupples & Leon to drop the price of his books to fifty cents. Cupples & Leon may have been shocked to discover an author willing to take a smaller royalty per book, but they soon learned that the mass production of fifty-centers increased total sales almost beyond belief. One gimmick used by Cupples & Leon brought the company a steady supply of potential customers.

> Cupples decided to compile a colossal list of children's names. Included on the jacket of its books was a coupon which, when filled out with the names and addresses of ten friends, entitled the whole group to Cupples' illustrated catalogue. The catalogue was an insidious narcotic with the habit-forming properties of opium. In it were printed fetching bits from the more popular series. Cupples estimates that all in all 500,000 names have been on that list.[3]

Presumably, that technique and the mass production of the fifty-centers contributed to the popularity and sales of yet another Stratemeyer series, *The Motor Boys,* published under the pen name of Clarence Young. The twenty-two novels in this series, published between 1906 and 1924 sold something in excess of 4,000,000 copies.

Around 1906, Stratemeyer evolved the idea of his Literary Syndicate which was perhaps loosely modeled after Dumas' syndicate. It must have been obvious to him by this time that his brain teemed with prolific ideas for plots and series, and the twenty-four hour day simply wasn't long enough. Details of the evolution of the Stratemeyer Syndicate (frequently and unkindly called Stratemeyer's Fiction Factory) are lacking, but the operational plan is clear. Stratemeyer sent aspiring writers three-page sketches detailing settings and characters and a chapter-by-chapter outline of the plot. Writers were given from one week to six weeks to fill in the outline. When the copy arrived at Stratemeyer's office, he edited and tightened the prose and checked for discrepancies with earlier volumes in the series. Then the manuscript was off to the printer. Writers were paid flat sums, from $50.00 to $100.00, depending upon the importance of the series.

In a recent autobiography,[4] Leslie McFarlane, author of the first twenty-six *Hardy Boys,* tells how he first encountered the Stratemeyer Syndicate. The trade journal *Editor and Publisher* ran an advertisement:

EXPERIENCED FICTION WRITER WANTED
TO WORK FROM
PUBLISHER'S OUTLINES

It was 1926 and McFarlane was a newly hired reporter for the *Springfield Republican* with no great hopes for money. He replied. The letter he soon received asked McFarlane to try his hand at developing a couple of sample chapters of either a *Dave Fearless* or *Nat Ridley Rapid Fire Detective* series book from an enclosed outline like this.

> CHAP. 1—Dave and Bob cruising off Long Island in launch Amos run into fog—mention first and second volumes of series—engine fails—ring reminds Bob of adventures on Volcano Island—mention other volumes—boys discuss Lem and Bart Hankers, believed dead—sound of foghorn is heard— ocean liner looms out of fog—collision seems inevitable.
>
> CHAP. 2—Ship veers off in nick of time—boys hear warning bell and see lighthouse—fix engine—almost pile up on danger- ous reef—night and darkness—searchlight suddenly reveals mass of wreckage dead ahead—launch crashes into wreckage and catches fire—boys dive into water—boat blows up—Dave looks for Bob.[5]

Later in 1926 (after McFarlane passed the test), he wrote the first *Hardy Boys* book, *The Twoer Treasure,* under what became a popular Syndicate house name: Franklin W. Dixon. The mark of his success in that first *Hardy Boys* book arrived in the form of an envelope from Stratemeyer containing outlines for the next two *Hardy Boys* books—*The House on the Cliff* and *The Secret of the Old Mill.* But with the outline,

There was also a letter, a check and a document that looked vaguely legal. The document, a contract, was very simple—it covered everything. It was a release form absolving me of any rights to any volumes already written or any that might be written in the future for the Stratemeyer Syndicate. It covered the plots, the titles, the Roy Rockwood name, the name of Franklin W. Dixon and the manuscripts, forever and ever. Furthermore, it included a promise that I would never under any circumstances divulge to anyone the fact that I had ever written a Dave Fearless book or a Hardy Boys book under any title or pen name for anyone.

The penalty for such a revelation wasn't spelled out, I assumed that it had something to do with boiling in oil.

I had no hesitation in signing this document. As a matter of fact, I had been doing a little thinking about the matter. The release saved me the trouble of asking Stratemeyer to do me a similar favor. No sworn affidavits—merely his signature to a promise that he would never tell anyone I ever wrote books for him.[6]

Since McFarlane had accepted in a weak and poverty-stricken moment Stratemeyer's suggestion that he try his hand at three books of the *Dana Girls* series, one can sympathize with his last paragraph. One seemingly capricious but carefully planned Stratemeyer idiosyncrasy was his desire to keep Syndicate authors unaware of each other's existence. McFarlane tells us it would have been difficult to locate other Stratemeyer ghosts.

> Nor would it have helped to seek out a companion spook and compare notes. They were anonymous, invisible, un-identifiable, impossible to find. I met one of them quite by accident years later and he said Stratemeyer conferred with writers only by appointment and that he took good care to see that appointments were judiciously spaced. No two spooks ever found themselves waiting side by side on the bench and in a position to compare notes or even to discover that each was Roy Rockwood or even (God forbid) Laura Lee Hope, renowned since 1906 as authoress of the Bobbsey Twins.[7]

Tom Swift was the first series to appear after the creation of the Stratemeyer Syndicate; this series outsold all earlier ones except *The Bobbsey Twins*. Using the Syndicate house name of Victor Appleton, the *Tom Swift* books began in 1910 and ended with the publication of the fortieth volume in 1941; total sales for the series

was something like 15,000,000 copies.

Different as they appeared at first glance, series books had common elements. Early in the opening chapter of all books following the initial volume would appear some hook to the previous volume or volumes, a hook that would make any kid aware that he had missed at least one terribly exciting book. In the last paragraph or so of the last chapter would be another hook, this time suggesting that if the present book was a thriller, then the reader had even greater excitement awaiting him. Andrew Svenson, a late partner of Stratemeyer's daughter in the Syndicate, caught the essence of series books:

> The trick in writing children's books is to set up danger, mystery and excitement on page one. Force the kid to turn the page. I've written page one as many as 20 times. Then in the middle of each chapter there's a dramatic point of excitement and, at chapter's end, a cliffhanger.[8]

Any reader of the *Hardy Boys* or *Nancy Drew* will remember those cliffhanging moments of "Watch out, Frank" (or Nancy). Finally, about halfway through the second chapter of most series books, action was temporarily interrupted, allowing the writer to remind readers of the entire series so far. In *Baseball Joe, Pitching Wizard,* the fourteenth and last of the once popular *Baseball Joe* series, Joe and his friend Jim Barclay see a man fall over the edge of a ravine. They rush to him, find him still alive, recognize in him a villain from previous books, and then as they talk over the unconscious body, writer Lester Chadwick interrupts with a wrap-up of the previous thirteen books, everything from *Baseball Joe of the Silver Stars* to *Baseball Joe, Club Owner:*

> While they stand there in utter bewilderment, it may be well, for the benefit of those who have not read the preceding volumes of this series, to tell who Baseball Joe was and what had been his adventures up to the time this story opens.
>
> Joe Matson had been brought up in Riverside, a small but thriving town. His parents were estimable people of moderate means whose lives were bound up in their two children, Joe and his younger sister, Clara.
>
> Joe grew up a strong and vigorous youth, frank, manly and courageous. He excelled in all boyish sports, but was especially drawn toward baseball. All the time he could spare from his school and home duties found him playing in some of the vacant lots that the boys frequented.
>
> It soon appeared that Joe Matson had a natural aptitude for pitching, and before long he had at his command a collection of curves and slants which made him feared by the teams that came to measure strength with the town nine.
>
> How he became the mainstay in the box of his home team, what difficulties he met and surmounted, how the envy of rivals sought to discredit him, how in spite of all obstacles he won victory after victory, is told in the first volume of this series, entitled 'Baseball Joe of the Silver Stars.'
>
> Later on he went to boarding school, where his outstanding work on the school nine won recognition for him, despite the tactics of the bully of the institution.
>
> Following his graduation he entered Yale. Here the unwritten law that gave the preference to veterans and held the freshmen in the background kept him for some time from having a chance to show his ability on the diamond. But such a light as Joe Matson's could not be long hidden under a bushel, and in a time of great stress his opportunity came and he registered a glorious victory for Yale. Nor was it the last, for he eventually became one of the greatest college boxmen that Yale had ever known.

His work in the box for Yale was so sensational that he received an offer to pitch for the Pittston team of the Central League. Here he made good from the start and soon became the leading twirler of that league. It was evident that he would not long remain in the sticks, and one of the keen-eyed scouts of the St. Louis Cardinals spotted him and he was signed up promptly.

Many players who are sensations in the bush circuit fall down lamentably when they get among the players of the major leagues. Only one who has the stuff can get by there.

Joe Matson got by in record time. One after the other he faced the doughty teams of the National League—the Giants, the Cubs, the Reds, the Dodgers, and all the rest of that famous aggregation. Many of them smiled when the comparatively untried stripling faced them for the first time, but they did not do much laughing after the game was over. Here was a youngster to be reckoned with.

No one realized this more keenly than McRae, the manager of the New York Giants. He was the keenest judge of baseball talent in the country, and he lost no time in acquiring Joe Matson for his team.

Now Baseball Joe felt that he had reached the very height of his ambition, the goal that is dreamed of by all young players. But not for a minute did he relax. He knew that he still had much to learn and from none could he get better teaching than from McRae. That shrewd old fox taught him all he knew, and what Baseball Joe once learned he never forgot. Before long he was universally acknowledged to be the king of pitchers.

But his strength lay not alone in the box, though that was his chosen throne. His batting was as remarkable as his twirling. He had the eye of a hawk in spotting the ball. His timing was perfect, and he met the ball at just the right fraction of a second to make every ounce of his strength tell. Before long he developed into the greatest batter in the game.

He became known as the home-run king, and people packed the parks all over the circuit in the hope of seeing Baseball Joe clout another homer. Again and again he led the league in home run hitting, and many a game was won thereby that would otherwise have been lost.

The Giants were a great team, but, outside of the pitcher's box, there were other teams quite as powerful. It was Joe's great pitching year after year that brought the championship of the league to New York and later on several world championships.

Second only to Joe as a pitcher was Jim Barclay, who had come to the team from Princeton. He had a great arm and a good head, and a warm friendship sprang up between he and Joe. The latter coached the young recruit until he became one of the mainstays of the nine in the box. This friendship between the two was still further cemented when Jim fell in love with and married Joe's sister, Clara.

Joe himself had met his fate some time earlier. On one occasion when his team was in the South Joe had been instrumental in saving a young girl, Mabel Varley, the daughter of a banker, when the horse she was driving ran away. Love between Mabel and the stalwart young athlete was not long in developing. They were married some time later and their wedded life had proved ideally happy.

Baseball Joe had not pursued his meteoric career without making enemies, and their machinations against him at times were very serious.

In the spring of the year before that in which this story opens his arm had gone wrong, owing to an injury inflicted by enemies the season before. He consulted eminent specialists who decreed that for a whole year he would have to withdraw from the game unless he wanted his arm to be entirely ruined. The consternation of McRae was great, and Joe Matson himself was shocked beyond measure by the fateful verdict. But there was no help for it and they had to yield.

Joe went back to Riverside to recuperate. He reached there just at the time that the local baseball club was placed on the market. Joe saw a chance to stay in the game he loved, if only as manager, and he bought the club. In doing so he incurred the bitter enmity of Moe Russnak, an unscrupulous Jew, who himself had intended to buy the team. Aided by Hupft and McCarney, two former Giants who had been thrown off the team for crooked work, Russnak worked up a scheme that came near costing Joe his life.

How Russnak overreached himself and was sent to jail, how Joe brought a club of tailenders up to the championship of the Valley League, the many thrilling and exciting incidents that attended his efforts, are told in the preceding volume of this series, entitled 'Baseball Joe, Club Owner.'[9]

After that whirlwind tour through the life of a truly amazing man, author Lester Chadwick returns us to the story, "Now to return to Joe and Jim as they stood amazed and perplexed at the recognition of Moe Russnak as the man who had fallen into the gully." They really don't write books like that anymore.

Who wrote for the Syndicate? Stratemeyer almost certainly wrote all the books which appeared under his own name or the names of Arthur M. Winfield and Captain Ralph Bonehill; Leslie McFarlane wrote the first twenty-six *Hardy Boys* and three of the *Dana Girls;* Howard Garis, better known as the author of the Uncle Wiggily stories, wrote the first thirty-five Tom Swift books (the prolific Garis family—father Howard, mother Lilian, and children Roger and Cleo wrote many Stratemeyer Syndicate books prior to their establishing their own Syndicate); Harriet Adams (Stratemeyer's daughter) wrote many of the *Dana Girls* and apparently all the *Nancy Drew* series; and Andrew Svenson wrote the *Happy Hollister* series. But the identities of many series writers are unknown and are likely to remain that way. Certain house names appeared over and over again, witness the *incomplete* list below.

BOYS' BOOKS—

Victor Appleton, *Tom Swift* series, *Don Sturdy* series, *Moving Picture Boys* series, *Moving Picture Chums* series

Victor Appleton II, *Tom Swift, Jr.* series

Charles Amory Beach, *Air Service Boys* series

Captain Ralph Bonehill, *Boy Hunters* series, *Flag of Freedom* series, *Frontiers* series, *Young Hunters* series, *Young Sportsman* series, *Mexican War* series, *The Outdoor* series

Lester Chadwick, *Baseball Joe* series, *College Sports* series

Allen Chapman, *Tom Fairfield* series, *Fred Fenton* series, *Boys of Business* series, *Radio Boys* series, *Ralph of the Railroad* series, *Darewell Chums* series

Elmer A. Dawson, *Garry Grayson* series, *Buck and Larry Baseball* series

Franklin W. Dixon, *Hardy Boys* series, *Ted Scott Flying* stories

James Cody Ferris, *X Bar X Boys* series

Grahame Forbes, *The Boys of Columbia High* series

Captain Wilbur Lawton, *The Boy Aviator* series

Lt. Howard Payson, *Boy Scout* series, *Motor Cycle Chums* series

Nat Ridley, Jr., *Nat Ridley Rapid Fire Detective* series

Roy Rockwood, *Speedwell Boys* series, *Dave Dashaway* series, *Great Marvel* series, *Bomba* series, *Dave Fearless* series, *Deep Sea* series, *Rambling Boys* series

Raymond Sperry, Jr., *White Ribbon Boys* series
Frank V. Webster, *Webster* series (Alger-like books)
Jerry West, *Happy Hollister* series
Marvin West, *The Motor Rangers* series
Arthur M. Winfield, *Rover Boys* series, *Putnam Hall* series, *Bright and Bold* series, *Winfield* series, *Silver Lake* series
Clarence Young, *Jack Ranger* series, *Motor Boys* series, *Racer Boys* series

GIRLS' BOOKS—
May Hollis Barton, *The Barton Books For Girls*
Annie Roe Carr, *Nan Sherwood* series
Alice B. Emerson, *Ruth Fielding* series, *Betty Gordon* series
Grace Gordon, *Patsy Carroll* series
Alice Dale Hardy, *Riddle Club* series
Mabel C. Hawley, *The Four Little Blossoms* series
Grace Brooks Hill, *The Corner House Girls* series
Laura Lee Hope, *Moving Picture Girls* series, *Outdoor Girls* series, *Bobbsey Twins* series, *Blythe Girls* series, *Six Little Bunkers* series, *Bunny Brown* series
Carolyn Keene, *Nancy Drew* series, *Dana Girls* series
Agnes Miller, *Linger-Not* series
Gertrude W. Morrison, *Girls of Central High* series
Margaret Penrose, *Radio Girls* series, *Motor Girls* series, *Dorothy Dale* series
Helen Louise Thorndike, *Honey Bunch* series
Edna Winfield, *Holly Library* series

An incredible number of series and an incredible number of books flowing from the mind of one man and the pens of heaven knows how many anonymous writers. Estimates of the total number of books produced by the Syndicate over the years vary from as few as 800 to as many as 1200. A reading of Leslie McFarlane's *Ghost of the Hardy Boys* suggests that it was all quite possible, and given Stratemeyer's operation and ambition it was not unlikely that a vast number of books could be produced.

Then in 1908, the Boy Scouts of America was established; a few years later Stratemeyer was to become highly disturbed by the BSA and their leaders. James E. West, Chief Scout Executive, was alarmed by the outpourings from the presses of books he deemed inferior:

The boys' taste is being constantly vitiated and exploited by the mass of cheap juvenile literature. To meet this grave peril the Library Commission of the Boy Scouts of America has been organized.[10]

Not long after, Franklin K. Mathiews, Chief Scout Librarian, visited Louis Reed of Grosset and Dunlap and proposed a mass reprinting of a list of better books for boys, making finer literature more widely and inexpensively available. Grosset and Dunlap, one of the two chief publishers of Stratemeyer's Syndicate, agreed, and on November 1, 1913, appeared a Boy Scouts of America publication "Safety First Week" announcing the list. By 1934, more than 2,000,000 copies of BSA-approved books had been sold. The list eventually included seventy-five titles: classics like Jack London's *Call of the Wild,* John Masefield's *Jim Davis,* and Jules Verne's *20,000 Leagues Under the Sea;* contemporary boys' books like William Heyliger's *Bartley, Freshman Pitcher,* Ralph Paine's *College Years,* and Ralph Henry Barbour's *For the Honor of the School;* and books about the Boy Scout movement, Percy Keese Fitzhugh's *Adventures of a Boy Scout,* Charles P. Burton's *Boy Scouts of Bob's Hill,* and William Heyliger's *Don Strong of the Wolf Patrol.* Announcements about the series were featured prominently in the ad sections at the back of Grosset and Dunlap books:

EVERY BOY'S LIBRARY
BOY SCOUT EDITION   Similar to This Volume
    The Boy Scouts of America in making up this Library, selected only such books as had been proven by a nationwide canvass to be most universally in demand among the boys themselves. Originally published in more expensive editions only, they are now, under the direction of the Scout's National Council, re-issued at a lower price so that all boys may have the advantage of reading and owning them. It is the only series of books published under the control of this great organization, whose sole object is the welfare and happiness of the boy himself. For the first time in history a *guaranteed* library is available, and at a price so low as to be within the reach of all.

If all this affected Stratemeyer and his Syndicate relatively little, the next BSA move disturbed him considerably more. In the November 18, 1914, *Outlook,* Franklin K. Mathiews, Chief Scout Librarian, delivered a stinging diatribe against Stratemeyer's Syndicate without once mentioning it by name. Mathiews began by noting that in most surveys of children's reading, inferior books, (defined as those not found in libraries), were widely read and probably as influential as the better books. Mathiews argued that Syndicate books were even more dishonest and inaccurate and inflammatory than the earlier and much-attacked dime novels.

> In almost all of this 'mile-a-minute fiction' some inflammable tale of improbable adventure is told. Boys move about in aeroplanes as easily as though on bicycles; criminals are captured by them with a facility that matches the ability of Sherlock Holmes; and when it comes to getting on in the world, the cleverness of these hustling boys is comparable only to those captains of industry and Napoleans of finance who have made millions in a minute. Insuperable difficulties and crushing circumstances are as easily overcome and conquered as in fairy tales. Indeed, no popular character of history or legend or mythological story was ever more wise, more brave, more resourceful, than some of these up-to-the-minute boy heroes are made to appear in the Sunday supplement juvenile stories.[11]

Mathiews' loud and angry title for his article, "Blowing Out the Boy's Brains," is underscored throughout, especially in these paragraphs:

> Because these cheap books do not develop criminals or lead boys, except very occasionally, to seek the Wild West, parents who buy such books think they do their boys no harm. The fact is, however, that the harm done is simply incalculable. I wish I could label each one of these books: 'Explosives! Guaranteed to Blow Your Boy's Brains Out.'
>
> . . . .
>
> The difference between a *Treasure Island* and a modern 'thriller' in its many editions is not a difference in the elements so much as the use each author makes of them. A Stevenson works with combustibles, but, as in the case of using the gasoline, he confines them, directs them with care and caution, always thinking of how he may use them in a way that will be of advantage to the boy. In the case of the modern 'thriller' the author works with the same materials, but with no moral purpose, with no real intelligence. No effort is made to confine or direct or control these highly explosive elements. The result is that, as some boys read such books, their imaginations are literally 'blown out,' and they go into life as terribly crippled

as though by some material explosion they had lost a hand or foot. For not only will the boy be greatly handicapped in business, but the whole world of art in its every form almost is closed to him. Why are there so few men readers of the really good books, or even of the passing novels, sometimes of real worth? Largely, I think, because the imagination of so many men as boys received such brutal treatment at the hands of those authors and publishers who give no concern as to what they write or publish so long as it returns constantly the expected financial gain.[12]

To support his contention that series books were objectionable, Mathiews cites the manager of a book section in a New England department store who read another article condemning cheap books. The manager, wanting to be sure that he was not retailing filth for children, "sent some of these books to the local children's librarian, whose report, of course, confirmed his fear that they were not wholesome."[13] Using librarians to establish the worthlessness of series books may be standard procedure today, but Mathiews' use of the gimmick was doubtless fresher then.

Mathiews attacked these "trashy" books for many reasons, one of the chief being that hack writers were employed in the cruel salt mines of Stratemeyer's Syndicate to produce money for one man. This was strange reasoning, since the implication seemed to be that if the books had not sold well, they would have been less deserving of attack. He concluded his article with a melodramatic incident readers today may find less than compelling:

Just as I am closing this article there comes to my desk a letter from a scoutmaster in Lansing, Michigan. To the letter a postal card is attached signed by the sheriff stating that "information is wanted relative to the whereabouts of Guy Arthur Phinisey, who left his home in Lansing, Michigan, on September 2, 1914,' etc. In the letter of the scoutmaster I find these significant words: 'From the information I have received there seems to be no reason for his leaving home of his own accord. He has a good home, and his parents seem quiet but thrifty. The only possible clue I can find is 'cheap reading.'"

Of course not every boy who indulges himself in 'cheap reading' will be so affected, but who of us is wise enough to know which one it is that will be so influenced?[14]

Determining how successful this article was is problematical; but a later account states that shortly after the appearance of "Blowing Out the Boy's Brains"

> Women in Portland Oregon, stood beside the counters of bookstores discouraging would-be buyers of fifty-centers. Disgusted booksellers packed up their *Tom Swifts* and shipped them back to the publishers.[15]

While Mathiews never attributed any of his ideas to Anthony Comstock, leading American censor of the time, some passages from Comstock's 1883 book *Traps for the Young* remind the reader more than a little of Mathiews' later words. Attacking the cheaper literature of the 1870's and 1880's, Comstock said,

> Light literature, then, is a devil-trap to captivate the child by perverting taste and fancy. It turns aside from the pursuit of useful knowledge and prevents the full development in man or woman of the wonderful possibilities locked up in the child![16]
>
> Take further instances of the effect of this class of publications, and then say if my language is too strong. Does it startle and offend? To startle, to awaken, to put you on your guard, to arouse you to your duty over your own children is my earnest purpose. *Your child is in danger of having its pure mind cursed for life.*
>
> A few months ago, in a small town in Massachusetts, I arrested a young man about twenty-one years of age, for sending most obscene and foul matter by mail. He was in the field with his father at work at the time of arrest. He desired to go to his room to change his apparel before going to court. While in his room, and up to the moment of the finding of a pile of these vile five-cent story-papers in one corner, he had been perfectly cool and stolid. When these were discovered, he started as though a nest of adders had been opened, and said with great feeling, 'There! that's what has cursed me! That has brought me to this!'[17]

In addition to creating the list of better boys' books, Mathiews persuaded Percy Keese Fitzhugh to develop several series presenting boy scout life in a far more realistic light. Fitzhugh's seven series sold approximately 3,000,000 copies, and the *Tom Slade* series (1915-1930), the *Boy Scout* series (1913-1915), the *Buddy Books for Boys* series (1927), the *Flying Stories* series (1930-1932), the *Pee Wee Harris* series (1922-1930), the *Roy Blakeley* series (1920-1931), and the *Westy Martin* series (1924-1931) did offer competi-

tion to Stratemeyer's Syndicate, though they never equalled the sales or the popularity of Stratemeyer's books.

Mathiews made a final effort to destroy Stratemeyer's Syndicate in 1919. He "persuaded Frederic G. Melcher and the American Association of Book Publishers to establish the first National Children's Book Week 'to bring together in common cause the many groups which had a deep interest in the reading of children—librarians, teachers, publishers, artists, authors, scout leaders, and the like.'"[18]

The overall effect of the campaign against Stratemeyer was probably minimal. Certainly Mathiews was deadly serious about Stratemeyer, and Stratemeyer increasingly took Mathiews seriously; but little emerged out of this extended squabble. Stratemeyer may temporarily have lost some sales, and when he challenged Grosset & Dunlap about the appearance of the competing *Every Boy's Library,* Grosset & Dunlap made it clear that they had no desire to become embroiled in the argument and even if they did, they were not at all sure whose side they might take. Stratemeyer wisely let the matter drop. He may have "toned down dangers, thrills, and violence in favor of well-researched instruction" in later volumes, as Arthur Prager suggests,[19] but in the long run the only winners were boys who continued to buy and read Stratemeyer's books and could now find other books available as well in a less expensive format. Financial losses must have been temporary, because by 1934 Grosset & Dunlap was selling about 3,000,000 Stratemeyer Syndicate books yearly, while Cupples & Leon sold another 1,000,000 copies.

The effectiveness of Mathiews' challenge is open to question in light of the data compiled by Carleton Washburne and Mabel Vogel in their *Winnetka Graded Book List*. The authors polled 36,750 children in thirty-four cities throughout the country to determine what books were read and liked. Using the responses, the authors compiled a list of 700 books reported at least twenty-five or more times. In their original publication, the authors excluded from the graded list "books that are not recommended because of low literary value" (e.g., *Bobbsey Twins, Honey Bunch, Shifting for Himself, Mystery at Number Six, Adventures of Reddy Fox*) and "books that are not recommended because of subject content" (e.g., *The Harvester, The Circular Staircase, The Hound of the Baskervilles, When a Man's a Man*) based on the evaluations of selected librarians. Commenting upon the ambiguous nature of the phrase "literary value," the authors wrote:

> The books of one series—seventeen of them—were unanimously rated trashy by our expert librarians and almost unanimously (98%) liked by the 900 children who read them. On the other hand, of the ten most popular books, not one was rated trashy by the judging librarians (although one librarian so considered *Huckleberry Finn!*). For the most part the children's tastes do not appear to be very far wrong. If a group of children's librarians, selected as among the most expert in the United States, differ among themselves as to what books have high literary merit and what ones are trashy does it not show that none of us are able to set up as yet any final and generally acceptable standard of literary merit? If we adults do not agree on what books are 'literary' should literary merit be a primary determining factor in selecting and recommending books for children? Is it not more important to know what books are likely to be thoroughly enjoyed by children of various ages and degrees of reading ability?[20]

Presumably to appease their own consciences and possibly to satisfy the curiosity of teachers and librarians, Washburne and Vogel published two supplements to their original booklist, showing books previously excluded. Stratemeyer must have been pleased and Mathiews horrified to learn that seventeen Bobbsey Twins books, six Tom Swifts, and several other titles from other Stratemeyer books were listed.[21]

When World War II broke out, the Stratemeyer Syndicate dropped several of its series, partly because paper was difficult to get, partly because several of the series were obviously losing readership. The most famous early Stratemeyer series ended (or so it seemed at the time) in 1941 with the publication of the fortieth Tom Swift book. Apparently, by that time young boys had lost interest in the wild adventures of this great hero. But in 1954, *Tom Swift* was transformed into the *Tom Swift, Jr.* series, written by Victor Appleton II. But even the casual reader must have noted the change, for *Tom Swift* was clearly not *Tom Swift, Jr.;* the earlier books were primarily adventure books and the newer series mixed adventure with genuine science.

Two popular Stratemeyer series survived World War II and they may endure forever, English teachers and librarians notwithstanding. The Hardy Boys first appeared in 1926 in *The Tower Treasure,* and that one title had sold more than 1,500,000 copies by 1973. Number 51 in the series, *The Naked Monkey,* appeared in 1972 and sold more than 60,000 copies that year. In 1975 alone, 1,670,000 *Hardy Boys* books were sold—not a bad record for a series few people thought would last. Ed Zuckerman's recent article[22] amusingly details changes in the series from its beginnings, particularly the changes that have taken place through the rewriting and updating of older volumes for today's boys.

But if the *Hardy Boys* had their fans, no fans were and are more dedicated and faithful than the readers of *Nancy Drew. The Secret of the Old Clock* appeared in 1930 and since that time fifty-two more mysteries and one *Nancy Drew* cookbook have been published. Estimates of the total sales of *Nancy Drew* books range between 55,000,000 and 60,000,000, a healthy figure indeed for the clean-cut, blonde teenager from River Heights. But Nancy's popularity with readers was guaranteed when she first appeared in print. Even the first book in the series made clear what a super-girl, super-detective she would become.

Older *Nancy Drew* books have been revised and updated, and to compare the 1930 *The Secret of the Old Clock* with the 1959 revision is to find intriguing changes, though none of them fundamentally alter Nancy's personality or ability. In the printings after the 1959 copyright, this legend appeared on the reverse of the title page.

> This new story for today's readers is based on the original of the same title.

A recent printing of the 1959 edition no longer contains that message. The 1930 edition presented Nancy as 16 years old, the 1959 revision as 18 years old. The plot of both editions are much alike, but structurally there are odd, if not significant, changes. More interesting changes can be found in smaller matters. The "negro caretaker Jeff Tucker" with his Uncle Tom-ish "humorous" dialect of the 1930 edition is replaced by "Jeff Tucker, the caretaker, the tallest, skinniest man I've ever seen outside a circus," in the later edition. As the series continues and earlier volumes are revised, villains lose distinct ethnic characteristics, and the strange/humorous dialects of earlier minor characters become more and more Anglo-Saxon. Ardent feminists have joyously gathered Nancy into the fold as an early prototype of the liberated young woman. Jane Ginsburg, writing in *Ms. Magazine,* wrote,

> Nancy Drew, whose mystery-solving exploits have filled the contents of 50 books, is one heroine who qualifies in many ways as a role-model for young feminists. Unlike the patient and self-sacrificing protagonists of the nurse books, Nancy is brave and active. She seldom needs strong-arm male assistance.[23]

And Bobbie Ann Mason asked,

> Where would women's liberation be without Nancy Drew and Judy Bolton and Beverly Gray and Cherry Ames? Nancy Drew alone has been crucial to the lives of millions of girls (no one can count how many) since 1929 . . . She was the first official girl sleuth, and the rest came tumbling after.[24]

If Mason later notes some qualifications in her enthusiasm for Nancy Drew, she still retains more than nostalgic enthusiasm for Nancy.

English teachers and librarians have opposed Stratemeyer's Syndicate almost since Stratemeyer began writing. Mathiews maligned Stratemeyer and temporarily may have hurt sales, but the attack was soon forgotten. Stratemeyer may have lost sales because of the *Winnetka Graded Book List* and its supplements, may have cost Stratemeyer some sales but likely very few since his books were never intended for the library. His readers would have paid no attention to the attack even if they had ever heard of it. The violent feelings some critics have harbored for Stratemeyer is puzzling and surprising. In a 1934 article, librarian Hope White called Stratemeyer an "arch-fiend."[25] In 1956, librarian Janie Smith quoted Mathiews approvingly and launched yet another attack on Stratemeyer.[26] And in 1964, librarian Margaret Beckman triumphantly announced three major reasons why *Nancy Drew* or the *Bobbsey Twins* did not deserve a place in the library:

> In the first place, it is a matter of cost . . . If it is the responsibility of teachers and librarians to provide the best there is for our children, then surely no public funds should be spent on this sort of trash. The second reason is a matter of time . . . I disagree most strenuously that there is no harm done in reading the Bobbsey Twins and Nancy Drew, etc. There are only six to eight years in which a child can read, *as a child,* and there are so many wonderful books to be read he will never have time to read them all. To waste these few precious years reading the less than worthwhile is really a crime . . . The final reason is the effect of Bobbsey Twin reading on youthful minds. Certainly I know there are some children who are omnivorous readers, who will read, unencouraged, everything they can find and jump easily from the Hardy Boys to *Treasure Island.* But this is where the newspaper experts make their mistake. They assume all children can or will do this, because some of the few children with whom they are familiar have been able to.[27]

Some English teachers and librarians still apparently believe it is their duty to attack *Nancy Drew* and the *Hardy Boys*. Future attacks appear to be as unpromising and futile as they are inevitable. Perhaps some people genuinely enjoy modeling their lives after Don Quixote.

It is frequently said that the Stratemeyer books have limited literary value, and of course that's true as far as it goes. Any adult reader can discover this through even a limited acquaintance with a Nancy Drew or Hardy Boys book. But that is also true of most adolescent literature, most adult literature, most science fiction, most mysteries, most books generally. And true or not, the assertion begs the question. The Syndicate never pretended it was creating imperishable literature. More to the point, young boys and girls rarely look for those qualities that may help to create great or enduring literature. Young people look for rapid action and humor and excitement, and Syndicate books certainly provided that. But more important to Stratemeyer were the moral lessons his books purveyed. Whether boys and girls listened to the morality in the midst of all the action may be a moot point, but there *was* morality in abundance. And, no matter what the book or what the series, Stratemeyer's books preached the same moral lessons over and over.

(1) The Protestant Ethic: hard work is good in and of and for itself, but rigorously applied it will be rewarded here on earth, if not in affluence at least in gaining a higher rung on the ladder of respectability.

(2) The Godly and manly virtues of cleanliness, thrift, righteousness, and abstinence (from gambling, drinking, smoking, gossiping, frivolity, and evil thoughts) are essential for the good man or woman.

(3) The hallmarks of the good American are Yankee ingenuity and tenacity; he/she can do anything or discover anything he/she wants to.

(4) Education and sports are essential to young people and both should be taken seriously, since they will make a good person a better person.

(5) The outdoor life is beneficial to young people, psychologically and spiritually as well as physically.

(6) Evil and good are clearly and easily distinguishable to the good person; rarely do gray or doubtful areas lie between evil and good.

(7) All young people must respect the law, the church, the school, adults, and authority in general, for in the final analysis, society is wiser than the individual.

(8) America is truly the land of promise for all, abounding in opportunities for the young person who watches for them and follows through with his/her innate drive.

One question about the Syndicate books persists, a question, which by its existence perhaps assumes an answer unfavorable to *Nancy Drew* and the *Hardy Boys*. Will reading series books permanently impair young readers? I sincerely believe the answer must be a resounding NO! My daughter went from Nancy Drew (or more accurately, all of the Nancy Drews) to Beverly Cleary's *Ellen Tebbits* and from there on to Betty Smith's *A Tree Grows in Brooklyn*. Each in turn became a literary touchstone used by Sherri for several years, then abandoned. Why I should have been so surprised at that time now escapes me, for I went through much the same process with different books. I read every sports story and every series book I could get my hands on in the small public library of Clarinda, Iowa. The librarian paid no attention to me, treating me with almost total disdain. That may have been the nicest gift she could have given me—she left me totally alone, totally free to determine my own reading for my own tastes, perverted and childish as they must have appeared to her. I read all the Tarzan and Zane Grey books the library owned, and somewhere around my tenth or eleventh year I began to buy all the twenty-five cent books I could afford at the local Woolworth or J. C. Penney stores during Christmas season. The books had no particular literary value, but they were exciting and mysterious and horrible and fun and all the good stuff reading has always represented to me, all the stuff that school for many years thereafter never represented. But my progress in reading should be no particular surprise, for most of us librarians and English teachers read widely and indiscriminately for much of our youth. And we survived and we grew because of our reading, all of it, the bad and the worst mixed with a little of the good, *not* despite it but because of it.

On May 10, 1930, Edward Stratemeyer died of pneumonia. But his Syndicate continued. Mrs. Harriet Adams and Mrs. Edna Squier, Stratemeyer's daughters, carried on. Mrs. Squier became an inactive partner in 1942. Andrew E. Svenson joined the Syndicate in 1948, and was a full partner from 1961 until his death in 1975. The number of series published has shrunk to seven: Hardy Boys, Nancy Drew, Dana Girls, Bobbsey Twins, Cherry Ames, Tom Swift, Jr., and Wynn and Lonny. But the sales continue, at an almost unbelievable rate—approximately 6,000,000 copies a year—led by Drew's 2,300,000 last year.

The Stratemeyer Syndicate goes on.[28] Harriet Adams is now 83, but Grosset & Dunlap has made arrangements for others to take over the work of the Syndicate when there is no longer a Stratemeyer left. The Syndicate goes on, and the readers become older and are replaced by the newly young, and the Syndicate goes on and on and on. It may go on forever. I hope it does. More important, so do thousands of young people today. So will thousands of young people tomorrow.

NOTES

1. New York: Grosset & Dunlap, 1899.
2. New York: Grosset & Dunlap, 1926.
3. "For It Was Indeed He," *Fortune*, April 1934, p. 193.
4. *Ghost of the Hardy Boys* (New York: Two Continents, 1976).
5. *ibid.*, p. 22.
6. *ibid.*, p. 72.
7. *ibid.*, pp. 188-189.
8. Ed Zuckerman, "The Great Hardy Boys' Whodunit," *Rolling Stone*, September 9, 1976, p. 39.
9. Lester Chadwick, *Baseball Joe, Pitching Wizard* (New York: Cupples & Leon, 1928), pp. 11-16.
10. Quoted in John F. Sullivan, "The Do Good Boys and the Grave Peril of Percy Keese Hits the Trail," *Boys' Book Collector*, Spring 1972, p. 290.
11. Franklin K. Mathiews, "Blowing Out the Boy's Brains," *Outlook*, November 18, 1914, p. 652.
12. *ibid.*, p. 653.
13. *ibid.*, p. 654.
14. *ibid.*
15. "For It Was Indeed He," *Fortune*, April 1934, p. 209.
16. Anthony Comstock, *Traps for the Young*, ed. Robert Bremner (Cambridge: Harvard University Press, 1967; first published in 1883), p. 12.
17. *ibid.*, pp. 28-29.
18. Dora V. Smith, *Fifty Years of Children's Books 1910-1960: Trends, Backgrounds, Influences* (Champaign, Illinois: National Council of Teachers of English, 1963), p. 6.
19. Arthur Prager, "Edward Stratemeyer and His Book Machine," *Saturday Review*, July 10, 1971, p. 53.
20. Carlton Washburne and Mabel Vogel, *Winetka Graded Book List* (Chicago: American Library Association, 1926), p. 44.
21. Carlton Washburne and Mabel Vogel, "Supplement to the Winetka Graded Book List," *Elementary English Review*, February 1927, pp. 47-52 and March 1927, pp. 66-73.
22. "The Great Hardy Boys' Whodunit," *Rolling Stone*, September 9, 1976, pp. 36-40.
23. Jane Ginsburg, "And Then There Is Good Old Nancy Drew," *Ms.*, January 1974, p. 93.
24. Bobbie Ann Mason, *The Girl Sleuth: A Feminist Guide* (Old Westbury; New York: The Feminist Press, 1975), p. 6.
25. Hope White, "For It Was Indeed He," *Illinois Libraries*, October 1934, pp. 113-116.
26. Janie Smith, "History of the Bobbsey Twins," *South Carolina Library Bulletin*, May 1956, pp. 3-4.
27. Margaret Beckman, "Why Not the Bobbsey Twins?" *Library Journal*, November 15, 1964, pp. 4612-4613, 4627.
28. If much remains unknown about the Stratemeyer Syndicate, much more has been written than the casual reader might expect. Anyone interested in

further mining the Stratemeyer lode should consult the following among other sources: Robert Cantwell, "A Sneering Laugh with the Bases Loaded," *Sports Illustrated*, April 23, 1962, pp. 67-70, 73-76; Sol Cohen, "Minority Stereotypes in Children's Literature: The Bobbsey Twins, 1904-1968," *Educational Forum*, November 1969, pp. 119-125; Paul C. Deane, "The Persistence of Uncle Tom: An Examination of the Images of the Negro in Children's Fiction Series," *Journal of Negro Education*, Spring 1968, pp. 140-145; John T. Dizer, Jr., "Fortune and the Syndicate," *Boys' Book Collector*, Fall 1970, pp. 146-153 and Winter 1971, pp. 178-186; John T. Dizer, Jr., "Serials and Boys' Books by Edward Stratemeyer," *Dime Novel Round-Up*, December 1975, pp. 126-148; John T. Dizer, Jr., "Stratemeyer and the Blacks," *Dime Novel Round-Up*, October 1975, pp. 90-117; John T. Dizer, Jr., "Stratemeyer and Science Fiction," *Dime Novel Round-Up*, July 15, 1975, pp. 66-81 and August 1976, pp. 74-90; Roger Garis, *My Father Was Uncle Wiggily*, New York: McGraw-Hill, 1966; Harry K. Hudson, *A Bibliography of Hard-Cover Boys' Books*, Clearwater, Florida: Jiffy Blueprint Company, 1965-1966; James P. Jones, "Nancy Drew, WASP Super Girl of the 1930's," *Journal of Popular Culture*, Spring 1973, pp. 707-717; James P. Jones, "Negro Stereotypes in Children's Literature: The Case of Nancy Drew," *Journal of Negro Education*, Spring 1971, pp. 121-125; J. Frederick MacDonald, " 'The Foreigner' in Juvenile Series Fiction, 1900-1945," *Journal of Popular Culture*, Winter 1974, pp. 534-548; Russel Nye, *The Unembarrassed Muse: The Popular Arts in America*, New York: Dial, 1970, especially Chapter 3; Arthur Prager, *Rascals at Large, or, The Clue in the Old Nostalgia*, Garden City: Doubleday, 1971; Peter Soderbergh, "The Stratemeyer Strain: Educators and the Juvenile Series Book, 1900-1974," *Journal of Popular Culture*, Spring 1974, pp. 864-872; Edna Yost, "The Fifty Cent Juveniles," *Publishers Weekly*, June 18, 1932, pp. 2405-2408; Edna Yost, "Who Writes the Fifty-Cent Juveniles?" *Publishers Weekly*, May 20, 1933, pp. 1595-1598.

WHAT MAKES A BAD BOOK GOOD:
ELSIE DINSMORE

Jacqueline Jackson and Philip Kendall

Prologue

Item: One co-author of this article found a pack of Old Maid cards drawn by her three daughters. The pairs were daintily dressed Victorian children of no particular literary background: Jamie and Janie, Nancy and Norma, standing for their portraits with their hoops and sand pails. Except for one pair, drawn by daughter #2: a child labeled Enna maliciously smashing a doll, and its mate, a crumpled heap of a child labelled Elsie.

Item: Daughter #1, with swollen eyes, laughing and crying simultaneously, "I get so mad at myself every time I read *Elsie Dinsmore!* I know it's an awful, soupy book but I always weep buckets just the same!"

Item: The co-author, realizing her daughters were near Biblical illiterates, undertook to read some Bible to them one night, starting with the story of Joseph. She did not recall that Joseph is left languishing in the pit while the story of Judah and his daughter-in-law Tamar is interpolated. Suddenly into it, she plowed bravely ahead, providing exegesis on such matters as Hebrew law in respect to brothers fathering children for the deceased, spilling seed on the ground, harlots, the double standard which would have allowed Judah to send Tamar to the torch for adultery, while he went scot-free, and finally the birth of twins, one of whom thrust an arm from the womb, was quickly tagged as first born with a red thread, and then inexplicably was delivered second. It took half an hour to cover thirty verses, and at the end there was silence for the space of several moments. Then daughter #3, age ten, turned from staring into the darkened backyard and said, "Do you mean to tell me Elsie Dinsmore read *that*?"

Daughter #2 did not draw Frank and Joe Hardy as the only literary figures on the Old Maid cards. Daughter #1 did not say, "I know *Pollyanna* is a bad book but I weep buckets." Daughter #3 did not exclaim, "Did Nancy Drew read *that*?" No. The bad book whose power all these items attest to, the bad book that had become such a part of their lives was *Elsie Dinsmore*. On the basis of this evidence, along with testimony too numerous to quote from readers of *Elsie* both young and old, as well as their own fascination with the story, the co-authors maintain that any book as bad as *Elsie Dinsmore* must have something good about it to exert such power.

There is an honorable tradition of making a good book bad: *Gulliver* is bowdlerized. *Uncle Remus* speaks BBC English. *Tom Sawyer* is abridged, or straitjacketed into 3rd grade word lists, or cast into a comic book so one can almost avoid reading entirely. *The Little House on the Prairie* indeed finishes the process, by becoming a bad TV show.

In this paper our interest lies in the opposite direction. Are there any patently bad books that are good? And good in and of themselves, without outside tampering or mutilation? Perchance are there any *great* bad books, so transcendental in their badness that they will survive the ages? Friends, there is one. The authors maintain that *Elsie Dinsmore* is such a classic. Unfortunately, *Elsie Dinsmore* has been out of print more than a generation, and if remembered in critical works it is only as an object of ridicule. We hope however, that once we have brought this literary injustice to your attention, all of us, true to the Modern Language Association motto, *Ex obscuritate, lux!* will help to restore *Elsie* to her rightful pedestal in American letters.[1]

It was in part this MLA tradition which narrowed our selection from the wide range of better-known dreadful books. *Black Beauty* is available in every dime store, and Horatio Alger is enjoying a revival on the paperback racks. But *Elsie* surpasses Alger in badness, and is, in addition, a *woman*. Ah, you say, but that still leaves *Black Beauty*. One co-author, a social historian, did seriously urge as our model that epitome of cruelty and injustice to women, until a closer reading of the text revealed Black Beauty to be male.[2]

Before we go further, for the sake of the uninitiated, it behooves us to establish our initial assumption, that *Elsie* is indeed a bad book. We could cite numerous critics,[3] but instead let us quote a random passage:[4]

"Dear papa," she whispered, "God will take care of us."
"I would give all I am worth to have you safe at home," he

Two of the Old Maid cards drawn by the co-author's daughter, inspired by *Elsie Dinsmore*.

Martha Finley creator of the "Elsie Dinsmore" books. *Elsie and Her Loved Ones* by Martha Finley, 1903.

answered, hoarsely, pressing her closer and closer to him.

O! even in that moment of fearful peril, when death seemed just at hand, those words, and the affectionate clasp of her father's arm, sent a thrill of intense joy to the love-famished heart of the little girl.

But destruction seemed inevitable. Lora was leaning back, half fainting with terror, Adelaide scarcely less alarmed, while Enna clung to her, sobbing most bitterly.

Elsie alone preserved a cheerful serenity. She had built her house upon the rock, and knew that it would stand. Her destiny was in her Heavenly Father's hands, and she was content to leave it there. Even death had no terrors to the simple, unquestioning faith of the little child who had put her trust in Jesus.

But they were not to perish thus; for at that moment a powerful negro, who was walking along the road, hearing an unusual sound, turned about, caught sight of the vehicle coming toward him at such a rapid rate, and instantly comprehending the peril of the travelers, planted himself in the middle of the road, and, at the risk of life and limb, caught the horses by the bridle—the sudden and unexpected check throwing them upon their haunches, and bringing the carriage to an instant standstill.[5]

We let the work speak for itself. We are sure you now need no argument from us to agree that *Elsie Dinsmore* is a bad book. We do hasten to add at the outset that we are well aware of its flagrant racism:[6]

> "How do you do, Aunt Chloe? I am very glad to know you, since Elsie tells me you are a servant of the same blessed Master whom I love and try to serve," said Rose, putting her small white hand cordially into Chloe's dusky one.
>
> "Deed I hope I is, missus," replied Chloe, pressing it fervently in both of hers. "I'se only a poor old black sinner, but de good Lord Jesus, He loves me jes' de same as if I was white, and I love Him an' all his chillun with all my heart."

We beg indulgence for *Elsie* by reason of the age and ethos which produced it.

Elsie Dinsmore was published in 1868, the work of Martha Farquharson Finley (1828-1909), a maiden lady long in good works for the Lord, mainly through the means (till *Elsie*) of the Presbyterian Publication Committee in Philadelphia. The child of first cousins, she spent her childhood in Ohio and Indiana, was educated in private schools in Indiana and Philadelphia, taught school in Indiana for two years, returned to Philadelphia for her work with the Presbyterians, bought (in 1876) a home in nearby Maryland and remained there until her death. Her output, not counting Sunday School books, totaled forty-seven volumes, of which thirty-nine were juvenile novels, twenty-eight being *Elsie* books with the last Elsie, *Elsie and Her Namesakes,* completed a scant four years before her death. The other eight were adult novels or biographies.

The sketch in the biographical dictionary whence we gleaned the above facts[7] is sneeringly negative, which at least lends interest to the review of an otherwise uneventful life:

> There seems, indeed, to have been no excuse for the immense and long-continuing sale of the Elsie books or of Miss Finley's other juvenile stories; no reason, why, forty years after their inception, they should still have outsold any other juveniles except Louisa May Alcott's (which are, of course, in a different category)—and yet that was the case. It is only within the present century that children have stopped reading about Elsie, weeping over her, and perhaps praying for her. The secret of her success lay hidden within the mind of the quiet little old lady with spectacles, a rather grim mouth, and soft primly arranged white hair. One wonders if after all it was the children who made Elsie's and, in lesser degree, Mildred's public. Could it have been the parents who chose and insinuated the books, and inculcations of a Victorian ideal? Certainly when the children exposed to Elsie grew up to be parents themselves, confronted with a clear-eyed and realistic brood of youngsters hungry for stronger stuff, the sale of the Elsie books slumped suddenly, never again to be revived.[8]

Clearly the biographer did not feel himself up to the task which we have set for ourselves: "There is no excuse," "no reason why," "the secret of her success lay hidden within the mind of that quiet little old lady." May we point out that *Elsie Dinsmore,* with its continuation-sequel *Elsie's Holidays at Roselands,* contains the whole of that secret, and that the author, age thirty-nine at the publication of those volumes, seems to be struggling with problems most little old ladies have long put to rest.

We emphatically disagree that parents were the cause of *Elsie's* popularity, noting its electrical impact on more present-day

children than those cited in the prologue, and our singular lack of
success in forcing enough exemplary reading matter on children of
our own acquaintance to make any difference in sales figures, even
if assisted by a multitude of parents. That the parents themselves
might also be avidly reading *Elsie* is a possibility that apparently
does not occur to our bemused biographer. And as to his "clear
eyed and realistic brood of youngsters hungry for stronger stuff,"
as the rest of this paper will demonstrate, what can be stronger
than Elsie?

What, then, are the ingredients of the fascination which differen-
tiate *Elsie Dinsmore* from the morass of undistinguished bad books,
now justly sunk into obscurity?[9] To begin, Elsie is beautiful; we
are told at our first encounter in the schoolroom at Roselands that
she has "large, soft eyes of the darkest hazel," and shortly thereafter, she is compared with a miniature of her deceased mother:
"she was very beautiful, with a sweet, gentle, winning countenance,
the same soft hazel eyes and golden brown curls that the little Elsie
possessed; the same regular features, pure complexion, and sweet
smile." Beauty, as for Snow White and many others, causes
problems: "The truth is, I believe we are a little jealous of her; she
is so extremely beautiful, and heiress to such an immense fortune.
Mamma often frets, and says that one of these days she will quite
eclipse her younger daughters." This beauty poses problems for her
father, too: "The darling!" he murmured to himself; "she is lovely
as an angel, and she is *mine,* mine only, mine own precious one;
and loves me with her whole soul." But more of Horace Dinsmore's
problem anon.

In addition, Elsie is fabulously rich through her mother, and
though her fortune is being held in trust for her, she has a generous
allowance. This great wealth also causes complexities: her youthful
spendthrift Uncle Arthur constantly wants to borrow, and her
grandfather dislikes her because her maternal grandfather, "that
Grayson!" made his money in trade instead of land.

Elsie is also gentle, loving, kind, compassionate, suffers all injustice patiently, never stoops to deceit, returns good for evil, frees
humming birds, entertains smaller guests ignored by the rest of the
Dinsmore children, and gives expensive presents to the help. You
would think that these exemplary virtues would make her appreciated and loved in return. But except for the help, this is not
the case: "Elsie," exclaimed Louise, "I have no patience with you!

such ridiculous scruples as you are always raising. I shall not pity
you one bit if you are obliged to stay at home," and:

> "She is an odd child," said Adelaide; ". . . she is so meek
> and patient she will fairly let you trample upon her. It pro-
> vokes papa. He says she is no Dinsmore, or she would know
> how to stand up for her own rights; and yet she has a temper,
> I know, for once in a great while it shows itself for an in-
> stant . . . and then she grieves over it for days, as though she
> had committed some great crime; while the rest of us think
> nothing of getting angry half a dozen times in a day."

Elsie is, in fact, persecuted—albeit for righteousness' sake. Her
unique position in the family: a dead mother, an absentee father, a
grandfather and youthful stepgrandmother, and a group of aunts
and uncles the oldest of whom is seventeen, the youngest six or
seven; the isolated location (a southern plantation in an unspecified
state, but near the sea) where the children are taught at home; and
Elsie's own unfortunate personality traits make her the ideal victim.

Arthur maliciously joggles her elbow while she writes, making her
blot her copy book. Two hundred pages later he unlocks her desk
to do a more thorough job. Miss Day, unable to discipline the
unruly Dinsmores because of their mother's watchful eye, vents all
her rage on the patient and unprotected Elsie. Her grandfather
treats her "with entire neglect" and her grandmother with loathing.
But the hapless child has a solace, for

> . . . young as Elsie was, she had already a very lovely and
> well-developed Christian character . . . she/had/ very clear and
> correct views on almost every subject connected with her duty
> to God and her neighbor; was very truthful both in word and
> deed, very strict in her observance of the Sabbath . . . [and] . . . in
> spite of all her trials and vexations, little Elsie was the happiest
> person in the family; for she had in her heart that peace which
> the world can neither give nor take away; that joy which the
> Saviour gives to His own, and no man taketh from them. She
> constantly carried all her sorrows and troubles to Him, and the
> coldness and neglect of others seemed but to drive her nearer
> to the Heavenly Friend, until she felt that while possessed of
> His love she could not be unhappy, though treated with scorn
> and abuse by the whole world.

> "The good are better made by ill,
> As odors crushed are sweeter still."

And Elsie has a dream, by day and by night, that her absent and unknown father had come home, "that he had taken her to his heart, calling her 'his own darling child, his precious little Elsie' . . . But from month to month, and year to year, that longed-for return had been delayed until the little heart had grown sick with hope deferred . . ."

As the torments increase, the intensity of longing increases. When at last her father does return home, Elsie is quite unequal to the situation:

> She leaned against the wall, her heart throbbing so wildly she could scarcely breathe . . . So overwrought were the child's feelings that she nearly fainted; everything in the room seemed to be turning round, and for an instant she scarcely knew where she was.
>
> But a strange voice asked, "And who is this?" and looking up as her grandfather pronounced her name, she saw a stranger standing before her—very handsome, and very youthful-looking in spite of a heavy dark beard and mustache—who exclaimed hastily, "What! this great girl *my* child? Really it is enough to make a man feel old." (He is twenty-seven at the time)
>
> Then, taking her hand, he stooped and coldly kissed her lips.
>
> She was trembling violently, and the very depths of her feelings kept her silent and still; her hand lay still in his, cold and clammy.
>
> He held it an instant, at the same time gazing searchingly into her face; then dropped it, saying in a tone of displeasure, "I am not an ogre, that you need to be so afraid of me; but there, you may go; I will not keep you in terror any longer."

Elsie rushes to her room, flings herself upon the bed, and "with her crushed and bleeding heart, sobbing, mourning, weeping as though she would weep her very life away," she exclaims,

> "O papa, papa! . . . My own papa, you do not love me; me your own little girl. Oh! My heart will break. O mamma, mamma! if I could only go to you; for there is no one here to love me, and I am so lonely, oh, *so* lonely and desolate!"

From here on, Elsie's father takes over the persecution, and beside his machinations the relatives and the governess are amateurs. For Elsie expected little from them but injustices and cruelties, nor did she love them so dearly; while her own papa, whom she adores next to Jesus, plays with her as a cat with a mouse, now enflaming her hopes with a kind word or caress, now casting her into bleaker despair than heretofore by some new aloofness, disapproval, deprivation or punishment. Horace Dinsmore has no visible work, and his entire time is apparently spent, when he is not with his friends, in amusing himself with Elsie. Neither can Elsie name these cruelties for what they are, for are not they being done by her own beloved papa, and for her own good?

We have endured 218 grueling pages before we reach the first real breakthrough of her father's affection, when "for the first time he folded her in his arms and kissed her tenderly, saying, in a moved tone, 'I *do* love you, my darling, my own little daughter." Yet a scant four pages later, after Miss Day accuses Elsie of impertinence and contradiction, in response to Elsie's agonized entreaties he lays down a ruler and says, "No, I shall punish you by depriving you of your play this afternoon, and giving you only bread and water for your dinner. Sit down there," . . . and in a bit, as Elsie sobs and cries violently, he says, "Elsie, cease that noise; I have had quite enough of it." Horace's capricious cruelties lead finally to the famous piano stool scene, the high point in the first volume, where the proud father, wishing to bask before his friends in his daughter's accomplishments, asks her to play a secular song on the Sabbath:

"Will not tomorrow do, papa?" she asked in a low tremulous tone . . .

"Certainly not, Elsie," he said, we want it now . . ."

"O papa! I *cannot* sing it today; *please* let me wait until tomorrow."

"Elsie," he said, in his sternest tones, "sit down to the piano instantly, and do as I bid you, and let me hear no more of this nonsense."

Elsie pleads that she cannot break the Sabbath; Horace informs her that he is judge in what is breaking the Sabbath. The friends entreat him to release Elsie.

"No," he replied, "when I give my child a command, it is to be obeyed: I have *said* she should play it, and play it she *must;* she is not to suppose that she may set up her opinion of right and wrong against mine."

He orders her to sit on the piano stool until she obeys him, though it should be till tomorrow morning. His step-mother crows triumphantly (for she had warned her stepson not to ask Elsie): "I knew very well how it would end." Whereupon Horace rejoins,

"Her father's arm was around her, and she had been standing silently, with her face hidden in his shoulder, while these thoughts were passing through her mind." Saalfield edition, *Elsie Dinsmore*, 19——.

Elsie's belief that breaking the Sabbath was a sin is illustrated here in a famous eipsode. *Elsie Dinsmore* by Martha Finley, 1867.

"Excuse me, but it has *not* ended; and ere it does, I think she will learn that she has a stronger will than her own to deal with."

This final line leads us to the delineation of the major theme and conflict that underlies the first two *Elsie* books.[10]

Elsie's father is intent on breaking Elsie's will. This is not of itself cruel, for those familiar with nineteenth-century social history will know that the breaking of the will was as necessary a step in child-rearing as were weaning and toilet training, and in sequence followed shortly after the latter. So it is Horace Dinsmore's parental duty, as God's vice-regent on earth, to break Elsie's will, and to save her from a life of spoiled self-indulgence.

The catch here is that he has been too long abroad, returning to his home when Elsie is already eight years old, and in his absence one greater than he has already accomplished this necessary task. Elsie's first four orphaned years were attended by her black mammy, Chloe, and Chloe, "though entirely uneducated, was a simple-minded, earnest Christian, and with a heart full of love to Jesus, had . . . early endeavored to lead the little one to Him . . ." But Martha Finley could not leave such grave responsibility completely to an untutored Negro slave, who in status and understanding is also only a child.[11] Therefore, at her original guardian's home, and for four more years at Roselands until a few months before the story begins, Elsie also had a housekeeper. Mrs. Murray was an intelligent old Scotswoman, "and devoutly pious, and had carefully instructed this lonely little one, for whom she had almost a parent's affection, and her efforts to bring her to a saving knowledge of Christ had been signally owned and blessed of God and in answer to her earnest prayers, the Holy Spirit had vouchsafed His teachings, without which all human instruction must ever be in vain."[31] Here is a more fitting person for the guardianship of Elsie's soul, a free, white, educated Calvinist Scotswoman (remember Finley's own religious persuasion), better than whom no other would understand the necessities of the early submission of one's will to God and the dangers implicit in not doing so.

Elsie has already demonstrated this total submission to the reader's utter conviction, long before her father comes home. Do not be misled into thinking that Mrs. Murray has been the will-breaker. No, it is the third of the trio of teachers, the Holy Ghost, God, or specifically, Jesus that has done this, and the task has been accomplished not by force but through love.

The major mistake, and cause of conflict in the book, is not only Horace's but everyone's believing that Elsie has a will, when in fact she has none. In everything and to everyone, from Arthur to her father, Elsie is totally submissive—except when their will conflicts with the will of God. Therefore Elsie will not lie or cheat to please Arthur, nor play a secular piece on the Sabbath to please her father. We say *will* not,, but the truth is, she *cannot,* for she has no will to *will* not. The suspense in the book is not, *will* Elsie play the secular piece, (or in the second book, read the secular story). No, the reader hasn't the slightest shadow of a doubt that Elsie might recant. The suspense is entirely in how much abuse the little sufferer can endure before she faints—or even dies, for her faith. For though God *cannot* lose—it is not a possibility in the Christian fable—the earthly vessel may be shattered before it goes to its eternal reward.

So the contest is not really between Elsie's will and her father's will, but between God, through the vessel of Elsie, and God's vice-regent on earth—who in nineteenth-century tradition, *should* be the very one to break Elsie's will to God. Instead Horace, himself unsaved, must needs represent Satan, since he is intent on making the child go against God's will. It is this stupendous theme that in part accounts for the fantastic power of the book.

But only in part, for there is another theme that heightens the story still further. For Elsie does not recognize the devil in Horace, but adores her papa with a passion scarce surpassed by her love of Jesus. There is a difference. Jesus can be prayed to, sung to, communed with, His sweet presence felt; but Martha Finley does not go so far as to make Him available to physical touch, not even in Elsie's frequently overactive imagination.

Not so Horace Dinsmore. Before his arrival, Elsie dreams, will he "take me on his knee and pet me?" When at long last she achieves that desired pinnacle, we have the first real mutual love scene between father and daughter:

> With a sudden impulse she threw her arms around his neck, and pressed her lips to his cheek; then dropping her head on his breast, she sobbed: "O papa! *dear* papa, I *do love* you so *very* dearly! will you not love me? O papa! love me a *little.* I know I've been naughty very often, but I will *try* to be good."
> Then for the first time he folded her in his arms and kissed her tenderly, saying, in a moved tone, "I *do* love you, my

darling, my own little daughter."

Oh! the words were sweeter to Elsie's ear than the most delicious music! Her joy was too great for words, for anything but tears.

"Why do you cry so, my darling?" he asked, soothingly, stroking her hair, and kissing her again and again.

"O papa! because I am so happy, so *very* happy!" she sobbed. "Do you indeed care so much for my love?" he asked. "Then, my daughter, you must not tremble or turn pale whenever I speak to you, as though I were a cruel tyrant."

"O papa! I cannot help it, when you look and speak so sternly. I love you so dearly I cannot bear to have you angry with me; but I'm not afraid of you now."

"That is right" he said, caressing her again. "But there is the tea bell."

Consider several other passages. In the first one, let us get Elsie off the piano stool, where we have kept her quite as cruelly as Horace Dinsmore did. She faints, of course, striking her head, and

was a pitiable sight indeed, with her fair face, her curls, and her white dress all dabbled in blood . . . It was some time ere consciousness returned and the father trembled with the agonizing fear that the gentle spirit had taken its flight. But at length the soft eyes unclosed and, gazing with a troubled look into his face, bent so anxiously over her, she asked, "Dear papa, are you angry with me?" "No, darling," he replied, in tones made tremulous with emotion, "not at all."

The doctor recommends immediate bed and Horace carries her there, "kissing her lips;" after her prayers (said at her insistence) "he again raised her in his arms, kissed her tenderly several times and then laid her carefully on the bed." There ensues a brief discussion while he tries to get her to say she loves him better than anybody else, and then "with a half sigh turned away . . . not quite willing that she should love even her Saviour better than himself."

At a later point he murmurs, "Ah! I would I could be *all—everything* to her, as she is fast becoming to me. I cannot feel satisfied, and yet I believe few daughters love their fathers as well as she loves me."

On a return from a trip, "he sprang out and caught her in his arms the instant the carriage stopped. 'My darling, darling child!' he cried, kissing her over and over again, and pressing her fondly to his heart, 'how glad I am to have you in my arms again!'" And the next day:

> "Come with me," he said, "I want you."
> "What do you want me for, papa?" she asked as he sat down and took her on his knee.
> "What for? why to keep, to love, and to look at," he said, laughing. "I have been away from my little girl so long, that now I want her close by my side, or on my knee, all the time . . ." He fondled her, and chatted with her for some time; then still keeping her on his knee, took up a book and begun to read.

And a final passage:

> Then, picking her up, he tossed her over his shoulder, and carried her upstairs, as easily as though she had been a baby, she clinging to him and laughing merrily . . . "Ah!" he said, smiling, "and which is my present? . . ."
> "There is none here for you, sir," she replied, looking up into his face with an arch smile. "I would give you the bundle you carried upstairs, just now, but I'm afraid you would say that it was not mine to give, because it belongs to you already."
> "Indeed it does, and I feel richer in that possession than all the gold of California could make me," he said, pressing her to his heart . . .
> "My own papa! I'm so glad I do belong to you . . ."

In this last exchange especially there is very little of the father-daughter relationship. The "arch smile" gives it away: it is a lover's look. Though it would shock her to the core, Martha Finley has depicted Elsie and Horace as lovers. So added to God-through-Elsie vs. Satan-through-Horace locked in eternal combat for Elsie's soul is Elsie's and Horace's erotic passion for each other; the incest that every reader, young or old, Victorian or modern, is subconsciously aware of glossed over as filial and parental affection. Not strong enough stuff, Mr. Reviewer? What could be stronger than the knotting and reknotting of these sizzling themes?

And though one can't imagine it possible, they get more potent yet in *Elsie's Holidays at Roselands*.[12] This continuation-sequel is a parallel story to *Elsie Dinsmore,* the action again Papa trying to break Elsie's will; it might be repetitious if it were not painted on a grander canvas. The decibels increase in intensity as the story is cranked up another notch, another, and yet another. The crying becomes more agonized with shrieks added to the moans, the caresses even more passionate, and the mental cruelty sufficient to cause breakdown.

Here are the parallels:

In *Elsie* she is banished to the piano stool until she will obey; in *Holidays,* she is banished from her father's presence and affections till she will obey. In *Elsie,* the time of the banishment is an afternoon and an evening, causing fainting, resulting in Horace's remorse. In *Holidays,* the time of the banishment is many months, causing illness and death, and resulting in Horace's conversion.

We will slip in here a sub-theme running through both books and contributing its power to the main stream, which you will recognize when we tell you Elsie rises from the dead. After a long decline, towards the end of which her eyes were "sunken deep in her head, and their soft light changed to a glare of insanity," and "with a wild shriek of mortal terror" at her returning papa she cried out, "Oh save me! Save me! He's coming to take me away to the Inquisition! Go away! Go away!"[13] She sinks into a coma and succumbs—but only long enough for her stricken father to be told the news, and then is revived by the doctor, but not soon enough to save papa from salvation. For in his feverish working over her, the doctor forgets to let Horace know that a miracle has happened. This gives Horace time, in his several hours bereavement, to read Elsie's farewell letter to him, to caress her lock of hair, to read her tattered and tear-stained Bible, "to long with an *unutterable* longing for one caress, one word of love from those sweet lips that should never speak again," and to submit his groaning spirit to God. Thus Elsie is a Christ figure, or at least an imitation-of-Christ, for in the first book we catch echoes, both with her meek and humble spirit, and at the child-in-the-temple scene when she sits on her father's knee at a party, talking learned theology with his friends, to their wonderment; while in the second book she is so persecuted that she goes through Gethsemane (called just that), dies, is revived, but by her death and resurrection saves her father—and in later books, multitudes of others—to Eternity.

In *Holidays,* the incest theme is also greatly heightened, with heavy caressing through the start of the book, until Elsie's refusal to read papa a novel on the Sabbath. Then begin Horace's sadistic steps in breaking Elsie's will:

"Elsie, I expect from my daughter entire, unquestioning obedience, and until you are ready to render it, I shall cease to treat you as my child. I shall banish you from my presence, and my affections. This is the alternative I set before you. I will give you ten minutes to consider it. At the end of that time, if you are ready to obey me, well and good—if not, you will leave this room, not to enter it again until you are ready to acknowledge your fault, ask forgiveness, and promise implicit obedience in the future."

The "presence" prohibition starts out to mean in his apartment, with him ignoring her when he sees her about the rest of the house; but it becomes total later when he leaves the plantation to travel in the North. Meanwhile, he has bought a nearby estate and equipped it with everything for a honeymoon cottage: if such can be called a manor house with housekeeper, slaves, and apartment suites within it, with adjoining bedrooms for Elsie and himself. At Horace's command Elsie is led through The Oaks, a letter from him having told her of the pleasant home they would have together, her suite of rooms close to his own apartment, and the peaceful, happy life that they would lead . . . on condition of entire, unconditional submission on her part.

When Elsie recovers her reason after her descent into death and finally remembers the sad events that led her to madness, she bursts into tears and asks if once she is well, must she then go away. But Horace kneels, and with her pale head on his breast (in tones tremulous with emotion) says, "The Lord do so to me, and more also, if aught but death part me and thee."

He talks to her of "when we get into our own home," and when she is strong enough to be moved, takes her on a mystery ride ("he was unusually eager to get her into the carriage") ending at the new plantation, where, "giving her a rapturous kiss," he exclaims, "welcome home, my darling! Welcome to your father's house," and lifting her into his arms he carries her over the threshold.

Elsie looks forward to many pleasures. "It will be delightful to dine together in our own house. May I always dine with you?" "I hope so," he said smiling. "I am not fond of eating alone." After the meal Elsie, still in a weakened condition from her illness, reclines on her little bed in the arms of her father, he leading the discussion on obedience to an earthly father when it is not in conflict with God's will. Elsie whispers, "I will, papa," and hugs him "tighter and tighter." And then,

They were quiet again for a little while. She was running her fingers through his hair . . . Taking her in his arms, /he/ held her close to his heart. It was beating very fast . . . He pressed her closer and closer, caressing her silently with a heart too full for words . . . They sat thus for some time . . .

Shall we here rest the case? "Arch smile," in Book One, a lover's look. "Running fingers through his hair" while locked in long embrace, a lover's motion. Martha Finley may not have known what she was writing,[14] but she has written it, and the authors surmise that while she penned these lines, her own heart was feeling vicarious rapture.

Let us return to a lower key for a moment, to examine this admittedly bad writer's artistry with words; how she orchestrates the tears of Elsie's agonies against the fondlings that bespeak her fulfillment. Elsie cries, sobs, chokes, wails and weeps her way through over seven hundred fifty pages of the combined books. The authors[15] have made a count of these tears, the methodology being to count every tear reference, including compound references, as one if contained in a separate sentence or, if sufficiently separated in a single sentence to merit being considered as fresh tears. Thus, "The little Elsie fell upon her knees, weeping and sobbing" is counted as one reference, while "her happiness was too deep for words—for anything but tears; and putting her little arms around his neck she sobbed her joy and gratitude upon his heart" for two. We had an additional problem with the tear-count not found in the caress-count (which parallel study we will describe below) in that Elsie's tears, as above indicated, are sometimes tears of joy, occasionally tears of compassion, or even a complex of emotion, as when she weeps with the realization that Jesus suffered on the cross for *her*. Because close analysis revealed much tear-ambiguity, we decided to classify all tears together. Thus the tear-count in Chapter I of *Elsie Dinsmore* came out to be 11; Chapter II, 14; Chapter III, 15; Chapter IV, 30; Chapter V, 4 (but a very short chapter); Chapter VI, 18; Chapter VII, 19; Chapter VIII, 4; Chapter IX, 14; Chapter X, 7 (but she is unconscious for a large section of this chapter); Chapter XI, 4½ (we included a mournful gaze); Chapter XII, 15—but you may refer for the rest of the figures to the appendices to this paper.

Nor did we stop with the simple count; we also surveyed the

varieties of ways in which Elsie cried, for this much crying might become tedious to the reader under a less skillful pen. While sobs (243) and tears (347) were the most recurring words, we found different ways Finley shows Elsie's nuances of emotion while in the throes of weeping. A dozen or so examples will suffice:

— Soft eyes filled with tears of wounded feeling
— There to weep, mourn and pray
— Pouring out sobs and prayers
— Ah! Many a silent tear
— Pale and tearful
— Crying and sobbing violently
— Struggles to surpress her sobs
— Tears again fell like rain
— Bursting into tears and sobbing violently
— Hastily brushing away a tear that would come into her eye
— Hard struggle to keep down a rising sob
— Wept, sobbed, and wrung her hands in such grief and terror
— The paper was blistered with Elsie's tears
— A low cry of utter despair broke from Elsie's lips
— Sobbed convulsively

In addition, we made a sub-count to this study of the amount that Elsie trembles, when not connected with tears, and of the phrase, "she said in a low, tremulous voice." This combined count equals 61. Breakdown figures for the entire tear-count and sub-groupings, as well as the caress-count, may be found in the appendices.

The caress-count presented other difficulties other than those posed in the tear-count. While again, we counted as only one caress a reference in one sentence no matter how many fondlings, caressings, or kissings were found therein (i.e. "kissing her again and again and hugging her in his arms" would have a score of one in the caress-count, since we found it impossible to determine *how many* kisses or hugs), we were in this phase of the study confronted with *imagined, desired,* or *dreamed of* caresses, as well as *actual* caresses bestowed upon a *rival* (Horace's small sister Enna) while the stricken Elsie looks on. You will note that on our caress-graph, Appendix C, these are called rival-caresses, or "r" while the other three categories are grouped as unfulfilled caresses, designated by the small "i." Thus in Chapter I we have no real caresses but 3 imagined ones; in Chapter II, 4 imagined; Chapter III, 6 imagined and desired, 1 actual (though cold); Chapter IV, 12 desired, 4 rival caresses; and in the breakthrough chapter, Chapter X, 27 actual caresses.

Again let us pause to examine the versatility of Ms. Finley in expressing this sheer volume of caressing:

— Pressing his hand to her lips
— Passed hand caressingly
— Passed arm affectionately
— Kissed her cheek
— Pressed his lips to her brow
— Held up her face for another, and he kissed her lips
— Lucy got such a caress from her father as Elsie dreamed in vain for
— Longed to sit on his knee
— Dwelt with lingering delight on everything approaching to a caress
— Lingered in vain hope of obtaining a smile or caress
— Folded her in his arms and kissed her tenderly
— There on his knee caressing her more tenderly than ever before
— Filled with expressions of the tenderest affection
— He only answered with a kiss
— Caught her in his arms
— Took on knee
— Fondled

You will see, in Appendix D, that when our two graphs are superimposed, the tear-count (in blue) is extremely high when the caresscount (in red) is either absent or imaginary (shown by dotted line) or falls below four-to-a-chapter, while conversely, the tear-count drops as the reality-caress-count mounts. The tear-count is always present, however, even in chapters given to excessive realitycaressing; this is explained, the reader will recall, by Elsie's proclivity to cry the harder and more extreme her happiness.

The reader will readily grasp the importance of this study to the meaning of the entire paper.

What of the remaining twenty-six volumes of the *Elsie* series? After papa's conversion and the consummation of the union, so to speak, at The Oaks, the interest lags. Indeed *Holidays* does not conclude with Papa and Elsie in each other's arms, all differences resolved, but with an interminable honeymoon trip to Revolutionary War sites while Horace plays Uncle George to Elsie's Rollo.

Book II, *Elsie's Girlhood,* holds up well with a perennial but plow-horse theme: Papa's courtship and marriage to Elsie's dear old friend, Miss Rose, and Papa's scotching of two romances of Elsie's, the first with Herbert, a cripple first met in Book I (and on that account) and the second with Tom Jackson, a charming ne'er-do-well. The book ends with Papa bestowing her hand upon Mr. Travilla, his bachelor best friend who has waited patiently for Elsie since she was eight. This is something more than an echo of the incest theme, for all readers well know that Mr. Travilla is but a father surrogate.

In *Elsie's Womanhood* Elsie marries, and the high point of this volume is Papa's rage when she returns from her honeymoon calling Mr. Travilla, in his only insistence of obedience, "Edward."

The happy couple, incidentally, spend the entire Civil War abroad, thus freeing Martha Finley from any concern with social issues. They both wish the Union well, but being Southern their sympathies are naturally with the South. They mouth routine platitudes about Lincoln, and Roselands, Ion (Mr. Travilla's estate) and The Oaks are gracious about freeing their slaves, allowing them all to stay on at the old plantations if they wish to—and of course all do.

Mr. Travilla remains long enough in *Elsie's Motherhood* and *Elsie's Children* to provide Elsie with seven children. One is not quite sure how, since Elsie behaves "shyly"[16] with her husband, and her courtship, at any rate, "was disturbed by no feverish heat of passion."[17] He then conveniently dies in *Elsie's Widowhood,* allowing her to return to her true love, Horace Dinsmore. The remaining books dwindle to lengthy visits back and forth from estate to estate, with much sermonizing from the aging Elsie, and a grandchild brought in for young interest in *The Two Elsies.*

These themes range from bonfires to match flares compared to the volcanos Martha Finley uncapped in her first two volumes.

The whole strength of the Christian story, the world's best seller, is implicit in one theme of *Elsie* and *Elsie's Holidays,* and tied to this is an Oedipal love affair with the devil. It is our conviction that it is the intersection of these two themes, producing an idealistically Christian, sadomasochistic, incestuous-erotic work for children which, in spite of its being a thoroughly bad book, gives *Elsie Dinsmore* its compelling and abiding power, which elevates it to the supreme height of a great bad classic.

NOTES

1. How high the pedestal once was is indicated by the critics: "The series was admired and condemned, revered and ridiculed, recommended and rejected by the most eminent authorities and, more important, read by millions. With the exception of Mark Twain's Huckleberry Finn, Elsie Dinsmore is probably the best known character ever to appear in American fiction," Helen Papashzily, *All The Happy Endings,* (New York: Harper, 1956), p. 170; "Many years ago there was born in a remote corner of our land a little girl-child endowed by the angels and Martha Finley with every qualification for a perfect heroine of fiction . . . She was entered according to Act of Congress in the year 1868, but in 1927 she is still to be found in flourishing state and new bindings, while she will never cease to haunt the minds of millions of women. The name of the child was Elsie Dinsmore," Ruth Suckow, "Elsie Dinsmore: A Study in Perfection," *The Bookman,* October 27, 1927, p. 126; ". . . forty years after their inception, they [the *Elsie* books] . . . still have outsold any other juveniles except Louisa May Alcott's," anonymous biographer, *American Authors 1600-1900,* ed. Stanley Kunitz and Howard Haycraft, (New York: Wilson, 1938), p. 273; "Elsie is, without question, the most popular female character ever to have appeared in American juvenile literature," Janet E. Brown, *The Saga of Elsie Dinsmore, The University of Buffalo Studies, Monographs in English, No. 4,* Vol. 7, No. 3, July 1945, p. 75.

2. Both authors, however, firmly believe that Black Beauty is in reality a mare, and that the author was confused in her genders. Interpret, if you will, that equine coming-of-age, the breaking of Black Beauty to the bit: ". . . now I was to have a bit and bridle; my master gave me some oats as usual, and after a good deal of coaxing he got the bit into my mouth, and the bridle fixed, but it was a nasty thing! Those who have never had a bit in their mouths cannot think how bad it feels; a great piece of cold hard steel as thick as man's finger to be pushed into one's mouth, between one's teeth, and over one's tongue, with the ends coming out at the corner of your mouth, and held fast there by straps over your head, under your throat, round your nose, and under your chin; so that no way in the world can you get rid of the nasty thing; it is very bad! yes, very bad! at least I thought so; but I knew my mother always wore one when she went out, and all horses did when they were grown up; and so, what with the nice oats, and what with my master's pats, kinds words, and gentle ways, I got to wear my bit and bridle," Anna Sewell, *Black Beauty,* (New York: Grossett and Dunlap, 1949), p. 15.

3. Such as the unidentified biographer in the *American Writers 1600-1900,* op.cit. p. 272, "It is difficult to understand how even Victorian children could be persuaded to swallow this 'compound of sentimentality and masochism' and clamor for more, up to twenty-eight volumes. Obedience, piety, and smugness are the keynotes of the whole twenty-eight, and *Elsie* eternally 'bursting into tears,' would seem to a present-day child what she *is,* a nauseous little prig; her dear papa a tyrant of the type of Mrs. Browning's father, with trimmings that make him the silliest sort of caricature of the stock 'Southern gentleman'; while Mr. Travilla, who plays 'stooge' to Mr. Dinsmore in the earlier volumes and obligingly marries Elsie . . . is a mere

cardboard shadow of a man. A breath of fresh air would have blown the whole lot down," or Leslie McFarlane in *The Ghost of the Hardy Boys,* (London: Methuen/Two Continents, 1956), p. 160, ". . . in the Himalayas of junk turned out by writers of juvenile fiction the Elsie Books stand like Everest as the worst ever written by anybody, and that Elsie Dinsmore is without peer the Most Nauseating Heroine of all time,"·or Janet E. Brown in *The Saga of Elsie Dinsmore,* op.cit., pp. 76-77, "Miss Finley did not ever come under the influence of a serious British novelist, nor did she, strangely, imbibe any small hints on how to write good prose from her intimate acquaintance with the grand style of the King James Bible. She was not, unlike Miss Alcott, burdened with any sense of social responsibility towards her fellow men. In an age filled with voices crying unheeded in one wilderness or another, she was deaf to them all, and wrote about Revolutionary atrocities or outrages of naval impressments, long past. Her craftsmanship was elementary, even of its kind; her stories are made up of descriptive generalities, and conversation of the he-said and then-she-said variety. There is never any attempt to build up a background, to analyse emotions or motives, or to justify the behavior of one individual in his relation to another. Miss Finley goes from fact to fact, and leaves the reader to wonder if she—or her characters—ever gave any consideration to the possible value of thoughtful reflection. She was not learned; she had never 'with grave studies vexed a sprightly brain.' In fact, she abstained completely from ambitious scholarship."

4. We thank Professor Douglas Kindschi, cliomatrician at Sangamon State University, for producing the three random digits that resulted in our selection.

5. Martha Finley, *Elsie Dinsmore,* (New York: Dodd, Mead, 1868), pp. 184-185.

6. And has been read by some commentators as sexist as well. The co-authors feel this latter accusation to be unjustified, since Elsie is the strongest heroine we know, and totally successful in all her earthly and heavenly endeavors.

7. *American Authors 1600-1900,* op.cit., p. 272.

8. Ibid., p. 273.

9. Such as the two-hundred volumes of Jacob Abbott, forgotten by all but one co-author who wrote his dissertation on this first American mass-producer of juvenile literature, and by his students who must read a *Rollo* book as a requirement of History of Children's Literature 485.

10. These two books comprise one artistic unit in our eyes as indeed in the eyes of the author, who makes no more than a chapter break between the last paragraph of *Elsie Dinsmore* and the first paragraph of *Elsie's Holidays at Roselands,* (New York: Dodd, Mead, 1868).

11. Although Finley never has Chloe refer to herself as a child, on several occasions an adult houseboy, Pompey, does so: "Dis am *drefful* poor fare, Miss Elsie, . . . but if you say so, dis chile tell ole Phoebe to send up somethin' better 'fore Massa Horace gits through his dinner," p. 224.

12. Dodd, Mead, 1868.

13. In Elsie's insanity is her only recognition of Horace as the devil. Even then she does not utter the name, but to Elsie, the Pope was the anti-Christ, the Roman Church the epitome of evil, and anyone coming to take her to the Inquisition must needs be, if not the devil, then a soul in Satan's employ.

Elsie's sturdy sanity withstood all of Horace's calculated mental cruelty, including his threat to send her away to school, *until* he wrote that he was sending her to a convent school, and this put her over the edge. ". . . they will try to make me go to mass, and pray to the Virgin, and bow to the crucifixes; and when I refuse, they will put me in a dungeon and torture me . . . They will hide me from papa when he comes, and tell him that I want to take the veil, and refuse to see him; or else they will say that I am dead and buried. Oh, Aunt Adelaide, beg him not to put me there! I shall go crazy! I feel as if I were going crazy now!" *Holidays,* pp. 196-197.

14. Although perchance she does suspect, and attempts denial: In *Elsie's Womanhood,* (New York: Dodd, Mead and Company, 1875), Elsie and Mr. Travilla spend much time on their honeymoon discussing Elsie's favorite subject, Horace Dinsmore, and Elsie says, "I doubt if even you, my friend, have ever known all that papa has been and is to me: father, mother, everything—but husband," she added with a blush and smile, as her eyes met the kindly, tender look in his," pp. 138-139.

15. Our thanks to Professor Norman Hinton, medievalist at Sangamon State University, for his help with the computer skills needed for this section of our study.

16. *Elsie's Womanhood,* p. 137.

17. ibid.

PERRAULT'S "LITTLE RED RIDING HOOD": VICTIM OF THE REVISERS

Carole and D. T. Hanks Jr.

Until very recently American children have been carefully sheltered from "the facts of life," specifically from the facts of sexuality and death. Perhaps an unrecognized benefit of television programming has been to show that these facts are so all-engrossing to adults that there is no way to hide them from children. Of course we never successfully hid them anyway — we merely enmeshed our children in the conspiracy not to talk about them.

Children's literature is emerging from this conspiracy, reflecting our adult awareness that children are not only capable of coping with sexuality and death, but that they must cope with them if they are to mature. Modern children's books such as Judy Blume's *Then Again, Maybe I Won't* or Virginia Lee's *Magic Moth* reflect this new awareness of our children's capabilities and needs in these two areas.

This new awareness has not yet illuminated the American editions of a children's classic, "Little Red Riding Hood." Charles Perrault's *"Le petit chaperon rouge"* is centered on an erotic metaphor and ends tragically; yet neither of these elements of the tale figure in modern translations of the story.

Perrault's tale provides a classic example of the bowdlerizing which all too often afflicts children's literature. Derived from the German version, *"Rotkäppchen,"* (Grimm No. 26), American versions of the tale have been sanitized to the point where the erotic element disappears and the tragic ending becomes comic. This approach emasculates a powerful story, one which unrevised is a metaphor for the maturing process. It will be suggested, mostly between the lines, that much of the considerable literary value of the tale disappears in the revisions.

"Le petit chaperon rouge" is a brief tale composed of sixty-one lines of prose and a fifteen-line rhymed *"Moralité."*[1] The "moral" warns children, especially attractive young girls, against listening to all men *("toutes sortes de gens")*. Some of them, seemingly gentle, are actually wolves.

"Le petit chaperon rouge" has been so popular since Perrault

wrote it, that some folklorists have felt it must be part of the European oral tradition. Most students of the fairy tale, however, and some of the most eminent scholars of folklore, suggest that the tale originated with Perrault.[2] Be that as it may, Perrault's tale is classic in its simplicity and finality.

LITTLE RED RIDING HOOD

A Story

Once there was a little village girl, the prettiest that was ever seen. Her mother doted on her, and her grandmother doted still more. Indeed, this good woman made for her a little red hood which became her so well that everyone called her "Little Red Riding Hood."

One day her mother, having baked some shortcakes, said to Little Red Riding Hood, "Go see how your grandmother is feeling; someone told me that she was ill. Take her a shortcake and this little pot of butter." Little Red Riding Hood left immediately for the house of her grandmother, who lived in another village.

Entering into a wood, she met Sly Wolf, who very much wished to eat her but did not dare for fear of some woodcutters who were in the forest. He asked her where she was going; the poor child, who had not yet learned that it is dangerous to stop to listen to a wolf, said to him, "I am going to see my grandmother and take her a short-cake, along with a little pot of butter that my mother is sending her."

"Does she live very far away?" the wolf asked her.

"Oh, yes!" said Little Red Riding Hood. "It's by the mill which you see right over there; over there, it's the first house in the village."

"Well now," said the wolf to her, "I want to go there and see her too. I will go by this road here, and you by that road there; we will see who will be there sooner."

The wolf began to run with all his strength along the shorter road, and the little girl walked on by the longer one, amusing herself by picking hazelnuts, running after butterflies, and making bouquets of the little flowers that she came across.

It was not long before the wolf arrived at the home of the grandmother. He knocked at her door, "toc, toc."

"Who's there?"

"It's your granddaughter, Little Red Riding Hood," said the wolf, disguising his voice. "I'm bringing you a shortcake along with a little pot of butter that my mother is sending you."

The good grandmother, who was in her bed because she felt slightly ill, called out, "Pull back the bolt, the latch will open."

The wolf pulled the bolt and the door opened; he threw himself upon the good woman immediately and consumed her in less than no time, for it had been three days since he had eaten.

Then he closed the door and lay down in the grandmother's bed to wait for Little Red Riding Hood. A moment later she came knocking at the door: "toc, toc."

"WHO'S THERE?"

Little Red Riding Hood, hearing the wolf's deep voice, was afraid at first. But, thinking that her grandmother must have a sore throat, she replied, "It's your granddaughter, Little Red Riding Hood; I'm bringing you a shortcake along with a little pot of butter that my mother is sending you."

The wolf called out, softening his voice a little, "Pull back the bolt, the latch will open."

Little Red Riding Hood pulled back the bolt and the door of the house opened. The wolf, seeing her enter, said from within the bed where he was concealing himself under the covers, "Put the shortcake and the little pot of butter on the cupboard and come to bed with me."

Little Red Riding Hood took off her clothes and went to get into the bed, where she was greatly astonished to see how her grandmother looked in her night clothes. She said, "Grandmother, what big arms you have!"

"The better to embrace you, my child," the wolf replied.

"Grandmother, what big legs you have!"

"The better to run, my child."

"Grandmother, what big ears you have!"

"The better to hear, my child."

"Grandmother, what big eyes you have!"

"The better to see, my child."

"Grandmother, what big teeth you have!"

"TO EAT YOU!" And saying these words, that wicked wolf threw himself on Little Red Riding Hood and ate her.

Moral

One sees here that young children,
And especially young girls

Who are pretty, well-formed, and pleasing,
Are wrong to listen to all sorts of men,
And that it is not a strange thing
That there are so many of them whom the wolf eats.
I say *the* wolf, because all wolves
Are not of the same kind;
Some of them have a pleasing air,
Not noisy, not sarcastic, not wrathful,
Are self-effacing, obliging, and pleasant,
Following the young ladies
Into dwellings as well as in the streets.
But alas! for her who does not know that these pleasant wolves
Are of all wolves the most dangerous.

The End

(Note: Perrault cast his "moralité" into verse; we have not attempted to versify him in English. The text for the translation is *"Le petit chaperon rouge,"* contained in Jacques Barchilon's reproduction of "The 1695 Manuscript" with his addition of the 1697 revisions, in *Perrault's Tales of Mother Goose,* I [New York: Pierpont Morgan Library, 1956], 131-34.)

The tale's brevity makes it clear that Perrault is here unconcerned with character development or an elaborate plot (*cf.* the thirteen pages — 289 lines — of *"La belle au bois dormant,"* pp. 117-29 in Barchilon). He establishes his protagonist in two sentences: she is a young village girl, the prettiest ever; her mother and grandmother dote on her; she wears a red cap, or hood, which the loving grandmother has made for her.[3] After this point we learn only three more elements of the little girl's character: she is to make an independent journey away from her mother; she has not learned that it is dangerous to listen or talk to a wolf; and she enjoys hazelnuts, butterflies, and flowers. With these carefully-selected details Perrault sketches the prototypical innocent little girl leaving the home. She is both beautiful and beloved, and customarily inhabits a secure and exclusively female world; she does not fear the Outsider, and she is identified with the natural beauties of nuts, flowers, and butterflies.

Perrault employs his other human characters simply as devices.

They establish Little Red Riding Hood's lovable quality and provide
the motivation for her journey. They are not otherwise important
in the story, except of course as a grandmotherly *hors d'oeuvre.*

The wolf is the other major character. He is personified menace,
and Perrault selects only the details necessary to establish his
role in Little Red Riding Hood's world. His simply being a wolf
is probably sufficient to support his menace, since wolves are
widely slandered in European (and American) tradition. Perrault
also introduces him as *"compere le Loup"* (Wolf, the deceiver) in
his initial meeting with Little Red Riding Hood, and adds immediately that he "very much wished to eat" the little girl. The wolf is
firmly established as the villain and as the only male in the story;[4]
the working-out of the plot is inevitable.

Inevitable and classic. Given an innocent who has not learned to
fear wolves, her initial deception is a matter of course, as is her final
destruction. All that is necessary is for the two central characters to
meet again, in surroundings where the wolf need not fear the intervention of woodcutters. Perrault brings the two together in just
such circumstances in the grandmother's home. He then underscores the destructively treacherous nature of the wolf by having
him engage in a metaphorical seduction: he tells Little Red Riding
Hood to join him in bed and she does so, first disrobing. The stage
is set and the major action of the tragedy is set in motion. Perrault
brings about the dénoument, and reinforces the essential natures of
wolf and little girl in his closing dialogue. This famous antiphon
indicates the little girl's innocent wonder at her "grandmother's"
size and, at the same time, re-establishes the wolfishness which that
size actually manifests. All that is then required, or artistically
appropriate, is to end dialogue and tale with:

> *"Ma mere grand, que vous avez de grandes dents!"*
> *"C'est pour te manger!" Et en disant ces mots, ce méchant*
> *Loup se jetta sur le petit chaperon rouge, & la mangea.*[5]

The tale's central metaphor and theme seem fairly clear. Perrault
saw fit to underline them, nonetheless, in his closing *"Moralité"*:
pretty young girls should not listen to "all sorts of men," he warns,
lest they be devoured by *"le Loup."* Obviously, Perrault uses "the
Wolf" as a metaphor, if not for *"toutes sortes de gens"* at any rate
for those whom he characterizes as quiet, self-effacing, anxious to
please, and *"les plus dangereux."*

This is not to say, however, that the tale is simply a metaphorical seduction — even though the wolf does indeed lure Little Red Riding Hood out of her clothes and into bed. Perrault wrought better than that, perhaps better than he knew. "Little Red Riding Hood" is the tale of the innocent who leaves home, meets the betrayer, doffs her family gift of warmth and protection (the *"chaperon"*), and is destroyed.[6] It is in a way the ultimate tragedy, if that is not too grandiose a term for a three-page fairy tale; youth and innocence leave home only to be destroyed guiltless. Something similar happened to Job's children.

Indeed, the basic theme of the tale is akin to that of *Job;* innocence, beauty, and goodness are destroyed by their opposites. In "Little Red Riding Hood" this theme is embodied in the tale of the child who leaves parent and home in order to engage in an independent action. The child commits no wrong, but the world of the forest deceives and destroys her. It is probably unnecessary to point out that such occurrences are facts of life. The continued popularity of Perrault's tale in France testifies to children's willing reception of the grim finality of the tale.

That grim finality is almost entirely missing from American versions of the tale. Most of them — even those which attribute the story to Perrault — delete the erotic element, provide a "moral" absent from Perrault's story, and deliver Little Red Riding Hood and her grandmother unharmed from the depths of the wolf. In short, most American retellings of the tale transmute it to the version which the brothers Grimm published as Number 26 in their *Märchen: "Rotkäppchen."*[7]

"Rotkäppchen," ironically, appears to be derived from Perrault's tale rather than from the "oral tradition," as the Grimms believed.[8] The tale suffered major revisions as it crossed the border; since the same revisions appear in most American versions, the important ones are presented here in some detail:

1. The mother's directions to *Rotkäppchen* in the Grimm story are quite detailed, and moreover provide the inception of the moral of the story: *"so geh hübsch sittsam und lauf nicht vom Wege ab"* ("walk along nicely and don't leave the path." *Kinder- und Hausmärchen*, p. 383).

2. There are no woodcutters nearby when the wolf meets *Rotkäppchen*, but he spares her in order to later consume both the child and the grandmother. He tells himself, *"Du musst es*

listig anfangen, damit du beide erschnappst" ("You must manage this slyly, so that you can snap them both up" — p. 384).

3. The wolf tempts *Rotkäppchen* to delay in order to pick flowers and listen to the birds. She leaves the path in order to do so.

4. The erotic element vanishes; the wolf conceals himself in the bed, but *Rotkäppchen* begins her series of "Grandmother what big . . ." exclamations from alongside it, and the wolf leaps out of it to devour her.

5. The tale ends as comedy rather than tragedy. When the wolf has consumed both the grandmother and *Rotkäppchen,* he returns to the bed, sleeps, and snores. A passing huntsman investigates the loud snoring and surgically rescues the women from the wolf's belly as the wolf sleeps on. They fill the resulting cavity with stones, the weight of which kills the wolf when he awakens and tries to spring up. Everyone is happy; the huntsman takes the wolf's pelt, the grandmother takes the cake and wine, and *Rotkäppchen* takes the moral, as she tells herself, *"Du willst dein Lebtag nicht wieder allein vom Wege ab in den Wald laufen, wenn dir's die Mutter verboten hat"* ("Never again in your life will you have a mind to leave the path to go off alone into the forest, when your mother has forbidden it to you" — p. 386).

These revisions "clean up" and reverse the theme of Perrault's tale. In the Grimm tale, the point is that someone will always take care of the child — even if she steps off the path. There will always be someone there, and youth and innocence — having learnt its lesson — will be rescued unchanged, resolved henceforth to mind Mother. The revised tale denies that the child can leave home and find destruction — instead, its point is "Mind your mother."

Perrault's tale, on the other hand, points out that leaving home, becoming independent of the parent, is a risky undertaking. It may result in disaster, not through the child's fault but because that's the way the world is. Its point is, "The wolf awaits."[9]

"The wolf awaits" is not a popular moral among American translators and publishers of *"Le petit . . ."* The overwhelming majority of American editions of "Little Red Riding Hood" in our local library, in the University of Minnesota education library, and in the Kerlan collection of children's books at the University of Minnesota, repress the central erotic metaphor and replace the tragic ending with the Grimm's happy ending. This occurs even when the tale is attributed to Perrault. (See Appendix)

In short, the American publishers of "Little Red Riding Hood" have protected their audience — our children — from the sexuality and violent death which Perrault built into his tale. They have revised away sex and death from a story which is a metaphoric rendering of the maturation process; they have denied the maturing process. Their heroine is rescued by an obvious father figure, and she resolves never again to "step off the path" to disobey the mother. Her independent action is portrayed as an aberration which automatically receives punishment. Independence is bad. Dependence is good. Remain a child.

Perrault's tale does not urge the child to remain immature, nor does it urge the opposite. His tale takes it for granted that a child will mature, that it will leave the home and the parent to engage in an independent task. But Perrault's tale points out that maturing is risky; there *are* dangers in the forest — if the maturing person makes a misstep (not necessarily through any personal fault), then he or she may perish. It's unjust, of course — as Job pointed out long ago, yet it is a fact. It is an important fact for those who plan to grow up; we do our children a disservice by protecting them from it. We also provide them with an inferior literary experience. The shocking ending, the injustice of Perrault's tale hits home; it prompts us to think further about the story we have just read. The Grimm tale, on the other hand, has no such impact. We can relax as we finish it; disaster has been averted, huntsmen will always providentially pass by, and Little Red Riding Hood will not step off the path again.

APPENDIX

"Little Red Riding Hood"
American Editions

In preparing the following table, we exhausted the resources of the Kerlan Collection at the University of Minnesota, of the children's literature collection of the University of Minnesota, and of the children's literature collection of the St. Paul, MN, public library.

The story has fared much better in England. The first known English translation was penned by one Robert Samber in 1729 (not by "G.M.," as was once thought; see Iona and Peter Opie, *The Oxford Dictionary of Nursery Rhymes* [Oxford: Clarendon Press, 1951], pp. 39-40, n. 1). It lumbers and makes rather free with Perrault in places, but is by and large a faithful translation. Now that it has been enshrined in the Opies' authoritative *Classic Fairy Tales* (London, New York, and Toronto: Oxford Univ. Press, 1974), it bids fair to continue for some time as the reigning British translation.

I. *Literal translations:*

(Translator not named). *Perrault's Classic French Fairy Tales.* New York:
  Meredith, 1967.
Walsh, Charles, trans. "Little Red Riding Hood." *One Hundred Favorite Folktales.*
  Ed. Stith Thompson. Bloomington and London: Indiana Univ. Press, 1968.
  Pages 76-8.

II. *Verse translation:*

Hogrogian, Nonny. *The Renowned History of Little Red Riding Hood.* New
  York: Crowell, 1967.
     An anonymous nineteenth-century version in jingly couplets, illustrated
  by Hogrogian.

III. *Grimm version attributed to Perrault:*

Goulden, Shirley, trans. *Sleeping Beauty and Other Tales.* New York: Grosset and
  Dunlap, n.d.
Haviland, Virginia, trans. *Fairy Tale Treasury.* New York: Coward, McCann, and
  Geoghegan, 1972.
Ponsot, Marie, trans. *The Fairy Tale Book.* New York: Simon and Schuster, 1958.
  (Deluxe Golden Book).
Stone, David, trans. *Famous French Fairy Tales: Collected and Adapted from the
  Original Perrault.* New York: Watts; London: Mayflower, 1959.

IV. *Translations which suppress erotic element:*

Johnson, A. E., trans. *Perrault's Complete Fairy Tales.* New York: Dodd,
  Mead, 1961.
Lines, Kathleen, ed. *The Little Red Riding Hood.* New York: Walck, 1972.
Untermeyer, Louis, trans. *French Fairy Tales by Charles Perrault.* New York:
  Didier, 1945.
N. B. The Grimm versions of the tale — which are legion — have been here
  ignored. (e.g., Elisabeth Orton Jones's twenty-nine-cent Golden Book, *Little
  Red Riding Hood* [New York: Golden Press, 1948; rpt. 1968]), also the *Little
  Red Riding Hood* "adapted by Andrew Lang" (New York: Golden Press,
  1967), which is actually "Little Golden Hood" from Lang's *Red Fairy Book.*

NOTES

1. The French text of *"Le petit chaperon rouge"* appears in Jacques Barchilon's
   reproduction of "The 1695 Manuscript [of Perrault's *Contes*]" with the 1697
   revisions; it appears in Perrault's *Tales of Mother Goose,* I (New York:
   Pierpont Morgan Library, 1956), 131-34.
2. Paul Delarue notes in his *Borzoi Book of French Folk Tales,* trans. E. Fife
   (New York: Knopf, 1956), that *"Rotkäppchen"* was derived from Perrault's
   "Le petit . . ." and recounted to Grimm by "a storyteller of French descent"
   (p. 381). He adds that a tale he reproduces, "The Story of Grandmother"
   (pp. 230-3), is the ancestor of Perrault's version of the tale and thus of the
   Grimm story. He states that this putative ancestor was collected *ca.* 1885; he

does not explain why he feels a tale collected in the late nineteenth century is the ancestor of a tale written in the late seventeenth century. Lee Burns, in her "Red Riding Hood" in *Children's Literature*, I (1972), 31, accepts Delarue's assertion without question.

An imposing array of authorities questions the idea that Perrault was indebted to any source other than his own imagination for *"Le petit . . ."* Thus Maria Leach's *Dictionary of Folklore, Mythology, and Legend* (New York: Funk and Wagnalls, 1949) states that "The story is not popular (directly from oral tradition) but seems literary . . ." (p. 636). Geoffrey Brereton, translator of the Penguin classic edition of Perrault's *Fairy Tales* (Harmondsworth, Eng.: Penguin, 1957) reports that Perrault's is the "first known version" of the tale (p. xxiv). Jacques Barchilon and Henry Pettit go so far as to suggest in *The Authentic Mother Goose Fairy Tales and Nursery Rhymes* (Denver: Alan Swallow, 1960) that Perrault "may well be the tale's inventor" (p. 13); Stith Thompson seems to follow suit in *One Hundred Favorite Folktales* (Bloomington and London: Indiana Univ. Press, 1968), where he writes that "Little Red Riding Hood" is "Literary" rather than part of the oral tradition (he attributes it to Perrault; see his "Notes and Sources" to the tale, which appear on pp. 76-8). Iona and Peter Opie, in *The Classic Fairy Tales* (London, New York, and Toronto: Oxford Univ. Press, 1974), content themselves with the statement that "No version of the story has been found prior to Perrault's manuscript of 1695, and its subsequent publication in *Histoires ou Contes du temps passé,* 1697" (p. 93).

3. Perrault's *"chaperon"* was the cap-like headdress into which the hood of the Middle Ages evolved. It was never a "riding hood" for Perrault, but that translation of the term is now fixed beyond changing.

4. The woodcutters are of course male, but they cannot be said to be "present" in any meaningful sense.

5. Barchilon, p. 133. Punctuation and paragraphing are modernized; the last sentence is Perrault's 1967 revision of the 1695 MS.

6. Lee Burns suggests that the betrayal here is of a child's "deepest desire and trust" since it involves Little Red Riding Hood's intimacy with a (grand)parental body, an intimacy which embodies "a tactile desire . . . far deeper than the desire for heterosexual intercourse" [see "Red Riding Hood," *Children's Literature,* I (1972) p. 31].

7. Jakob and Wilhelm Grimm, *Kinder- und Hausmärchen* (Berlin and Vienna: Harz, n.d.), pp. 383-7.

8. See note 2. See also Harry de V. Velten's "The Influence of Charles Perrault's *'Contes de ma Mère L'Oie'* on German Folklore," *Germanic Review,* 5 (January 1930), 14-16, 18.

9. This interpretation of the story is partly inspired by Bruno Bettelheim's fascinating *The Uses of Enchantment* (New York: Knopf, 1976). We do not mean to imply that he would agree with this interpretation; he regards Perrault's version of the tale as having robbed the story of much of its meaning, and prefers the Grimm version (pp. 167-183). We do not agree.

ALICE'S JOURNEY FROM ALIEN TO ARTIST

James Suchan

Alice's puzzling and complex actions in the Wonderland books have provided critics with enough ammunition to maintain a steady salvo of charges and countercharges in their attempts to decide what her actions mean.[1] William Empson manages to sidestep some of the critical crossfire without destroying the complexity of Carroll's work by stating that the Alice books are about growing-up.[2] The implications of Empson's statement are by no means simplistic; he recognizes what psychologists have long recognized, that a child must undergo severe emotional and physical stress before reaching maturity. The Alice books, as some critics believe, are not about a typically pristine and angelic Victorian heroine; Empson correctly calls Alice the "child become Judge."[3] But the Pigeon in Wonderland may be more accurate in saying that Alice is "a serpent; and there's no use denying it."[4] However, the Unicorn in *Through the Looking Glass* is most observant in exclaiming, "It's a fabulous monster" (p. 288). If the Unicorn is right in his assessment of Alice, she belongs more to the lineage of fictional heroes and heroines like Heathcliff, Cathy, and Becky Sharp than with innocent waifs like Little Dorrit, Sissy Jupe, and Oliver Twist.

The perplexing and crucial debate whether Alice is a "monster," a "serpent," a "child-judge," or simply a little girl clearly reflects the ambivalent attitude that Victorian adults held about children. Jan Gordon argues persuasively that adult conflicts about children emerge more freely in literature than in life:

> The most amazing feature of, say, Dickens' treatment of children is how quickly they are transformed into monsters (by adults) . . . One effect of this identification with evil adults . . . is that the only way of approaching childhood is by way of the opposite of satanic monstrosities — namely, the golden world of an edenic Wonderland whose pastoral dimensions give it the status of a primal scene.[5]

Gordon goes on to state that children in Victorian literature are often allied with the depraved and the Satanic — a view which originated in the writings of John Calvin. Typically, children can escape this alien status by "working out the brute" and thus eventually evolving to a higher spiritual plane which insures their social acceptance and identity. Unfortunately, the child's customary way of gaining social acceptance — identification with an adult spiritual guide who is part of that social structure and wise about the ways in which it operates — is closed because the mercantile values which the Fagins, Bounderbys, Murdstones, and Pumblechooks embrace are not suitable values for children to copy. Victorian culture does offer the child a way — though an unsatisfactory one — of attaining social acceptance. Innocent children like Oliver Twist, Sissy Jupe, and Paul Dombey possess pastoral values that cannot be corrupted by adult mercantile values; this type of child inhabits Gordon's "golden world of an edenic Wonderland." On the other hand, depraved children can "work out the brute" only with the help of an adult spiritual guide who is not part of the social structure. For example, Magwitch, a transported criminal, teaches Pip love and compassion by his own unselfish love of Pip. But Alice defies being relegated to the role of a simple, innocent child, and she will not accept a "spiritual guide" to lead her through the Wonderland environment   she chooses to stumble through her dream experience on her own. She tries to attain an adult-like identity and social acceptance in a unique way; she attempts to balance the adult need for order and logic with the child's need for uncontrolled, spontaneous play. Alice is able to maintain this balance by taking the brutal aspects of her Wonderland dream as well as its disturbing psychic sources, and, in her role as artist, transform these forbidden, socially destructive, "monstrous" impulses into a highly organized work of art — the Looking Glass story.

The Wonderland animals' belief that Alice is more of a monster than a little girl equates her with the "monster-boys," and makes her as much an alien in Wonderland as the depraved, Satanic, and often orphaned boys were alien to the Victorian social structure. However, there's a major twist to this relationship; the values that make Alice an alien in Wonderland are the values that guarantee the stability of Victorian social structure. Alice's sadistic treatment of the Wonderland animals, her refusal to accept the nonsense and chaos which is a "given" in Wonderland, and her persistence in interjecting rational, above-ground values into the Wonderland environment cause the animals to reject her. At least children like

Pip, David Copperfield, and Tom Brown can escape their alien
status by rejecting their "childish" values and embracing adult
values; unfortunately, Alice does not have this choice in Wonderland and winds up bringing her adult values there. Moreover, she
remains an alien because she keeps on offending the animals. Alice
never does learn from her mistakes and remains a static character
throughout most of her journey. She must destroy her dream and
return to the aboveground world to escape her estranged situation.
Even in the aboveground world Alice is more of an adult than a
child; she is alienated from typical child-like attitudes, and she can't
attain her fundamental wish to escape adult restrictions. She
escapes this double-bind by becoming a "teller of tales," an artist
who retells her Wonderland dream to her sister. Becoming an artist
alleviates the boredom and restriction Alice finds in the adult
world, and, at the same time, allows her to assume a socially
acceptable role by recounting to her sister the intricately structured
Through the Looking Glass tale. However, Alice's experiences can
be approached by others only through the organized story-book
framework of "once upon a time," not by following the rabbit
down the hole. In her role as artist, Alice can at least control her
Wonderland experience and feel confident that she's neither a
monster nor a child, but an adult recapturing and structuring a
potentially dangerous past. Emanuel Schwartz, in an excellent
study of the structural elements of the fairy tale, argues that these
stories, like dreams, are "problem solving mechanisms,"[6] attempts
to gain relief from the insoluble problems of living. Through her
symbolic control of the real world, Alice can overcome her
estranged condition in *both* the real and Wonderland worlds and
establish a much needed sense of identity.

Alice's Adventures in Wonderland begins with Alice's escape into
the world of the White Rabbit; it is an escape because she is bored
by the story her sister is reading to her. Undoubtedly, the book that
Alice finds uninteresting is one of those popular-with-adults but
painfully dull, didactic children's books written by a Mrs. Fairchild
or a Mrs. Sherwood. Alice's pursuit of the rabbit represents a rejection of those sombre, civilized values of the aboveground world
symbolized by the book that "has no pictures or conversations in it."
She pursues the rabbit to his hole and rashly follows him down
until the tunnel drops out and she unexpectedly finds herself in
free-fall. This transition from aboveground to underground does not

result in Alice's loss or rejection of her aboveground values. She tries to curtsy during her fall, and, after taking a jar of marmalade from one of the shelves she passes, she exhibits an adult-like concern that she might injure or even kill someone underneath her if she drops the jar. She even wonders about the longitude and latitude of her location and about winding up on the other side of the earth where people (Alice calls them "Antipathies") "walk with their heads downward." The concern for these geographic details indicates that Alice has been adversely affected by dull, educational books and has accepted the attitudes and values of the adult world. Alice is not a child with a "tabula rasa" innocence and natural curiosity about the workings of the world; she is more like a literal-minded adult who expects the world to operate according to the logic and rules she has learned.

Ironically, Alice is an orphan and alien in a world she herself has dreamed; in this world she lacks a reliable set of authority figures (parents) to back up her assertions to the animals about logic and order. The animals are born from Alice's salty tears; however, she is so lacking in confidence and confused about her own identity that she doesn't realize she is the creator-"parent" of the animals. The animals insist that everyone wins at the end of the Caucus Race, and demand that Alice, the benevolent "provider," supply the prizes. They recognize Alice's superior status in Wonderland and solemnly present her with an elegant thimble; even the "provider" is given an award at the communal prize ceremony. Alice is discomfited by this "childish" display of emotion, and promptly asks the mouse to relate his history, thus rejecting the sense of community implied by the reward. Alice believes she can discover her own origins and destiny in Wonderland by examining the "histories" of the animals she meets. Unfortunately, she is so puzzled by the double-"entendre" on "tale" that she doesn't pay close attention to the mouse's story which does reveal the history of Wonderland. Alice doesn't realize that her own history and identity are inextricably bound to the Wonderland animals — in effect, they are her alter-ego.[7]

The reader first discovers that Alice is troubled about her origins and identity when she glances through a small door, spots the pastoral garden, but is puzzled about how to enter: "Oh, how I wish I could shut up like a telescope! I think I could if I only knew how to begin" (30). Alice's goal, similar to that of many Victorian heroes and heroines, is to reach the pastoral garden and (though not in any self-conscious manner) to find the source of her identity. She is completely unaware that her origins are located in an unpredictable, illogical, and chaotic universe which violates her orderly, adult-like attitude to the world. Since Wonderland lacks a coherent temporal and spatial organization, Alice can't employ the traditional means — overcoming a series of obstacles or trials — to gain the object of her quest. Consequently, in chapter IV, one-third of the way through Wonderland, Alice still has not formulated a plan to reach the garden, perhaps does not even know how to begin to formulate one:

> "The first thing I've got to do," said Alice to herself as she wandered about in the wood, "is to grow to my right size again; and the second thing is to find my way into that lovely garden. I think that will be the best plan."
> It sounded like an excellent plan, no doubt, and very neatly and simply arranged: the only difficulty was that she had not the smallest idea how to set about it. (64)

Neat and simple plans don't work in the chaotic Wonderland landscape. Even after her spat with the pigeon about her identity Alice is still trying, with very little success, to organize her quest to reach the garden: "I've got back to my right size: the next thing is, to get into that beautiful garden — how *is* that to be done I wonder?" (77) She still doesn't realize that adult rational strategies don't work in Wonderland and that the best plan to reach the garden is to have no plan at all.

Alice's inability to implement a plan to reach the garden is symptomatic of a larger problem, her inability to establish a stable identity. Her abrupt changes in size so confuse her that she constantly complains that she doesn't know who she is from one moment to the next. The fall into Wonderland proves to be a fall from identity or self, and the result is a fragmentation and disorientation of the self.[8] Alice exhibits this fall from selfhood early in her Wonderland journey just after she has tasted the contents of the bottle labelled "Drink Me":

> She generally gave herself very good advice, (though she very seldom followed it), and sometimes she scolded herself so severely as to bring tears into her eyes; and once she remembered trying to box her own ears for having cheated herself in a game of croquet she was playing against herself, for this curious

child was very fond of pretending to be two people! (32-3)

Alice is not sure whether she exists as subject or object; she is capable of acting as both judge and defendant when she commits a transgression. Her self-punishment — she scolds herself and boxes her ears — reveals Alice as a judge who treats herself as an object. Later in her Wonderland journey she converts that masochism into sadism when she treats the animals as objects. Alice's identity problems increase her self-punishment. When she changes size and becomes increasingly confused about her identity, she cries, but then she severely chastizes herself for her tears: "a great girl like you to go on crying in this way! Stop this moment, I tell you!" (36) Following this incident, Alice asks the ontological question that all orphans either consciously or unconsciously ask: "Who in the world am I? Ah, that's the great puzzle!" (37) In an attempt to validate her identity, she turns to logical, common-sensical, aboveground methods which are doomed to fail in Wonderland. She starts evaluating her physical appearance and decides that she is not Ada because Ada's hair has ringlets and her hair is straight. Next she determines that she can't be Mabel because she's more intelligent than Mabel. Frustrated by her identity checklist, Alice exclaims, "she's she and I'm I" (37-8); however, even tautological statements don't prove that she's Alice and they don't alleviate her identity crisis. She then checks how much she really does know, and finds that her school knowledge fails her. She concludes with the same question that began her self-interrogation: "Who am I?" She decides she very well could be Mabel, but is distraught by the possibility. It never occurs to Alice that reversals or confusions of identity are much more appropriate in Wonderland than a stable identity.

Throughout most of her journey Alice is troubled by these identity problems. The Caterpillar's question, "Who are you?" echoes the question Alice has repeatedly asked herself. Even at this late point in her journey she still hasn't found a satisfactory answer. She's sure who she was when she woke up, but she's certain that she's changed several times since then, and readily admits to the caterpillar that she can't explain herself "because I'm not myself" (67). In her encounter with the pigeon, Alice, long neck and all, manages to stammer rather doubtfully that she's a little girl; but the pigeon is convinced that she's "inventing something," and that she's really a serpent. Alice's meeting with the Cheshire cat and their discussion about the proper direction to travel and the sanity of the characters in those directions temporarily deflect her identity problems.

What actions or what sorts of emotional responses are possible for an orphan whose identity and origins are blurred? Alice's emotions in response to her fluctuations in size shift from mild annoyance to irritation, and finally to rage. The unfortunate Wonderland animals are victimized by the violence that results from her anger. Paul Schilder correctly notices that in the Alice books "there is very little love and tenderness and little regard for the existence of others."[9] Schilder's generalization may be a bit simplistic, but coupled with Empson's observation that death is not far from sight in the Alice books and that the books are littered with jokes about death, one begins to see the grim, dark relationship between Alice and the Wonderland animals.

Alice cannot place blame, or, in a more general sense, find a causal relationship between her problems and the source of those problems. At first she blames herself, cries several times, then, after shrinking to less than two feet tall, falls into her own tears: "'I wish I hadn't cried so much!' said Alice, as she swam about, trying to find her way out. 'I shall be punished for it now, I suppose, by being drowned in my own tears!'" (40-41) Drowning in her tears would be the perfect exit, an unconscious suicide, for someone with masochistic tendencies; but instead, unaware that her tears have created the Wonderland menagerie, she spots a mouse and asks it a series of frightening questions:[10]

> "Ou est ma chatte?" which was the first sentence in her French lesson-book. The mouse gave a sudden leap out of the water and seemed to quiver all over with fright. "Oh, I beg your pardon!" cried Alice hastily, afraid that she had hurt the poor animal's feelings. "I quite forgot you didn't like cats."
> . . . "Are you — are you fond — of — of dogs . . . He (a farmer) says it kills all the rats and — oh dear!" cried Alice in a sorrowful tone, "I'm afraid I've offended it again!" (42-43)

Alice doesn't deliberately offend the mouse, but her conversations with him are filled with sadistic references to his predators and to predatory values. Despite having been taught "proper," aboveground behavior, Alice can't consistently obey these rules any more than she can learn from her experiences in Wonderland. After the caucus race she proudly announces that Dinah is adept at catching mice and is a regular bird hawk; the large population of birds move off in a hurry. It is doubtful that Alice matures at all during her Wonderland journey; her urgent need to cling to her aboveground values almost forces her to treat the animals cruelly.

Alice's cruelty stems from the conflict between her desire to escape the repressive order of the aboveground world and her allegiance to civilized values. A repressive society surely would not allow a child to openly question its values; consequently, the Wonderland dream is the suitable terrain for Alice to work out her conflicts. The poems that Alice recites provide further proof that her cruelty is primarily unconscious. When Alice tries to repeat "How doth the little busy bee" in an attempt to affirm her identity by using her memory of aboveground lessons, the poem is strangely altered:

> How cheerfully he (crocodile) seems to grin,
>   How neatly spreads his claws,
> And welcomes little fishes in
>   With gently smiling jaws! (38)

Alice is sure that these are not the right words to the poem, but is significantly unaware that the poem's gruesome ending echoes the predatory remarks that she has made to the mouse and the birds. She also fails to remember "You are old, Father William"; the poem she does recite ends with a grumpy Father William threatening to kick a young man down the stairs if he dares to ask any more questions. Southey's didactic poem about a hearty, righteous, God-fearing father who is fond of giving advice to his son is transformed into a poem about an argumentative, cagey old man who is not beyond using violence to silence a young boy. Even when Alice attempts late in her Wonderland journey to repeat the Lobster-Quadrille, the words come out "very queer." The poem ends with a reference to one of the lobster's predators:

> When the sands are all dry, he is gay as a lark,
> And will talk in contemptuous tones of the Shark.
> But when the tide rises and sharks are around,
> His voice has a timid and tremulous sound. (139)

It is easy to see Alice's cruelty to the animals as a turning outward of her past cruelty to herself — her masochism is transformed into sadism. After she has created her Wonderland family, she no longer chastizes herself, but regularly directs her aggression toward the animals. And since the Wonderland animals are an extension of Alice's self, much as a child is an extension of his mother, the punishment of the animals is still a self-punishment. Alice extends and amplifies the self-alienation she felt at the beginning of her journey by viewing herself as a projection of the animals.

The transformation of masochism into sadism is unconscious on Alice's, or, more accurately, on Lewis Carroll's part.[11] The dynamics of projection best explain the transformation in Wonderland from masochism to sadism; children often identify themselves with their aggressors to escape further punishment, and in effect become child-adults. We get a brief hint of some of the causes which contribute to Alice's insistence on aboveground order in Wonderland when she determines that the bottle labeled "Drink Me" was not poison but quite safe to drink:

> "No, I'll look first," she said, "and see whether it's marked 'poison' or not"; for she had read several nice little stories about children who had got burn't, and eaten up by wild beasts, and other unpleasant things, all because they would not remember the simple rules their friends had taught them . . . (31)

The "nice little stories" that Alice has read are clearly the moral, didactic novels like Christina Rossetti's *Speaking Likenesses,* whose plot resembles *Alice's Adventures in Wonderland,* Dorothy Kilner's *The Village School,* Charles Kingsley's *The Water Babies,* and Mrs. Sherwood's *History of the Fairchild Family.* All these "children's" books gloated over the grotesque and emphasized that physical suffering "saved" the moral values of the child and thus placed him on the proper road toward salvation. The purpose of these instructional books was to quickly change the child into an adult. But these writers' emphasis on physical punishment represents a psychologically sinister means of accomplishing this goal. By identifying with their aggressors, children show their unconscious belief that most adults would find it impossible to punish someone who conforms to adult values: an adult will not punish himself or an obvious replica of himself. However Alice, due to her self alienation — an adult-like mind in a child's body — finds it easy to punish herself because she sees herself as an "other"; her creation of the Wonderland animals shows a *further* dissociation of child from adult. Consequently, Alice's masochism, prevalent in the early part of the story, only appears to be transformed into sadism in her treatment of the animals. These complex patterns of projections intensify Alice's confusion about her identity. When she falls down the rabbit hole to escape the boredom of the aboveground world, her identity as a child is closed to her because she has already assumed adult values; her only alternative to escape adult values is to seek a symbolic childhood — the edenic garden which promises preconscious innocence. But in Wonderland, as Alice painfully discovers, one opens doors only to find more doors.

Alice's quest to reach the garden involves a collage of fortuitous experiences. She rigidly tries to enforce civilized rules in Wonderland to gain some direction in her quest, but finds that most of the animals ignore her commands. Only the Cheshire cat is unlike the other Wonderland animals, and is therefore Alice's only real ally. His head detached from his body and his grin represent the sort of intellectual detachment which the "adult" Alice finds to her liking — the cat could supply Alice with a solution to her identity problems. However, Alice rejects the solution because it seems illogical to her:

> "We're all mad here. I'm mad. You're mad."
> "How do you know I'm mad?" said Alice.
> "You must be," said the Cat, "or you wouldn't have come here."
> Alice didn't think that proved it at all. (89)

The Cheshire Cat realizes that chaos is the ordinary order of events in Wonderland, and, his relegating everyone there to a state of madness is not a joke or a moral judgement, but simply an accurate description of the animals' actions. Obviously the animals don't think that their actions are strange because they lack self-consciousness, and the anarchy of their kingdom constantly reaffirms the irrationality of their behavior. Because Alice always relies on her reason and her memories of a logical, coherent aboveground world, she cannot evaluate her Wonderland experiences from the animals' point of view. She is incapable of realizing that there may be some connection between the animals' peculiar behavior and the curious events in Wonderland. If Alice could accept the "madness" of Wonderland, she could escape her alienated condition by becoming all child, a member of the Wonderland kingdom, and not a constant opponent of its nonsensical values.

At the Mad Hatter's tea party Alice still persists in imposing her old notions of sanity on the "mad" actions of the March Hare, the Mad Hatter, and the Dormouse. Alice is not amused by the puns, the riddles without answers, and the uncivil treatment she receives at the tea party. Indeed, she is so uncomfortable that she tries to enforce her aboveground social decorum on the maniacal gathering:

> "Your hair wants cutting," said the Hatter. He had been looking at Alice for some time with great curiosity, and this was his first speech.
> "You should learn not to make remarks," Alice said with some severity; "It's very rude." (94)

The Hatter, unconcerned about his lack of social graces, changes the subject and asks Alice a riddle that has no answer. But Alice and the Hatter soon start squabbling about meaning and about the logic of syllogisms. A decorous tea party so typical in the aboveground world turns into a discourteous, argumentative, cruel meeting which Alice finds distasteful. But even more disturbing to her than the impropriety and cruelty of the Hatter and the Hare is the eradication of time. Time had been dead for some time before Alice joined the interminable tea party. After the Hatter's rude comments and the discussion of syllogisms, the Hatter suddenly asks Alice, "What day of the month is it?" What follows is a series of puns and absurd comments on watches and time. Alice and the Hatter resurrect Time (the Hatter murdered him at the great concert given by the Queen of Hearts), but they beat and waste him through a series of nonsensical personifications. Time rebels: "he won't do a thing I ask! It's always six o-clock now" (99) the Hatter complains, and one of the absolute, taken-for-granted forms of nineteenth-century order is subverted.

The "A Mad Tea Party" chapter contains the most subversive affront to Alice's system of aboveground values that she has yet faced. She finds her linear, progressive notion of time in as many pieces as Humpty Dumpty. For an orphan whose identity has been shaken by sudden changes in size, abrupt transformations in name, quick reversals in logic, and unexpected breakdowns in memory, the obliteration of time represents rock bottom in her quest for identity. Alice, very much like Little Jo in *Bleak House,* is a queer species in an alien environment: she has no past that she can accurately remember, no parents to rely on for direction, and no visible social models to imitate. Her search for the garden is the only activity that has any meaning for her, and despite her perplexing and troubling experiences, she never abandons that goal.

After deciding that she'll never again go to a tea party like the Hatter's, Alice spots a door in one of the trees, goes in, sees another smaller door, then nibbles a mushroom to shrink to the proper size, and finally enters the beautiful garden with the "bright flower-beds and the cool fountains." Ironically, she finds Five and Seven, two playing cards, painting the white roses red and arguing over the matter. The pastoral that Alice has finally reached is not a tranquil Utopia, but only a "painted," artificial garden filled with argumentative cards and a disagreeable Queen. This is not the garden that Alice sought; undoubtedly she expected the kind of garden found in many Jane Austen novels, where nature is regulated into neat patches of flowers, a picturesque fountain or grotto, and a well placed grove of trees. Despite her disappointment, the fact that she has reached her goal gives her knowledge that she has never before possessed. Alice is not intimidated by the harsh Queen of Hearts because, for the first time she is certain about her identity, confident of her worth, and aware that she's only dealing with playing cards: " 'My name is Alice, so please your majesty,' said Alice very politely; but she added to herself, 'why they're only a pack of cards, after all. I needn't be afraid of them' " (108)! In addition, Alice exerts her will by her rude comments to the Queen:

"How should I know," (who the cards are) said Alice, surprised at her own courage, "It's no business of mine."
The Queen turned crimson with fury, and after glaring at her for a moment like a wild beast, began screaming, "Off with her head! Off with _____ "
"Nonsense!" said Alice, very loudly and decidedly, and then the Queen was silent. (109)

Alice's rudeness is an important step toward her rejection and destruction of Wonderland (and a part of herself) to preserve her aboveground identity. Her recognition that the King and especially the Queen have no real power foreshadows her statement, "You're nothing but a pack of cards" (161), before she destroys her dream.

There are several reasons why Alice regains her identity when she realizes that Wonderland is a realm of "stuff and nonsense." First of all, there are many similarities between Alice and the Queen: both characters rule a large number of the Wonderland inhabitants, both are sadistic in their treatment of these inhabitants, both threaten brutality and never act on their threats, and both have rather arbitrary opinions about the appropriateness of order and disorder in their kingdoms. When Alice sees the Queen, she is in a sense seeing herself in an altered, reversed Wonderland form.[12] Alice feels cheated when she reaches the garden (actually the Queen's croquet ground), but she fails to realize that it is her imposition of civilized values on the chaotic garden that causes the disappointment. Alice's destruction of the dream, and obviously the animals, after her realization that the cards and the whole Wonderland world are "stuff and nonsense" is actually the destruction of her long-repressed, chaotic self that was partially freed in the uncivilized, free-form Wonderland environment. Perhaps Alice expected the garden to unite the self-alienating elements of her personality; instead, she is confronted with more of the nonsense she has been desperately trying to avoid.

The maddening trial that Alice is forced to attend heightens her need for stability and her old aboveground identity; her violent reaction to the turmoil is characteristic of her actions in any difficult situation she finds herself in. The destruction of the cards and the dream is a masochistic act similar to her actions in the aboveground world; often she scolded herself so severely for breaking the rules of croquet that she brought tears to her eyes. By obliterating her dream, Alice has punished and destroyed that part of herself that dares to break the rules created by repressive aboveground institutions. We have come full circle by the end of *Wonderland*. At the beginning of the dream Alice, who is fond of being two people, punishes herself for breaking rules; by the end of the dream she is still punishing herself, but that self is projected on a Queen who breaks the rules of croquet and trials.

What's the purpose of Alice's journey? Does she learn anything from her experiences in Wonderland? After she has destroyed the Wonderland dream, she runs off to tea, despite her experience at the Hatter's tea party. Her sister then redreams Alice's dream, taking such a great delight in it that "though she knew she had but to open them (her eyes) again, all would change to dull reality" (163). Alice's communication of her dream to her sister and her sister's belief that Alice "would gather about her other little children, and make *their* eyes bright and eager with many a strange tale, perhaps even with the dream of Wonderland" (164) makes Alice an artist. But the transformation of Wonderland into a story places linguistic and causal controls on Alice's experience. The

Wonderland story can only be experienced through Alice's point of view, and only through the limitations resulting from putting any experience into words. Consequently, Alice solves both her aboveground and Wonderland identity problems by assuming the role of an artist who is able to provide for others a non-destructive means of gratifying otherwise unacceptable impulses. However, the conclusion of the story implies that the terrifying, destructive aspects of Wonderland will be purged by the operation of time and memory; Alice, the "teller of tales," will remember her dream not as a nightmarish journey, but as one of the many simple joys of her childhood that took place on a happy summer day. By recreating her Wonderland experience in a fictionalized form, Alice has not rejected that experience because it was a product of idle fancy, but improved it and thus made it more palatable for children who share Alice's aboveground values.

To recapitulate, by the end of the Wonderland books Alice has changed from an alien in a madcap world into a "teller of tales" to future generations. Like Stephen Daedalus in *A Portrait of the Artist as a Young Man,* Alice tries to prove her worth and to improve her experience by molding this personal event into an understandable form which will please others.[13] The role of artist gives Alice a qualitatively different identity than the one she had at the beginning of the tale: she was subjected to the brutal domination of other fairy-tale writers, and now she is a creator of those tales. In "The Rabbit Sends in a Little Bill" chapter, Alice anticipates her role as an artist: "When I used to read fairy tales, I fancied that kind of thing never happened, and now here I am in the middle of one! There ought to be a book written about me, that there ought! And when I grow up, I'll write one . . ." (59). But how can one be sure that Alice's tales are not going to utilize the same tyrannical violence that her predecessors used? Even a cursory examination of *Through the Looking Glass,* a dream that Alice-as-artist consciously creates, reveals an over-concern about becoming Queen, a sadistic need to impose conventions on the Looking-Glass world.

In her role as artist, Alice tries to master her experience in Wonderland, but in the process largely destroys the original experience for the sake of her new identity. Perhaps the Unicorn was correct in saying that Alice is a monster, especially if one considers her treatment of the Wonderland animals, but without doubt the Pigeon is right when he accuses Alice of "trying to *invent* something."

NOTES

1. Paula Johnson's "Alice Among the Analysts," *Hartford Studies in Literature,*
   4, pp. 114-122 is a comprehensive survey of the various and contradictory
   views that psychoanalytic critics like Paul Schilder, Martin Grotjahn, and John
   Skinner hold about Alice. Robert Phillips has compiled many of the seminal
   essays on the Wonderland books in *Aspects of Alice* (New York: Vanguard
   Press, 1971). A reading of this group of essays reveals very little agreement
   among the critics about what Alice's actions mean.
2. William Empson, "The Child as Swain," *Some Versions of Pastoral* (New
   York: New Directions, 1968), p. 253.
3. Empson, p. 254
4. Martin Gardner, ed., *The Annotated Alice: Alice's Adventures in Wonderland
   & Through the Looking Glass* (New York: Bramhall House, 1960), p. 76. All
   subsequent page numbers in this edition are included within the essay.
5. Jan Gordon, "The Alice Books and the Metaphors of Victorian Childhood," in
   Aspects of Alice, ed. Robert Phillips (New York: Vanguard Press, 1971), p. 109.
6. Emanuel K. Schwartz, "A Psychoanalytic Study of the Fairy Tale," *American
   Journal of Psychotherapy,* 10 (1956), pp. 740-762.
7. Often fairy tales use animals who act in very human ways as "spiritual guides."
   These animals, often birds with golden feathers, talking fish, or a Cheshire cat,
   represent the hero's "other self."
8. Magnitude, or the size of the "self," of the body and the body parts, has
   special importance for children as well as for neurotics and psychotics. Since
   Alice acts more like an adult than a child in Wonderland, it seems appropriate
   to evaluate her actions, using adult criteria.
9. Paul Schilder, "Psychoanalytic Remarks on *Alice in Wonderland* and
   Lewis Carroll," *The Journal of Nervous and Mental Diseases,* LXXXVII
   (1938), p. 168.
10. Empson, pp. 271-273, explains some of the obvious Freudian symbolism in
    the early part of Wonderland.
11. I would hesitate to call Alice a realistic character in the same way I would
    consider Pip or David Copperfield to be realistic. Alice is a mouthpiece for
    Lewis Carroll, and the distinctions between Alice's and Carroll's concerns are
    often very difficult if not impossible to make.
12. In *Through the Looking Glass,* the sequel to Wonderland, Alice consciously
    desires to change from a pawn to a Queen. The similarities between Alice and
    the Queen in Wonderland foreshadow Alice's conscious desire to become
    Queen in *Through the Looking Glass.*
13. Breakdowns in communication and the destruction of the meanings of words
    constitute one of the main features of Wonderland. Ironically, Alice in her
    role of "teller of tales" ignores this fact and assumes, like a good Victorian,
    that ideas can be clearly and accurately communicated to an audience.

WHEN I WAS A CHILD I SPAKE LIKE A GREEK

William Sylvester

A private memory has, I believe, public implications.

During the weekly assembly, or meeting, at a Friend's school—the students called it a Quaker school—we were obliged to sit silently, and to wait. We were supposed to listen for the promptings of the inner light, and even then most of us sensed, however vaguely, that the notion of hearing was curiously mixed up with seeing. The confusion, if there were one, belonged to the inexplicable world of adults. Strictly speaking, any one of us should have been permitted to stand up and to speak. The inner light, however, was never to shine within us, but within a speaker chosen in advance. He was seated on a platform with other dignitaries and visitors, and the inner light almost invariable moved him to speak at exactly twenty minutes past the hour. Usually the speaker was on stage right, but we could never be sure which of the visitors had been designated. No matter who stood up and moved to center stage, the opening quotation was likely to be the same: "When I was a child, I spake like a child, but when I became a man, I put away childish things."

We sat bolt upright, partly from obedience and partly from resentment. We wanted to be out of there, away from concepts and confronted with things. We wanted noise and activity. We knew what we wanted, and that knowledge was paradoxically part of the experience. The adult world was there, and we had our privacy. As we sat waiting for the speaker to arise, we were alone and we knew it. Authority was literally above us, but out there, different from us. Nobody threatened us in the sense of claiming to understand us, and nobody made demands that we understand older people.

I take this experience to be emblematic of the time from the thirties through the early fifties. Ours was not the only school where the purpose of education, at heart, was to confront children with an adult otherness, an alien way of life to which we were supposed to become accustomed. The full implications are undoubtedly complex and far reaching but from the point of view of literature, one assumption, I believe, was clear: literature, real literature, belonged to an adult world. Latin, English and French were all "adult": Julius Caesar, Cicero, and Le Voyage de Monsieur Perrichon were equally difficult and equally good for us. The other literature, the books we read privately and for fun, were not "real." And in a sense they weren't: the adventures of Tom Swift, or of David Bimney Putnam were fantasies, or had the effect of fantasies, wish fulfillments, or undifferentiated sentimentality.

The fundamental assumption that reading for fun and reading for school were two separate activities had one immediate consequence; no creative activity was supposed to take place in an academic environment. Poetry was never written in school—except as an exercise—and poets never belonged to Universities. The voices in protest were infrequent but occasionally strident, as in Ezra Pound's correspondence with Professor Felix Schelling of the University of Pennsylvania.

The model for poetry, real poetry, poetry to be studied was the "well wrought," and the norm was the iambic pentameter, although one glanced briefly at the popularizers, such as Walt Whitman, Vachel Lindsay, or Carl Sandburg. These were the sanctified exceptions. The notion that poetry could be enjoyed, and also be studied in school—that, to me, was an astonishing proposition, particularly as it was offered by an eminently responsible person.

In the late 1940's, Henry Rago, before he became editor of *Poetry, A Magazine of Verse*, said in private conversation that he looked forward to the day when Marianne Moore's poetry would be read in high school.

It was a startling prediction, and in the light of subsequent experience, a rather tame one. When he was editor, the magazine was for all practical purposes the trade journal of poets, and all of the poetic revolutions were welcomed by him: Frank O'Hara's personalism, Robert Creeley, Black Mountain, New York, San Francisco. From this ferment has emerged a condition that seems like a state of permanent revolution: the establishment of a poetry that nominates, that presents, the poetry—as Kenneth Parchen claimed in 1947—belonging to the art that does not shed light, but IS light. The "radical" poetry of 1957-1960 became enshrined in textbooks for secondary schools in less than a decade, so that high school, junior high, and even younger students, read poetry by Ferlinghetti, Ginsberg, Pound, Lenore Kandel, Creeley, William Carlos Williams,

Corso, and many others. The speed of the acceptance has been ver-
tiginous, possibly because a poetry of "presentation" has at least a
few elements that are not "revolutionary" at all, but represent a
return to older ways of feeling. Charles Olson's penchant for archaeology in more than one sense of the word, William Carlos William's
translation of Sappho, Pound's interest in Greek, these and other
indicia suggest that we look to the Greeks for a poetry of presentation that would appeal to a wide range of ages, where indeed the
sense of age—child, adolescent, adult—would not be of primary
significance to the audience or to the performers.

One such poem, I have translated as follows:

> We come to the big house of a big man.
> He has made it.
> He's rich; he can roar out loud.
> Door,
> Open up automatically, door.
> People go through you door
> They get money and with money
> They swell up peacefully.
> Life is good if the vats are full
> The bread board high.
> Pile up the dough
> Bit by bit
> High as the hat on a Persian King . . .

> Δῶμα προσετραπόμεσθ᾽ ἀνδρὸς μέγα δυναμένοιο,
> ὃς μέγα μὲν δύναται, μέγα δὲ βρέμει ὄλβιος αἰεί·
> αὐταὶ ἀνακλίνεσθε, θύραι· πλοῦτος γὰρ ἔσεισι
> πολλός, σὺν πλούτῳ δὲ καὶ εὐφροσύνη τεθαλυῖα
> εἰρήνη τ᾽ ἀγαθή· ὅσα δ᾽ ἄγγεα, μεστὰ μὲν εἴη,
> κυρβασίη δ᾽ αἰεὶ μάζης κατὰ καρδόπου ἕρποι.
> νῦν μὲν κριθαίην εὐώπιδα σησαμόεσσαν

> .   .   .   .   .

> τοῦ παιδὸς δὲ γυνὴ κατὰ δίφρακα   βήσεται
>   ὕμμιν,
> ἡμίονοι δ᾽ ἄξουσι κραταίποδες ἐς τόδε δῶμα,
> αὐτὴ δ᾽ ἱστὸν ὑφαίνοι ἐπ᾽ ἠλέκτρῳ βεβαυῖα.
> νεῦμαί τοι νεῦμαι ἐνιαύσιος ὥστε χελιδών·
> ἕστηκ᾽ ἐν προθύροις ψιλὴ πόδας, ἀλλὰ φέρ᾽
>   αἶψα.
> ὑπέρ σε τ᾽Ὠπόλλωνος, ὦ γύναι τι δός·
> εἰ μέν τι δώσεις· εἰ δὲ μή, οὐχ ἑστήξομεν·
> οὐ γὰρ συνοικήσοντες ἐνθάδ᾽ ἤλθομεν.

The fragment comes down to us from the pseudo-Herodotean *Life of Homer*. But however vague our knowledge of the source, an important aspect of the poem emerges from two allegations— that the poem was sung by Homer himself, led around by children, and then later, as a begging song by children. The historical accuracy is not important for my purpose; we don't care whether Homer himself sang it, or whether children did. The age of the performer, or performers is not important, and the conclusion fits any age:

> Woman, give us something
> Good for you if you give us something.
> If you don't
> We'll go away
> We haven't come to live inside your house.

The poem presents both words and actions. The words provide a direct experience rather than the occasion for an interpretation. The words are acted out so that the rich people are as much a part of the begging scene as those who play the roles of beggars. All of the words point to immediate primary experience: wealth is "good," being poor is "bad," and food is "fun," the implications of the words "good," "bad," and "fun," being aesthetic rather than moral. We are not invited to ask, "What does the poem mean?" but rather "How does it relate to its society? Did this particular ritual really take place? Did Homer, blind, sing the song as he was led around by children?" The poem leads to questions about history, but we do not need history to interpret the poem.

The words of the poem present images, things, and these images imply ways of feeling that are common to people regardless of age, but the poem is also part of a ritual, and rituals sometimes make the distinction between childhood and adulthood irrelevant for the moment of the ritual itself. At Santo Domingo reservation, the day long dance is performed by men, women, and children of both sexes, and the reiterative stamping, the chanting, and the music consists of two lines, male and female, in gradations of size, from small children in the rear of the procession to the larger people at the front. All members, whatever their roles, share equally in the festival. In churches and temples, or in rituals within the home, the children are never read *at* during the ritual itself. The separation occurs during the sermon, and thus the sermon has a potentially unfavorable overtone.[2] If the children are specifically mentioned as children—as in a Seder—they nevertheless participate equally in the ritual partly because rituals name or present things rather than concepts.

Even if the children are named as children, they are not isolated from the ritual, as in the following begging song, preserved by Athenaeus.

> Ἦλθ᾽, ἦλθε χελιδὼν
> καλὰς ὥρας ἄγουσα
> καὶ καλοὺς ἐνιαυτοὺς
> ἐπὶ γαστέρα λευκὰ
> κἠπὶ νῶτα μέλαινα.
> παλάθαν σὺ προκύκλει
> ἐκ πίονος οἴκω
> οἴνω τε δέπαστρον
> τύρω τε κάνυστρον·
> καπυρῶνα χελιδὼν
> καὶ λεκιθίταν
> οὐκ ὠθεῖται.
> πότερ᾽ ἀπίωμες ἢ <τί σου> λαβώμεθα ;
> αἰ μέν τι δώσεις· αἰ δὲ μὴ, οὐκ ἐάσομες·
> ἢ τὰν θύραν φέρωμες ἢ θοὐπέρθυρον
> ἢ τὰν γυναῖκα τὰν ἔσω καθημέναν ;
> μικρὰ μέν ἐστι· ῥᾳδίως νιν οἴσομες.
> αἰ κα φέρῃς τι, μέγα τι δὴ <καὐτὸς> φέροις.
> ἄνοιγ᾽, ἄνοιγε τὰν θύραν χελιδόνι·
> οὐ γὰρ γέροντές εἰμες ἀλλὰ παιδία.

Here's a swallow, a swallow.
She brings beautiful weather
She brings a beautiful year
The belly is white
The back is black.
Bring out cookies with figs
From the rich house
A pitcher of wine
A box of cheese
Also wheat bread
And a pancake.

> The swallow will like that
> Are we to go away, or get something?
> We'll go if you give us something.
> If you don't, we'll stay.
> We'll take away the door or the doorstep
> Or the woman who sits inside.
> She's so small we can carry her easily.
> But if you bring us something
> Bring us something big.
> Open up
> Open up the door to the swallow.
> We are not grown ups, but children.

I suggest that we do not have to imagine real children performing the poem; adults pretending to be children would do just as well, because the poem is independent of vocal idiosyncrasies. Like the words associated with any festival or ritual, the assumptions about language—tacit but explicit—are often called an "oral tradition." But this tradition has very little (if anything) to do with a private interpretation of a uniquely endowed voice. To read a poem aloud is not to bring it into an "oral tradition" just as the destiny of the stage does not convert Aeschylus or Sophocles to an "oral tradition."

These two begging songs come down to us in written records about a reasonably well defined set of assumptions about poetry, about a particular class of poetry. The poems name things, proceed in chronological sequence, have no significant abstractions. They may not be Homeric in their scope or depth, but they share certain characteristics of Homer's poetry (those I have already named, following Eric Havelock, and, in a different context, Jahnheinz Jahn, and others). As in Homer, these poems assume that children are smaller versions of adults. There is no development of personality in Homer, no veerings of personality. People tend to be defined in their relationship to each other by having more or less power. Telemachus does not evolve into a full man, but instead events impinge upon him. Odysseus has a nurse, but his childhood does not stand in any explicating role to his immediate present. Everything in Homer, as Auerbach points out, occurs in the present. Changes in Homer tend to be aesthetic, of the senses, rather than moral. The *Iliad* begins with the anger of Achilles, and it ends with the death of Hector. The wrath is seen with greater or less intensity, with greater or less effect, but the choices are not moral, the shifts are not philosophical. There are laws in Homer, but no codes.

If we turn to the Aeneid, we enter a different world. Characters evolve; they change in their moral relationships to each other and they develop. Dido at the beginning of Aeneas's story is emotionally untouched, but after the story, she emerges passionately in love with him. Aeneas hesitates, not unlike Hamlet. He cannot bring himself to kill his enemy until he sees the spoils of his friend. Characters relate to each other through age, as well as through power—the aged Anchises, the child Ascanius—there is a sense of growth, even of dialectic in the *Aeneid*. The passion of Dido is heightened by her believing that the god on her lap is in fact Ascanius, so that the child is presented as having a special, complex and perhaps perplexing relationship to the passions of the adult world.

I run through these perhaps overly familiar differences between Homer and Vergil to stress a point of view that is perhaps less familiar: Homer is allied to an oral tradition, but Vergil to a vocal. One can read Homer, more or less effectively, but how one reads Vergil can alter the meaning, the interpretation drastically. For example: should one imagine a fiercely determined Aeneas, one who rejects his past dallying, and who intones proudly: "Sum pius Aeneas," or should we imagine an agonized Aeneas, one with reverence toward the sources of his being (pius) but following his duty reluctantly, and at a great emotional price? One can interpret the Aeneid, one can psychoanalyze Aeneas; one cannot psycho-analyze Achilles. Aeneas has problems; Achilles, encounters. Aeneas vacillates, his moods are at variance with his actions. Achilles changes his course, and he glows with greater or less intensity, perhaps burning up a river in the process.

From Homer, one could never derive concepts of either pacifism or patriotism in spite of some casual references to the Panhellenics. If you want to go to war, here is a speech by Odysseus; if you don't want to go to war, here is a speech by Achilles, and there is no meaningful paradox and no vocal rendition that will introduce nuances of interpretation or ironies.

The feeling of concepts is allied to the awareness of time, and the passing of time. Unlike the begging songs, the watchman in the opening scene of *Agamemmnon* judges his own work and his

relationship to this work. Because he is aware of himself as a
separate identity, he becomes aware of the passing of time.

> I beg the gods to let me go from this job
> Of keeping watch, the whole year long, my bed
> The rooftop of the Atreidae, resting on
> My arms, like a dog; I've come to know the crowds
> Of stars at night that bring both winter and summer
> To mortal men, the shining leaders, standing
> Out in the sky . . .
> . . . .
> I weep for the turn of fortune to this house,
> Not as it was before, when jobs were done
> In the very best way

Concepts can exist only in the process of time, and the concept of an age, of an identity, can exist only allied to the sense
of time. The watchman's prelude in *Agamemmnon* has its twentieth
century counterpart in studies of urban decay, and Vergil has his
counterpart in psychology and public pronunciamentos. We bring
to our sense of the begging songs our experience of non-fiction;
we respond to these songs with peculiar interest because we cannot
avoid being intellectual tourists. We turn to the begging songs,
to William Carlos Williams, to the festivals, the rituals and what
has generally been called "the tribal mode" with extraordinary
relief, where there are "no ideas, save in things."

And indeed there is a saving vitality in the mode of presentation.
The Homeric sense, as Hugh Kenner has pointed out, has been the
dominating force in two of the greatest and most experimental
of modern writers: the Odyssey inspired the opening of Pound's
Cantos, and is the groundwork for Joyce's *Ulysses*. In its fullest
flowering today, the mode of presentation is conscious of itself, a
periplum[1] that is both experienced and named, so that direct perception and the awareness of that perception tends to shade by chro-
matic nuances into complex and possibly cold abstractions. To be
naive today requires more than a letting go; it requires an effort of
the will, and shearing away of complexities. We do not return to
childhood; we create it.

We construct a childhood for the purposes of psychoanalysis.
Of whatever school or doctrine, the psychological stance assumes
that direct perception, if possible, is trivial. There is more to that

casual experience than meets the eye; the expression of anger
flows from a deep and hidden source, the laughter masks hostility.
Simple laughter, crying, joy and sorrow become minimal experiences gained at the expense of excluding a larger viewpoint. One
method of achieving naiveté—an assumption that is much larger
than any one mode of poetry today and tends to dominate them
all—is to write in a so-called colloquial or conversational style.

The assumption is constantly being rediscovered. Horace said
that he had a "pedestrian muse" and he was not being completely
self-deprecatory and ironic. The Renaissance notions of decorum,
Dryden's Preface to the *Fables*, and the Preface to the *Lyrical
Ballads*, in one way or another resorted to some standard of "real
speech." But every time the hypothesis is rediscovered, subsequent
generations reject the standards as being "artifical," or "stilted."

The colloquial, conversational tone that dominates poetry today
is in fact a highly stilted convention. If people are not consciously
trying to be poets, they will invariably move toward the highly
patterned forms of speech which are rejected today. Crowds chant
when they protest and when they riot; children tease in highly
rhythmic patterns, folk songs are usually highly regular in their
prosody. In rages or in passion, people instinctively distort speech
into regular and repetitive rhythms. Cockney rhyming slang,
proverbs, ghetto jargon and deep feelings emerge as a shaping
of language into regularity. The tom-tom, the booted foot, the
clapping hands, the expression of regular rhythms has generally
been associated with the primitive, the atavistic, the primeval. The
associations are of course not accurate, and charged with various
kinds of prejudice. But the associations do in fact exist and serve
to point out a curious assumption today: that regularity, specifically the iambic pentameter, is associated with abstractions, conceptual repressions of the emotions, in short—the Establishment,
a noun of generalized vituperative force.

I would like to suggest that the academic assumption lies not in
the iambic pentameter, but in the colloquial, conversational tone.
It is a style of poetry that is highly rarified and depends upon a vast
social upheaval, the extension of the university world. The tone
of contemporary poetry is colloquial only with respect to a narrow
sociological cut, and depends upon the highly sophisticated assumption that the isolation of words, or things, can be perceived as art.
The I.B.M. card in reality tends to be perceived as an annoyance;

it takes a rather special point of view to isolate the I.B.M. card and put it in a collage. The casual speech in a real conversation is not noticed as speech; to isolate it so that it is perceived as a poem requires a subtle complexity of conventions between the poet and the reader. One of the most misunderstood assumptions is this: in actual fact, poets avoid traditional prosody not because it inhibits emotion, but because it releases deep feelings. The drum beat stirs the blood, and if poets stir the blood, they run the risk of being psychoanalysed. For all of its affinities to the begging song, contemporary poetry lacks the rhythms, the interplay between pitch and quantitative stress—in short, the sense of splendor.

The model of a unanimity of response, of a shared experience, has many attractions and deep values; but when it dominates poetry and the poetry is brought into the class room, a curious uneasiness results. If the teachers and students are all sharing the same experience, there is nothing to rebel against, there is no *point d'appui* for the force, no rich person's house to march to.

If we go back to the image of children as objects of a sermon, we can perhaps sense certain advantages for the children. In that weekly meeting, our responses were idiosyncratic, and our mockery tended to be our own, to follow the configurations of our different personalities. The experience was not one that can be sentimentalized in retrospect: it was not fun by any means, but the tension involved growth and gave us even then a sense of our uniqueness.

And so I conclude with a dilemma: the poetry of interpretation offers conceptual freedom, but at the loss of emotive participation with others. The poetry of presentation offers emotional participation but at the loss of conceptual development and interplay.

We did not know that the ways of feeling we were searching for already existed in certain aspects of Greek literature; we did not know that in the late fifties we would get our wish.

We should be grateful for that poetry today which, like much Greek poetry, brings us back in touch with the intensely perceived object.

We should be.

We really should.

NOTES

1. *"Periplus,"* "a sailing around," as in Pound's Canto LIX: "Periplum, not as land looks on a map, but as sea foard seen by men sailing."
2. In any *rite de passage,* a ceremonial recognition of differences in age implies and enacts an equality of participation. A baby is an equal participant to a baptism.

THE EVOLUTION OF THE PIED PIPER

Bernard Queenan

In the English-speaking world, the Pied Piper of Hamelin has achieved status as a standard figure of reference. According to context, he can be cited as typifying the cheated journeyman who exacts a terrible revenge, the piper who must be paid by anyone who has called for a tune, the seducer of the young, or the mysterious and sinister sorcerer who lures the susceptible to disaster by the irresistible sweetness and charm of his spell.

His physical appearance, attributes, dress and background are likewise well established. Tall, swarthy, lean, blue-eyed, clean-shaven, clad in an old-fashioned costume of red and yellow, he is a poor wandering musician who earns the respect and patronage of the wealthy and powerful—Caliphs, Nizams, Chams and their like—for his extraordinary skills in the extermination of animal pests.

In the children's literature of other languages and cultures, the character and outward showing of the piper are more prosaic and less clearly marked. A flutist, ratcatcher, or run-of-the-mill magician, he simply appears from nowhere and departs again in the half-light of legend, without offering any information on his origins or background. He comes. He clears Hamelin of its rats. The townspeople fail to deliver the promised reward. The magus collects the children of the place and leads them to a nearby mountain. With the children, he passes into the mountain, never to be seen again.

The more vivid and circumstantial version of the story, and its widespread circulation in English, is undoubtedly due to its treatment by Robert Browning in the long poem that has become a classic of children's literature. Browning originally composed the work in 1842 for the amusement of a little boy who was confined to his room by illness. The child was William C. Macready, Junior, eldest son of William Macready, the highly popular and successful tragedian with whom Browning had long been friendly and for whom he had written several theatrical pieces. The poet intended Willie to use his verses as the subject of drawings or paintings in the production of which he had already shown some talent.

Three Pencil Drawings, by William Macready, Junior, illustrating "The Pied Piper of Hamelin." After seeing the boy's illustrations for "The Cardinal and the Dog" Browning sent him the Pied Piper poem and these drawings are the result. The drawings are labeled I, II, and III and represent Willy Macready's imaginative concept of various episodes in the story. Each of the drawings is about 7 1/4 inches (vertically) by 10 inches (horizontally). These drawings are reproduced with permission of Baylor University Browning Interests. Despite the poor quality of the reproductions, their direct association with the composition of Browning's poem makes their inclusion here of particular interest.

For source material, Browning apparently turned to a version of the legend printed in Nathaniel Wanley's "Wonders of the Little World" (1678). He may further have consulted Richard Verstegen's "Restitution of Decayed Intelligence in Antiquities," published in 1605. It is possible also that he added details picked up from verbal accounts narrated inside his own family circle, or taken down from story-tellers encountered during his journeys through Germany in 1834 and 1838. The accounts found in the publications of Wanley and Verstegen both repeat uncritically the substance of earlier printed works in German. The tradition of the Piper had attracted the attention of chroniclers and historians at the period when the printing press was giving circulation in fixed and permanent form to narratives which had up to that point mainly been current only in oral form.

The first known version of the story in print is in the "Wunder-zeichen" of the theologian Hiob Fincelius, which appeared in 1556. Fincelius reports that about 180 years before, the Devil had appeared in Hamelin and attracted many children, through his piping, to follow him to a hill where they were lost. This he considers to have been an awe-inspiring example of the wrath of God upon sin. He adds that the whole story is written in the Town Chronicle of Hamelin where many people of the better sort have read and heard it.

This reference to official town records suggests an obvious line of research for investigation of the origins and growth of the legend. Several studies have been written, and an admirably thorough and scholarly summary of their findings has been made by Dr. Heinrich Spanuth.[1] Dr. Spanuth opens his survey with a brief overview of the condition of Hamelin in the latter years of the thirteenth century. With an abbey dating from the eighth century, and a regular market from the tenth, it had become a Hansa town with full charter privileges granted in 1200. In 1259, it was purchased by Bishop Wedekind of Minden from the Abbot of Fulda for 500 marks of silver. The chronicles record that on July 28, 1260, the menfolk of the town sallied out on a military expedition against the town of Sedemünder and were, to a man, either killed or taken into captivity. The ecclesiastical registers indicate that a requiem mass was said yearly for the repose of their souls. Records also show that in 1277 the town lost its hard-earned privileges through the displeasure of the Lords of Braunschweig over the political stance adopted by the townspeople in the local power-struggles of the period.

Of the appearance of a piper in Hamelin on June 26, 1284, there is no contemporary report. On the other hand, a record has survived concerning the transfer, on July 23, 1284, the Eve of the Feast of St. John the Baptist, of a hide of land to the neighbouring hamlet of Honrode, and the names are recorded of the Burgomeister and his fellow signatories to the transaction. Only after the lapse of nearly a century does any record appear of an occurrence which might be construed as relating to the mysterious piper.

The reference is found as a note in the end-papers of a manuscript copy of the *Catena Aurea* of Heinrich von Herford which can be dated about 1370. Although the existence of this Luneburger Manuscript was noted in other textual references, the text itself was lost for centuries until located by Dr. Spanuth himself in 1936.

Written in Latin, with many of the conventional abbreviations and compressions typical of the style of the monkish scribe of the period, the text appears to read:—

> Notandum miraculum valde rarum quod accidit in opido hamelen mindense diocese anno domini M° cc° LXXXiiij ipso die johannis et pauli. Quidam adolescens de XXX annis pulcher et omnino bene vestitus ita quod omnes videntes eum in persona et in vestito eius admirabantur intrat per pontem et Wesere portem. Habens argenteam festulam mire forme incepit festulare per totum opidum et omnes pueri audientes illam festulam in numero CXXX sequebantur eum extra portam valuam origentalem quasi ad locum calvariae vel decollationis et evanuerunt et introesserunt quod nullus potuit investigare ubi unus eorum remansit. Matres vero puerorum currererunt de civitate ad civitatem et penitus nihil invenerunt. Unde vox in Rama audita est et quisque mater deplanxit filium suum. Et veteri computatur per annos domini vel per annum primum 2^m 3^m post jubilieum sic computaverunt in hamelen per primum 2^m 3^m annum post exitum et egressum puerorum. Ista reperi in uno antiquo libro. Et mater domini Johannis de Lude decani vidit pueros egredientes.

This text, as reproduced in reduced format in Dr. Spanuth's work, presents several interesting features not least of which is the juxtaposition of Roman and Arabic figures. In the fourteenth century, the new-fangled Arabic system of numeration was gradually spreading from Mediterranean bases throughout the centres of learning of

Northern and Western Europe. It is also noteworthy that the chronicler uses the phrase 'adolescens de XXX annis', in referring to the piper. If he was about 30 years old, and is described as 'adolescens', what is to be the translation of 'omnes pueri'? Boys? Children? Young people?

Leaving aside this and other niceties of translation, if this transcription of the Latin manuscript is accurate, a loose unpolished rendering into English would suggest the following narrative . . .

"To be noted is a marvellous and truly extraordinary event that occurred in the town of Hamelin in the diocese of Minden in the year of the Lord 1284, on the very feast-day of Saints John and Paul. A young man of 30 years, handsome and in all respects so finely dressed that all who saw him were awestruck by his person and clothing came in by way of the bridge and the Weser Gate. On a silver pipe which he had, of wonderful form, he began to play through the whole town, and all the children hearing him, to the number of 130, followed him beyond the eastern wall almost to the place of the Calvary or Gallows field, and vanished and disappeared so that nobody could find out where any one of them had gone. Indeed, the mothers of the children wandered from city to city and discovered nothing. A voice was heard in Rama and every mother bewailed her son.[2] And as people count by the years of the Lord or by the first, second and third after a jubilee, so they have counted in Hamelin by the first, second and third year after the exodus and departure of the children. This I have found in an old book. And the mother of Herr Johann de Lude, the deacon, saw the children going out."

Dr. Spanuth refers to the local church records of the period which contain references to a Deacon Johann von Lude who died on March 12, 1378. The allusion to his mother, as a little girl of perhaps ten years of age, seeing the children leave Hamelin in 1284, therefore seems acceptable as a statement of truth, rather than an improbable invention.

Other references to the passage of a piper are found among the surviving archives of the town. A Council Record Book known as 'De Brade', dating from the last years of the fourteenth century, contains an account of 130 children being lost, after following a piper dressed in multi-coloured clothing through the Eastern Gate of Hamelin on June 26, 1284. The same date, with some kind of allusion to the exodus of the children, was also reproduced in various inscriptions on buildings in the town. Some of these, on chimney-breasts or lintels, have been preserved. Others, such as a carved stone on an old Town Gate, have disappeared and are now known only from descriptions and sketches in literary texts left by observers.

With the passage of time, however, succeeding versions of the story tend to vary as to the day and year of the event, and to gain in embellishments of commentary and interpretation what they lack in historical precision.

Whether the story-tellers claim to have collected their accounts from conversations with the townspeople of Hamelin, or to have based their writings on older texts which they have consulted, they concur in colouring the events with overtones of magic, witchcraft and diabolic intervention. By the mid-sixteenth century, the accretion of narratives from folk-rhymes, quotations from chronicles and pious explanations, had solidified. It now becomes an account of wickedness attracting its merited punishment that encouraged chroniclers like Fincelius to formalize and repeat it for its exemplary message of the awesome visitation of the retribution that lies in wait for the froward and impenitent.

The seventeenth century saw a corresponding reaction, when the burghers of the prosperous and developing township attempted to redeem their reputation by denying the truthfulness and historical accuracy of the legend. Pamphleteers and historians were forthcoming who sought to discount the story of the piper and the children as a mere folk-fable without any greater factual substance than the unlikely invention of an ignorant, unlettered and superstitious populace seeking wonders and portents. Controversies and literary polemics developed, with exchanges of charges and counter-charges, assertions and challenges, accusations and denials. The ebb and flow of the debate makes for interesting and amusing reading, but the detail is of little value for the present survey. What is important is that the writers concerned were more intent on promoting their particular interpretations rather than on any systematic review of what objective evidence might still be accessible to scrutiny.

When the cooler intellectual climate of the Enlightenment arrived, writers of eighteenth century Western Europe were therefore content to repeat in different languages, and with varying details, the stories that they inherited as coherent narratives. Usually, the presentation was of a quaint old story — an unexplained curiosity of folk-tradition from the remote past.

The Romantic movement, with new attitudes to the heritage of the past and to the cultural treasury of popular traditions revived interest in the legend of the piper. In Germany, the brothers Grimm collected and published one account, and Johann Wolfgang Goethe made it the subject of a poem. Robert Browning was only one among many writers of the time to note the tale or to include a treatment in his literary output. The story also became the starting-point or inspiration for nineteenth century musical plays, songs and operas. Researchers who have sought some real event in history as the origin of the legend, have therefore had to contend with these many overlays of fictional exaggeration or outright falsification.

Some have seen the exodus of the young people of Hamelin as a distorted memory of an episode in the Children's Crusade of 1212, when the youth of Western Europe in their thousands followed Nicolas of Cologne to disaster along the shores of the Mediterranean. Others have argued that the children must have been carried off in some epidemic typical of the period. Exponents of this theory place the rats in the foreground of the story as carriers of the vermin that propagated diseases such as bubonic plague. When rats were plentiful, sickness and death would be widespread. The survivors from any outbreak of pestilence would develop some kind of immunity, from exposure to non-fatal attacks of the infection. At some later date, when rats returned and the plague with them, it would be chiefly the new generation of children who would have no developed resistance to the disease and who would therefore be borne away. The theorists who argue for some rational explanation along these lines suggest that the legend, in the form that Browning found and perpetuated, combines strands from different sources in the folk memory.

There are references, for example, in German popular tales to acts of revenge by sorcerers who are cheated out of what they consider to be their just dues. A story is found about the town of Lorch, which was beset by a plague of ants. A hermit arrived and was promised a fee for eliminating this nuisance. He led the ants away, but was not paid, so he took away all the pigs of the place, with a magic charm. The next year, a plague of crickets invaded Lorch. A charcoal burner was found who was promised money to rid the town of them. When he did, and was refused the agreed reward, he led away all the sheep. In the third year, came a plague of rats. An old man of the mountains arrived and promised to clear them for a price. When the rats disappeared and his payment was not forthcoming, he led all the children after him, playing on a pipe, to the Tannenberg.

The argument runs that if a migrant version of such a story were to be transferred to Hamelin, instead of Lorch, it would require little local colouring or associations for the story of the piper to become irrevocably linked to the name of the town. The fate of a Hamelin contingent vanishing in the Children's Crusade, or in the disastrous expedition to Sedemünder, or in the onset of some pestilence, would provide the necessary connection.

The children, or young people, might even have succumbed to an outbreak of the Dancing Madness, another frightening phenomenon of mediaeval Europe, in which dozens of the inhabitants of a locality would inexplicably be seized by a collective impulse to rise and roam together in a jerking, twisting frenzy, until they literally danced themselves into collapse and even death. Modern medical researchers suggest that the Dancing Madness, originated in the toxic effects of a fungus which infected growing grain crops, and which would survive and ferment to produce hallucinogenic substances such as ergot throughout the processes of being harvested, stored under unsatisfactory conditions, milled into flour and baked into bread. Instances have been investigated in recent years of similar outbreaks in country districts of Europe.

Against such ingenious and intriguing theories, however, stands the more prosaic and factual evidence of the note appended to the Luneburger Manuscript. There is no mention in this oldest reference either of any event requiring a supernatural explanation, nor any act of revenge for non-payment of an agreed price for banishing rats from Hamelin. Dr. Heinrich Spanuth points out that the scribe's account could refer in all respects to a visit to Hamelin by a herald or crier, acting as Lokator, or recruiting agent. It was a common practice at the period for the overlords of territories requiring immigrant populations to send a Lokator through their domains to preach the merits of far-off locations and invite those discontented with their present lot to venture out into the unknown in search of a brighter future. In 1284, Rudolph von Hapsburg, as Holy Roman Emperor, had recently acquired by

In 1888 Kate Greenaway made colour illustrations for *The Pied Piper of Hamelin* by Robert Browning, which became one of her best-known and most rewarding works. From THE KATE GREENAWAY BOOK: A Collection of Illustration, Verse and Text, edited by Brian Holme, Viking, 1976.

conquest extensive new possessions in Moravia. The Pied Piper of
Hamelin may therefore in fact have been one of Rudolph's
emissaries, clad in a colourful tabard carrying the heraldic blazon of
a coat-of-arms, and blowing flourishes on his trumpet to attract
onlookers. On that Monday, June 26, 1284, on the Feast of Saints
John and Paul, the little market-town held perhaps some two
thousand souls. The sudden and unexplained departure *en masse* of
one hundred and thirty young people must certainly have been a
grievous loss to the townspeople who remained.

It may well have been, however, that those who followed the
piper simply joined a convoy of emigrants waiting out of sight on
the road beyond the Koppelberg.

The suggestion contained in the Browning poem, that the
children of Hamelin became in time the ancestors of the inhabitants
of Saxon towns in Transylvania, or elsewhere in Eastern Europe,
may therefore reflect a historical fact.

NOTES

1. *Der Rattenfänger von Hamelin: Vom Werden und Sinn einer alten Sage*
   (Hamelin: Verlag C. W. Niemeyer, 1951).
2. Jeremiah 31:15
   Matthew 2:18

TOAD HALL REVISITED

Lois R. Kuznets

> "You like people. They interest you. But I am
> interested in places."
>
> Kenneth Grahame to his wife[1]

A wistful, bitter-sweet longing for the past, which goes by the name of "nostalgia" in modern times, is an oft-noted characteristic of Kenneth Grahame's *The Wind in the Willows.* Although we are unlikely to suspect or to want to nurture such nostalgia in a child under twelve, we may consider it merely one of the emotional bonuses of an adult reading of *The Wind in the Willows* and, as such, dismiss it as a peripheral concern.

Underlying the modern English connotation of the word "nostalgia," however, is the ancient denotation — a basic, "G-rated" emotion available to any age: homesickness, from the Greek *nostos* or "return home" and *algia* or "pain." In this study, I try to show that homesickness is not peripheral but central to *The Wind in the Willows* and is buried deep within its structure, as it is in the word "nostalgia"; Moreover, I argue that Grahame succeeds in transforming this basic homesickness (and its opposite extreme — wanderlust) into a more fruitful emotion for himself, his characters, and his responsive audience of any age: *Topophilia.* I borrow this term meaning love *(philia)* of place *(topos)* from Gaston Bachelard, who, in his book, *The Poetics of Space,* explores this phenomenon of the imagination.[2]

Bachelard, Sorbonne philosopher of science, wrote *The Experience of Space in Modern Physics;* in his more recent work of "phenomenological" criticism, he ruminates on various literary manifestations of topophilia. After an introduction in which he carefully detaches the consideration of certain poetic images from what he considers the reductionist tendencies of psychology and psychoanalysis, Bachelard examines what he calls "images of felicitous space." His chapters are provocatively titled: "The House from Cellar to Garret," "House and Universe," "Drawers, Chests, and Wardrobes," "Nests," "Shells," "Corners," "Miniature,"

"Intimate Immensity," "The Dialectics of Outside and Inside," "The Phenomenology of Roundness."

According to Bachelard, images of felicitous space in poetry (prominent in such writers as Rilke and Baudelaire) strike chords that reverberate in the reader. They send him back in his imagination not to the womb, as psychoanalysts may suggest, but rather to those places of his childhood that allowed him either in solitude or in the safe presence of loved ones to exercise his highest faculties of fantasizing and daydreaming. Felicitous space and its imagistic representations provide a secure center not *in* which to curl up in foetal position but *from* which one may safely venture out into the vast universe of thought and feeling. The womb, for Bachelard, is not a felicitous space; the house of one's childhood may be.

Grahame is only sometimes a poet; his topophilia is generally diffuse rather than distilled in single, striking, and reverberating images such as Bachelard explores. Grahame's sense of felicitous space appears in his leisurely, almost languid, descriptions of the general landscape of *The Wind in the Willows* and in the attention he pays to the particular habitats of his main characters. A sense of felicitous space, or better, a search for felicitous space, also permeates the structure of *The Wind in the Willows*. The tale has as its living center Mole's and Rat's vision of a wonderful place: The paradisal island of the weir in which the Great God Pan resides. Moreover, a series of crises determines the book's shape — crises through which each of the three main characters, Mole, Rat, and Toad, come to grips with their true homes, their true selves, and, to some extent, the universe at large.

In this study, attempting to show how topophilia pervades all, I shall consider first the geography of the universe of *The Wind in the Willows*, second the individual homes of each of the main characters, and finally the way in which their topophilic experiences form the structure of the book.[3]

Geography: River, Wild Wood, and Wide World

Grahame only vaguely maps out the geography of *The Wind in the Willows*. There can be no doubt, however, that the River is the center of that universe. We can note, remembering Bachelard, how Mole's and the reader's first glimpse of the River reflects not the physical sustenance it provides for the river animals, about which we have yet to learn, but rather imaginative sustenance, support, and inspiration:

> The Mole was bewitched, entranced, fascinated. By the side of
> the river he trotted as one trots, when very small, by the side
> of a man who holds one spellbound by exciting stories; and
> tired at last, he sat on the bank, while the river still chattered
> on to him, a babbling procession of the best stories in the
> world, sent from the heart of the earth to be told at last to the
> insatiable sea. (3-4)[4]

The River flows throughout the work, continuing to provide
imaginative inspiration. Especially in the winter, the River folk are
sustained by this flow. At that time, they indulge in "a good deal of
storytelling and comparing notes on the past summer and all its
doings" (44). The concern with the imaginative reshaping and
ritualizing of the River experience as it is recollected in tranquillity
is apparent also in an early passage. Here the narrator describes the
previous river season as a "rich chapter" with "highly coloured"
illustrations. He then moves into more active metaphors of artistic
creation so that the "chapter" becomes a "pageant" and a "stately
procession" "on the stage" as if announced by "string music" "in
stately chords that strayed into a gavotte" while various wild
flowers join the group so that "the play" could begin. (44-45)

In the center of the book and in the center of its central river
lives Pan, the Great Friend and Helper. Searching the River for
Otter's lost child, Portly, Mole and Rat move toward heavenly
music, aroused at every sensuous level. (133) As they approach
Pan's place, his paradisal island emerges through images of
roundness: the great weir is a "wide half-circle" that "closed in the
backwater." The island is "midmost of the stream, embraced in the
weir's shimmering arm-spread"; it is "fringed close with willow"; on
it is a lawn "set round with nature's own orchard-trees" (134).
Bachelard says that images of roundness tend to "help us collect
ourselves, permit us to confer an initial constitution on ourselves,
and confirm our being intimately, inside."[5] These embracing circles
certainly have that effect on Rat and Mole and, confirmed
intimately, Rat articulates a topophilic perception: "This is the
place of my song-dream, the place the music played to me" (134).
Grahame makes clear, however, that this inspirational place is not
to be revisited by either Rat or Mole, even in the imagination. (136)
This is perhaps because the island symbolizes the static perfection
of death and *The Wind in the Willows* celebrates life as it is depicted

in the unceasing flow of the River, the most available and general center of inspiration in the book.

On one side of the River, framing the water meadows, is the Wild Wood; Badger lives right in the heart of it. But as Rat points out about weasels, stoats, and foxes, the inhabitants of the Wild Wood," . . . you can't really trust them, and that's the fact" (11). In chapter three, we are also encouraged to feel that the Wild Woods are inhabited not only by these untrustworthy yet natural creatures, but also by evil spirits that threaten Mole. When Rat finds Mole at bay there, Rat claims mysteriously that one must have all sorts of occult knowledge to get through the Wild Wood safely. (53)

The Wild Wood as experienced by Mole and Rat in that scene has a hellish quality in contrast with the heavenly quality of the island of chapter seven. In the Wild Wood, Mole — less well-armed either materially or spiritually than Rat — is prey to a primal emotion, "The Terror of the Wild Wood." This terror drives him into a womblike but dubious shelter, "the deep dark hollow of an old beech tree" (50). The distinction that Bachelard makes between the uncreative retreat into the womb and the true topophilic experience is exemplified in the contrast between the island and the Wild Wood scene. Images of embracing roundness which are fulfilling in the former are here threatening: Mole ". . . penetrated to where the light was less, and the trees crouched nearer and nearer, and holes made ugly mouths at him on either side" (47).

It is impossible for one to be confirmed intimately inside the Wild Wood; the only felicitous space to be found there — until the end of the story when the Wild Wood is controlled — is Badger's buried residence. Badger's abode stands for a retreat into a buried past presided over by a stern but benign father-figure (see below). In contrast to the River, Badger's space is of limited inspirational value; but it is a controlled environment infinitely preferable to and comforting after the experience of the primal Terror of the Wild Wood.

Beyond the Wild Wood lies the Wide World with which Rat wants to have nothing to do. (12) Nevertheless, in chapter two, Rat and Mole, at the instigation of the worldly Toad, find themselves on the open road in Toad's mobile home, an unsteady caravan that is soon knocked into a ditch by that poop-pooping creation of restlessness, the motor car. The motor car becomes a prime symbol of the Wide World and its incursions on the world of nature; Toad, whose principal adventures take place in the Wide World, recognizes the motor car as a symbol of topo*phobia:* "Here today — in next week tomorrow! Villages skipped, towns and cities jumped — always somebody else's horizon . . ." (38).

There is some felicitous space in the Wide World, however, in one of these very villages that Toad would have skipped. In chapter five, returning to the River from a winter expedition, Rat and Mole at nightfall gaze upon human domesticity through a lighted window; the human inhabitants seem to have a "happy grace" (83). That domestic scene is clearly a human correlative for Mole's approaching reconciliation with his own home. Grahame here performs a highly sophisticated exercise in topophilic presentation, taking the rather commonplace image of felicitous space, the house in winter, and giving it double intensity and identification.[6] The passage describing and praising the interior scene continues for several pages and ends with a reminder of the freezing discomfort of the "outsiders," Rat and Mole, who are far away from home. (85) Here Grahame forces the reader to be both outside in the cold in imaginative alliance with Rat and Mole and inside, suddenly aware of how felicitous human space can be, how cozy the ones inside look from the outside.

The River, the Wild Wood, and the Wide World are the broad features of the universe of *The Wind in the Willows.* We do get glimpses of several other aspects of the Wide World through Toad's misadventures. For the most part, however, the Wide World places are not taken seriously. Descriptive passages are facetious or mildly satirical; the intensity of feeling projected into the space centered on the River becomes fainter the farther we move away from it into the Wide World. The Wide World as Grahame depicts it offers little opportunity for topophilic reflection; at its best it can be a funny, but not generally felicitous, place.

Homes — From Lowest to Highest

Grahame chooses a water rat, a mole, and a badger as animal characters for reasons that seem to have more to do with the positions of their natural homes than with the animals' natural propensities and physical characteristics. It is important that Rat, Badger, and Mole live at various depths in the earth. Badger lives deepest down; Mole lives just under the surface; Rat lives in a hole in the Riverbank open to the River's ebb and flow. While the interiors of their homes are no more naturalistic than the animals' characteristics, the general positions of their homes are. Only Toad's home is totally anthropomorphic and above ground, befitting the animal character that is going to have the most dealings with mankind; it is, however, in an artificial position for a toad, a reptile that would not erect a Tudor or Georgian mansion but would burrow into the mud.

As we discover in chapter four, Badger's home is not only deep, but is an amazing structure with massive architectural features. Being a natural underground dweller, Mole feels immediately at home there and he and Badger discover a natural rapport in their somewhat similar sense of felicitous space. They ally, at least temporarily, against the dwellings of Rat and Toad, making it clear that for some, as Badger says, "there's no security or peace or tranquillity except underground" (75).

Badger's home is a ruin and the storehouse of a bygone civilization; as such it is akin to the "cellar image" investigated by Bachelard.[7] Badger's description of the provenance of his home through forgotten civilizations, too long to quote here, imbues the topophilic image with shades of *ubi sunt*. Badger's protectiveness towards the little animals and his corrective severity towards Toad indicate the paternal role he plays in this story. Also, through his dwelling place which is linked with past generations, Badger becomes the archetypal father to Toad, who functions as the archetypal prodigal son; Badger's home is rooted deep in earth and past; Toad's is at the mercy of time and the elements.

The security of the underground cellar, while valuable, does not have the highest value in *The Wind in the Willows*. This, however, does not begin to come clear until we have read the "Dulce Domum" chapter. Mole's experience with his own underground home shows that Grahame considers the underground (in all of its shades of meaning) too narrow and confining to be felicitous space in the topophilic sense.

At the beginning of the book, in response to spring, Mole too hastily leaves his underground in the midst of spring cleaning. Bird songs call him away; "the mysterious fairy calls" of homesickness draw him back there at Christmas time. The season is significant: Mole's humble abode as shelter for weary, shivering travelers recalls the Nativity story. Mole, transformed into host, is permitted to dispense hospitality not only to Rat but to caroling field mice as well. Being a host is clearly one of the joys of having "one's own place," and the Christmas carol the field mice sing is almost a topophilic hymn linking those outside with those inside, animal with human, hospitality with spirituality. (98)

The welcoming of the field mice is a traditional social event, and Mole's deep appreciation of sociability distinguishes him from Badger, whose hospitality is accidental. Mole also lives closer to the surface and the narrowness of the underground is not sufficient for him. He leaves the underground again after Christmas. His vision of felicitous space expands in the course of the book and his character develops accordingly while Badger remains static, finally and limitedly grown up. Because it allows Mole to change and to respond to the inspirational River, I think we can say that Mole's earth home, though not as massive and impressive as Badger's, is one step "above" Badger's.

Badger may like to talk about his home, but Mole becomes positively lyrical when Rat asks him to "tell us all about it, and how you came to make it what it is" (95). To be physically in one's home is not enough; bonds are forged by talking about it. Talking about one's home becomes an emotional release and therapeutic action for Mole here, for Toad in the "grimmest dungeon" of chapter eight and for Rat when he hears a siren call. Homesickness is largely inarticulate and very close to a pain in the gut; topophilia starts somewhere in the imaginative faculty and moves to the vocal chords.

There is a natural link between this need to talk and Rat's finding inspiration for poetry in his River home. Badger fails to see this, or rather sees the position of Rat's home and his poetic faculty as equally untrustworthy. (76, 247) The entire topophilic direction of *The Wind in the Willows* confuses and intertwines Rat's poetic faculty with the position of his domicile on the banks of the River. But Badger's estimate of the value of Rat's position and his verbal occupation is clearly wrong. Part of Mole's development beyond Badger and the underground is caused by his acceptance of Rat's superior talents. Although both Rat and Mole see Pan, Mole says "You hear better than I . . . I can not catch the words" (140).

Rat's intimacy with the River is set out early in the book in the most positive terms imaginable. When his new acquaintance, Mole, says, "So—this—is—a River!" Rat replies, "*The* River," and goes on to emphasize that "what it hasn't got is not worth having" and "what it doesn't know is not worth knowing." (9-10) Rat's intimacy with the River is the source of his physical, emotional and spiritual life. Each reinforces the other.

Rat's dwelling place gives him a role as spiritual guide equal to or greater in importance than Badger's paternal role. This is symbolically indicated by Rat's rescue both of Mole and Toad from drowning in the River (19-20, 213). These could be baptismal scenes in which Rat is the agent both of physical rescue and spiritual baptism. Like Chaucer's intellectual clerk, however, not only would Rat "gladly teche" but also would he "gladly lerne." Later, when Rat must go through his own crisis and reconciliation with his home, his disciple, Mole, re-teaches him about the River and revives his essential topophilia.

I imagine an impatient Toad complaining: "And what about me, how do I fit in here?" "That's just the point," I reply, "You don't fit *in* at all. You sit on top of all this." "Good, that's just where I belong," shouts Toad, jumping up and down, knocking everything apart, and falling off in the bargain.

Toad Hall is an attractive excrescence on the face of the earth and Toad seems an equally attractive child-man figure playing with expensive toys. According to Badger, Toad Hall is as unstable as its owner, vulnerable to every natural disaster, and, as we see later, to social disasters as well. Badger is probably right: the most unstable character lives in the most unstable house and the fact that it is elegant does not necessarily make it felicitous space.

The contrary may be true. Although it might be easier to exercise topophilia when one's image of home is a mansion rather than a hole in the ground, Grahame shows this not to be the case. Again he agrees with Bachelard who speaks of how poets seek for some core of intimacy and have difficulty finding it in a castle.[8] Toad, in prison, fumbles around and makes a false start in describing his home to the sympathetic gaoler's daughter. He begins as if reciting a classified advertisement for "an eligible self-contained gentleman's residence" (146). The girl interrupts him and asks him to tell her "something *real*" about it.

He then launches a description which pivots on the image of Toad "when other animals were gathered round the table and Toad was at his best, singing songs, telling stories, carrying on generally" (147). Toad's topophilia as depicted here is not mere braggadocio; this topophilic image of the entertaining host is a common one.

The image of man's place there, from the great gabled hall of Beowulf, is associated with feasting and storytelling. Later in the story, Toad Hall, as vulnerable as other great halls, will be besieged by the forces of disorder. Toad, in addition to talking about his home, will have to earn it, clearing it like Ulysses of invaders. With the help of the others he will do so; but his true victory will be a non-material, topophilic one, reconciling himself to his "place."

Structuring Topophilic Experiences

A general sense of development and change in Toad, Rat, and Mole should lead us to feel that *The Wind in the Willows* is not "episodic"; intensive examination indeed shows Grahame's iron hand and its topophilic grasp. *The Wind in the Willows* begins with an abortive housecleaning and ends with a symbolic housecleaning. The center of the book is the centering experience of the island of the weir. The chapters in which Mole, Rat, and Toad have their respective final topophilic crisis, are not spaced symmetrically but are placed at progressively decreasing intervals. This suggests a pattern based on the timing and difficulty of development in the main characters and indicates the strong sense of structural control Grahame exerted on the tale.

The four major animal characters divide into two groups in terms of topophilic experiences. Mole and Rat assist one another in coming to different reconciliations with their homes, each suited not just to the temperament of the character, but also to the nature of his home. Badger does not go through a topophilic crisis himself but is an instrument in bringing Toad to topophilic fulfillment.

Mole's topophilic experience comes first. It is relatively simple; he returns to his formerly deserted home needing an imaginative recognition of a secure center. In his own bed that Christmas Eve, after the salutary and necessary experience of being host and of talking at length to Rat about his home, Mole realizes that his home "had long been unconsciously a part of him" and that he appreciates the "special value of some such anchorage in one's existence" (103). Of course, those very qualities that make Mole's home easy to return to — it is small, humble, unobtrusive, and safe underground — lead him again to desert it, to heed the call of the "upper world" and to "return to the larger stage." (103) Unlike some twentieth-century heroes, however, Mole can go home again and again, both physically and imaginatively, and receive the "same simple welcome" (103).

Rat's home is more complex and his topophilic crisis stranger and more ambivalent. The bustle and flurry surrounding the fall departure of migrating birds in "Wayfarers All," stimulates in Rat a restlessness and discontent that turns almost maniacal when he hears tales of exotic lands from a passing Sea Rat. For the moment, he loses touch with his vital center and is filled with wanderlust. As if possessed by the other Rat, with the "sea-grey eyes," he packs his satchel and starts off. He is, in some measure, like Toad, who was possessed by the motor car, and he must be treated with some of the same force: "Grappling with him strongly [Mole] dragged him inside, threw him down, and held him" (186). Ordinarily the essence of the topophilic man, intimate with and sustained by his set place (the felicitous space of the River), Rat is vulnerable in the extreme flexibility of his imagination. "The haunting sea voices that had sung to him" (187) sound very different from the poop-poop of the motor car; they offer an exoticism of place rather than a negation of place. But for Rat they won't do; he's a fresh-water Rat not a salt-water Rat.[9]

The title of this chapter, "Wayfarers All," suggests that life is a kind of pilgrimage. But the attempt to act out that image of life in physical terms is inappropriate for Rat: the farther he travels from the River into the Wide World, the farther away he goes from his true vision of his other-worldly Home, the island in the center of the River. The true pilgrimage for Rat is along that River into the sea of imagination, and Mole recognizes this. He first tries to make Rat talk about his home and then to write poetry. Rat at first rejects pencil and paper, but "sometime later, the Rat was absorbed and deaf to the world" (188). Mole has to open his own ears to the song of the birds; Rat, like Ulysses, has to deafen his ears. A hole in the ground isn't quite enough but all the world is too much for topophilia.

Given the anthropomorphic nature of Toad and his juvenile temperament, it is not surprising that his topophilic crisis takes longest to develop. His is the most complex and remains the least stable after resolution. He needs help and finds it most obviously in Badger, who, as already noted, functions differently from the three other main characters. Badger goes through no development or change himself but serves especially to stabilize restless Toad, with whom he is most contrasted, just as badgers in general are considered here (in their topo-longevity), to be in contrast with humans. Badger notes the topo-longevity of the badger species:

> "People come — they stay a while, they flourish, they
> build — and they go. It is their way. But we remain . . . We are
> an enduring lot, and we may move out for a time, but we wait
> and are patient and back we come." (78)

Badger has special knowledge denied to Toad — knowledge of a
secret, significantly underground passageway to Toad Hall. In his
possessing it and dispensing it to Toad at the proper moment,
Badger indicates most explicitly that he is the surrogate father and
guardian to Toad, who has yet to come into his inheritance in any
meaningful way. In addition, as an already formed character,
Badger is the main *re*forming force in Toad's life, a super-ego who
has not yet been internalized. The language of chapter six, where
the three friends attempt to keep Toad under house arrest, is shot
through with missionary fervor; it confirms Badger's instrumental
and dedicated role long before the final crisis.

In each chapter where we meet Toad — two, six, eight, ten and
eleven — he is someplace else; this confirms his restlessness. Most
times we meet him he seems worse off than before, suffering the
consequences of one folly and involving himself in a new one. Since
he seems little closer to maturity on his return from prison than he
was before, it is clear that he cannot alone recapture his rightful
place, Toad Hall. We are not surprised that he takes fourth place in
planning and executing the plot to overcome its usurpers. The
mock-epic quality of the chapter title, "The Return of Ulysses," is
in full force as far as this hero is concerned. Still, on the scene of
the action and spurred by the mocking weasels, Toad does manage
to acquit himself and later to thank his faithful friends with
some good grace.

But it is not really on the scene of the action that Toad undergoes his true crisis and comes into his own. After he has sent out
elaborate invitations to a banquet, his friends inform him that he
cannot feature himself as continual entertainment for his guests.
He then retires to his bedroom where he acts out for the benefit of
a semicircle of empty chairs the performance that he would have
given had he been permitted. (254-256) What is significant about
this scene in terms of its psychological import is that it is like the
previous scene, in which Toad acted out his motor car mania with
these same chairs. (112-113) That time he was under lock and key

and heavily guarded by his friends. This time, however, Toad himself locks his door and closes the curtains; it is a completely private act that includes the singing of a song beginning "When the Toad came home!"

Toad's crisis, like his two friends', is topophilic in that it is associated with a particular place and is imaginatively and creatively resolved. It was out of the handsome Tudor window that "formed such a feature of his bedroom" that Toad first escaped Toad Hall. Toad has a dream about this same bedroom while taking shelter in a hollow tree on his way home. His accommodation and sense of place is limited. We are not entirely sure yet that he is fit or grown-up enough to be master of the entire Hall, but he is getting there, working outward from the vital center of his home, his bedroom. He is in the terms of the child psychologist Fritz Redl, symbolically developing "controls from within."[10]

Toad, one of the first characters that Grahame created for his son's bedtime story, resolves his crisis in the one place in a house that a child might call his own. As undefinitive as his bedroom resolution may be, Toad's solution is surely reassuring for a child — indeed, for the child within all of us. Toad's small progress in self-control suggests that childish impulses are natural and recurrent and need not be repressed altogether. By contrast, Mole's and Rat's crises are largely adult and are not prolonged or difficult enough either for twentieth-century child or twentieth-century adult.

The series of topophilic crises leading up to an emotionally satisfying ending give a comforting pattern and shape to the total book. The prodigal-son theme played out by both Portly and Toad is comforting and topophilic; it implies that the welcome mat is always out on the doorstep of one's childhood home. Comforting and topophilic too is an epic level in *The Wind in the Willows* that is not merely mock. The recapture of Toad Hall from disorderly invaders, making the Wild Wood safe for everyone, is a securing and enlarging of the available felicitous space.[11] This feat makes Toad, Badger, Rat, and Mole true epic heroes and, as other epic heroes they become legendary not only within their own little world but in the Wide World as well.

The little world of *The Wind in the Willows* was the vital center from which Kenneth Grahame transformed his own nostalgia (and perhaps the homesickness of his son) into topophilia. Such love of place is really a love of ourselves at our most innocent and imaginative, and may be sustaining to us as we make our own way through the Wide World.

NOTES

1. Peter Green, *Kenneth Grahame, A Biography* (Cleveland: The World Publ. Co., 1969), p. 126, quotes Grahame's friend, Graham Robertson, quoting Grahame.
2. *The Poetics of Space,* trans. Maria Jolas (New York: Orion Press, 1964).
3. Reasons of space prevent me from continuing with an already prepared fourth section of this paper. It contemplates not only the beneficial aspects of topophilia for the characters in the book and its readers, but also the way in which topophilia can become topophil*ism* in its potential association with other, less attractive "isms." The felicitous space that Grahame creates and reveres is a stable and domestically comfortable environment that encourages a healthy concern for nature and for other beings. This environment, in turn, stimulates an imaginative sublimation of wayward impulses. The maintenance of this "felicitous space," however, partly depends upon deep-seated attitudes that I certainly would not embrace wholeheartedly, nor would want to encourage in my children. These are, in particular, paternalism, sexism, and political and social conservatism. I do not have time to consider these aspects here but I urge all critical readers of *The Wind in the Willows* to do so.
4. All quotations are from Kenneth Grahame, *The Wind in the Willows* (1908; rpt. New York: Charles Scribner's Sons, 1961). Page numbers of quotations and pertinent references are cited in the text.
5. Bachelard, p. 234.
6. Bachelard, pp. 38-40, examines a number of such images.
7. Bachelard, p. xxxiii, quotes from Jung's *Contributions of Analytical Psychology* an image depicting the human psyche as if it were a towering building onto which successive generations have added storeys; ". . . In the cellar we discover Roman foundation walls and under the cellar a filled-in cave, in the floor of which stone tools are found and remnants of glacial fauna in the layers below . . ." Later Bachelard makes clear that in spatial imagery the cellar is associated with the primitive, subconscious, and frightening, as well as with the foundations of civilization inherited from ancient man. Characteristic of Grahame here, as in his use of Pan, is that he strips the earth and nature images of many of their "forbidden" elements, associations with lust and death, and keeps the more benign and comforting ideas and feelings associated with these places.
8. "We must first look for centers of simplicity in houses with many rooms. For as Baudelaire said, in a palace, 'there is no place for intimacy.' " Bachelard, p. 29.
9. There is a temptation here and elsewhere in this paper to give biographical explanations for some of the choices Grahame makes and the symbols he uses. Those interested in Grahame's biography will find the nature of Rat's temptations very significant. I have tried not to yield to these or to psychoanalytical

temptations which would be totally out of keeping with Bachelard's thesis and approach.

10. Fritz Redl and David Wineman, *The Aggressive Child* (Glencoe, Ill.: Free Press, 1957).

11. This ending, of course, is also in keeping with a pastoral tradition, which always had within it an element of escape from and discontent with the real world, particularly after the Industrial Revolution and the social dislocations that accompanied it.

THE SANE, THE MAD, THE GOOD, THE BAD:
T. S. ELIOT'S OLD POSSUM'S BOOK OF PRACTICAL CATS

Marion C. Hodge

In general, T. S. Eliot's poetry is intellectual, subtle, static, lyrical. Nothing much happens in it. There are few characters, and they do little except think. Prufrock takes a walk, climbs stairs. Gerontion is "an old man in a dry mouth / Being read to by a boy, waiting for rain."[1] In *The Waste Land,* Madame Sosostris tells fortunes, Phlebas the Phoenician drowns, and, at the conclusion, the narrator sits "upon the shore / Fishing . . ." In *Ash-Wednesday* and *Four Quartets,* there are no characters at all, no activity; there is only meditation. The most vigorous narratives in Eliot's "serious" work are those concerning the sexual grubbiness of the typist and "the young man carbuncular" in *The Waste Land,* and that of Sweeney in several short poems. For the most part, then, Eliot's poetry is thought and symbol, state of mind, state of consciousness. His themes are commonly the emotional and moral sterility of modern civilization and the hope for the renewal of an abiding, satisfying faith, a mythology that will order the present chaos and evil. Implicit in these themes is a vision of humanity as vulgar, powerless, and depraved.

But when Eliot writes for children, some things are different. In *Old Possum's Book of Practical Cats* there is much more action, more narrative, little abstraction, no stream of consciousness. There are many characters in these poems, several of whom are criminals, and there is a great deal of violence, although Eliot here is less serious than in his other work: sometimes he is downright playful.

But even when writing for children, the moralist in Eliot cannot be suppressed. Just as he is drawn to the symbol in his "serious" poems, he is drawn to the fable in these poems for children. In *Prufrock,* in *The Waste Land,* in *Four Quartets,* he preaches to adults. In *Old Possum's Book of Practical Cats,* he preaches to children (and adults). He dispels any doubts about his intentions, any doubts that the cats he describes are not symbols for human beings, in the concluding poem of the series, "The Ad-dressing of Cats":

> You now have learned enough to see
> That Cats are much like you and me
> And other people whom we find
> Possessed of various types of mind.
> For some are sane and some are mad
> And some are good and some are bad. . .
>
> (11. 5-10)

Nor is Eliot's vision of mankind's depravity and violence changed. The most obvious theme of these beast fables is the imperfectibility of catkind/mankind. This theme is explored through the many criminals who are main characters, and, except for a few instances, through those cats who are not outlaws but are nevertheless subjects of satire rather than praise. The second important theme of *Practical Cats* is that of order in a violent, chaotic world.

The imperfectibility of mankind is a stated theme in three poems, "The Old Gumbie Cat," "The Rum Tum Tugger," and "Mungojerrie and Rumpelteazer."

"The Old Gumbie Cat" describes the attitudes and actions of Jennyanydots, a reformer of the "let's be up and doing," "learn a trade and become a productive member of society" school of thought. Part of the Gumbie Cat's nature is to be idle: "All day . . ./ She sits and sits and sits and sits" (11. 3-4), and so she seems to be an idle rich type. During the night she becomes active, and sneaks into the basement, being "deeply concerned with the ways of the mice"(1.9), cockroaches, and beetles who live there.

From what are these unsavory characters to be saved by their social and cultural superior? Well, Jennyanydots does not like the mice because "Their behaviour's not good and their manners not nice" (1.10) and because they "will not ever keep quiet" (1. 19). She is disgusted by the cockroaches' "idle and wanton destroy-ment" (1. 32). Jennyanydots, like many of her ilk, is prone to think in stereotypes.

Because the indictment of the mice, cockroaches, and beetles is no more serious or specific than this, and because the Gumbie Cat's solutions are quite specific, Eliot is satirizing the Gumbie Cat herself. He obviously does not agree with her that teaching the mice "music, crocheting, and tatting" (1. 12) will do any lasting good—neither will giving the cockroaches "employment" (1. 31), forming "from that lot of disorderly louts, / A troop of well-disciplined helpful boy-scouts . . ." (11. 33-34), or organizing the beetles into a tattoo (1. 36). If these activities work, why is it necessary for Jennyanydots to make visit after visit to the basement? Eliot knows that when the Gumbie Cat turns her back the mice and cockroaches and beetles will resume their boisterous destruction. He has chosen these creatures for symbols of the lower class specifically because of such hopeless activity. It is their nature. They cannot be improved. Eliot puts distance between himself and the Gumbie Cat when he says that *"she thinks* that the cockroaches just need employment" (1. 31, my italics). Moreover, he qualifies his statement on the effectiveness of her reforming activities: "So for Old Gumbie Cats let us now give three cheers—/ On whom well-ordered households depend, it appears" (11. 37-38). "It appears" shows the precariousness of Eliot's situation. Regarding this problem, he, like many of us, is in somewhat of a moral and intellectual bind, for he admires the Gumbie Cat's efforts to rehabilitate the basement-dwellers even while he smiles at her naiveté.

So while the Gumbie Cat receives faint praise, she is also damned. She is damned, above all, because she does not realize the depth of man's depravity; and secondly, because she thinks a few lessons in arts and crafts will be sufficient to alter the situation in the basement; and thirdly, because her efforts are superficial—she is not vitally interested in the mice and cockroaches, for if she were, she would not sit all day in the "warm and sunny spots" (1. 14) winding the curtain-cord and tying it into sailor-knots (1. 21), that is, doing nothing.

The imperfectibility of catkind/mankind is also a theme in "The Rum Tum Tugger." The Rum Tum Tugger is a "curious beast" (1. 23) and a terrible bore" (1. 12). He is a "bore" because he is not satisfied with anything:

> The Rum Tum Tugger is a Curious Cat:
> If you offer him pheasant he would rather have grouse.
> If you put him in a house he would much prefer a flat,
> If you put him in a flat then he'd rather have a house,
> If you set him on a mouse then he only wants a rat,
> If you set him on a rat then he'd rather chase a mouse.
>
> (11. 1-6)

He is a "beast" for several reasons: he is disobliging" (1. 24) and "artful and knowing" (1. 31), he is generally an unloving creature who "doesn't care for a cuddle" (1. 32) —a cuddle being something which satisfies both owner and cat—but who will sometimes selfishly "leap on your lap in the middle of your sewing" (1. 33). Also, he is a thoroughly modern and thoroughly democratic cat who "only likes what he finds for himself" (1. 28). We may infer that he doesn't appreciate the civilizing influences of such surrogate experience as is found in history and literature, Finally, the Rum Tum Tugger is a "beast" because he likes chaos: "there's nothing he enjoys like a horrible muddle" (1. 34). What can be done about such a cat? Can he be made to see his errors and to correct them? No, "For he will do / As he do do / And there's no doing anything about it!" (11. 9-11). In this poem, Eliot is more emphatic than elsewhere in the series about mankind's moral and spiritual sterility; he makes these words a refrain with which each stanza (and so the poem itself) concludes.

Similarly, the final line of "Mungojerrie and Rumpelteazer" shows Eliot's insistence that the crimes of these two "highly efficient cat-burglars" (1. 18) cannot be curtailed: "there's nothing at all to be done about that!" "Mungojerrie and Rumpelteazer" seems at first to be a playful poem, less serious than either "The Old Gumbie Cat" or "The Rum Tum Tugger," but it is a very serious poem indeed. For example, a cook, "in a voice that was *broken with sorrow*" (1. 25, my italics), announces to a family that they "must wait and have dinner *tomorrow!*" (1. 26) because the two thieves have stolen the "Argentine joint" (1. 27). If such cruelty is not bad enough, Eliot underscores the family's powerlessness. They are reduced to mere frustrated exclamation: "It's that horrible cat! / It was Mungojerrie—or Rumpelteazer!" (11. 28-29). Apparently having no recourse, or at least feeling they have none, "most of the time they left it at that" (11. 16, 29). This kind of detail makes the narrator's final statement even more poignant—a desperate cry of mixed rage, frustration and resignation in the face of man's depravity: "And there's nothing at all to be done about that!"

In *In Defense of Reason,* Yvor Winters has written that "Eliot's position is one of unmitigated determinism. . . [Eliot believes] that the individual lacks the private and personal power to achieve goodness in a corrupt society. . ."[2]. These three poems in particular, and the series of poems in general, corroborate Winters' contention. Eliot's often raucous versification and his vigorous

rhymes tend to muffle the pessimism of the moral, but it is there
nevertheless; and it is present as well in the several poems which
depict the activities of criminals.

"Growltiger's Last Stand" is a swiftly moving little narrative
which describes the violent death of Growltiger, "the roughest cat
that ever roamed at large" (1. 2). Growltiger is hated and feared so
much that his death at the hands of the Siamese is celebrated in
England as well as in Bangkok. At the beginning of the poem, the
narrator describes Growltiger's appearance, reputation, and belli-
erent personality. Growltiger is a rough-looking character, wearing
a "torn and seedy" coat and "baggy" trousers (1. 6). One ear has
been torn off in a fight and he is missing an eye (11. 7, 8). He has
such a terrible reputation that "people shuddered at his name"
(1. 10), and

> They would fortify the hen-house, lock up the silly goose,
> When the rumour ran along the shore: GROWLTIGER'S
>   ON THE LOOSE!

(11. 11-12)

Growltiger revels in his infamy, "Rejoicing in his title of 'The
'Terror of the Thames'" (1. 4). His title is accurate, for besides
being a thief, Growltiger is a brawler and murderer, preying on the
"weak canary" (1. 13), "pampered Pekinese" (1. 14), or "any Cat"
with whom he "came to grips!" (1. 16). Growltiger reserves his
greatest hatred for those "of foreign name and race" (1. 18), and
particularly the "Persian and the Siamese . . . / Because it was a
Siamese had mauled his missing ear" (11. 19-20).

Growltiger makes his last stand when one Gilbert leads "his
fierce Mongolian horde" in a surprise attack. Growltiger's defenses
have been relaxed on "a peaceful summer night" (1. 21) so that he
might enjoy the company of "the lady GRIDDLEBONE" (1. 30).
Growltiger's closest aides, Grumbuskin and Tumblebrutus, have
left the ship, and his crew is sleeping below deck.

As Growltiger and Griddlebone sing to each other, Gilbert and
his men slip aboard the ship and imprison Growltiger's sleeping
crew. Griddlebone slinks away when the attackers are discovered
and escapes, but Growltiger is forced to walk the plank. This is an
ironic punishment, Eliot points out, but one that is justified:

> He who a hundred victims had driven to that drop,

> At the end of all his crimes was forced to go ker-flip,
>   ker-flop.

(ll. 51-52)

The final stanza describes the international celebration which follows the death of Growltiger. In England Growltiger's death is cause for such acts as "dancing on the strand" (1. 54) and roasting whole rats (1. 55), while in Bangkok "a day of celebration was commanded" (1. 56).

What Eliot had in mind by writing "Growltiger's Last Stand" is difficult to say unless it was to present catkind in one of its most deplorable states. The very brevity of the poem argues against psychological or dramatic sophistication, and its superficiality of detail makes it unsatisfactory as a story. The characters possess little virtue and resort to violence to attain their goals. Growltiger is a thief, a murderer, and a bigot. His lover, Griddlebone, is another of Eliot's jaded females, being "Disposed to relaxation, and awaiting no surprise" (1. 35). She is also, as we have noted, a coward, obviously feeling no loyalty to Growltiger. Growltiger's best friends have abandoned him to drink and seek out more victims (11. 25-28). Gilbert and his men are as cruel, fierce, and ruthless as Growltiger. There is no evidence that they are motivated by anything other than simple revenge. The English are cowardly and ineffectual when confronted with Growltiger's crimes. The English and Asian are both small of soul, dancing at the criminal's death, rejoicing not in the triumph of justice so much as in their relief that an enemy has been eliminated. Thus, Eliot seems primarily concerned to present another pessimistic picture of catkind.

But as with his other "simple" children's poems, Eliot infuses into 'Growltiger's Last Stand" a measure of complexity. Growltiger is not entirely devoid of admirable qualities. He is sometimes "disposed to show his sentimental side" (1. 24). He apparently cares deeply for Griddlebone, and she is attracted to him by his singing ability:

> Growltiger had no eye or ear for aught but Griddlebone,
> And the Lady seemed enraptured by his manly baritone. . .

(11. 34-35)

But Eliot's tone in inconsistent. As much as he seems to deplore racial prejudice, Eliot allows his narrator to use the derogatory

term "Chink": "With a frightful burst of fireworks the Chinks
they swarmed aboard" (1. 42). This line also demonstrates the
narrator's stereotypical thinking. Why else would Chinese fireworks
be connected with such a military-like operation? Then there is the
narrator's lack of seriousness. Griddlebone is said to be "skeered"
(1. 45) when Gilbert attacks; and instead of a more forceful metaphor ffor walking the plank, Growltiger is said "to go ker-flip,
ker-flop" (1. 52).

These details make even clearer the depiction of catkind as mean
and despicable. Gilbert does not openly challenge Growltiger to do
battle, but instead attacks him when he least expects it, "on a
peaceful summer night" when "all nature seemed at play" (1. 21),
when the latter is enjoying what is surely a rare moment of respite
from the driving of his own desperate heart. That the narrator is a
bigot merely shows him to be similar in character to the other cats
in the poem. And finally, the narrator's use of slang for Griddlebone's cowardice and Growltiger's death shows him to possess the
same lack of depth and greatness of soul that characterizes the
populace in general.

Mungojerrie and Rumpelteazer are criminals too, but they are
not as vicious, not as hated as Growltiger. They are "very
notorious" (1. 1) as "highly efficient cat-burglars" (1. 18) with
remarkable skills as "knockabout clowns, quick-change comedians,
tight-rope walkers and acrobats" (1. 2). They are the kind of
criminal that society often tolerates and even admires to some
degree, "plausible fellows" (1. 20) who have "a very unusual gift
of the gab" (1. 17) and therefore will even "engage a friendly
policeman in conversation" (1. 20).

Unlike Growltiger, Mungojerrie and Rumpelteazer are not brutal
cats; they concentrate on the taking of property rather than the
taking of lives. And although their crimes, as we have already seen,
often cause their victims a good deal of grief, they cause no terror
or bodily harm. These two cats, however, are destructive, knocking
tiles "loose on the roof / Which presently ceased to be water-
proof. . ." (11. 9-10), smashing and crashing things in dining-room,
pantry, and library (11. 34-37). Moreover, they often steal from the
very people who can afford it least, the "family" to whom the loss
of a cut of meat means the loss of a meal, the family who buys
fake, cheap "Woolworth pearls" (1. 14).

In "Macavity: The Mystery Cat" we find a character much

more like Growltiger than either Mungojerrie or Rumpelteazer. T. S. Matthews may be right when he says that "It is possible to see the origin" of this poem "in a rarely fortunate day at the dentist's— *Macavity's not there!*"[3] But the cat that Eliot presents here is responsible for emotions quite different from the pride and relief one experiences after a favorable dental report. While his "powers of levitation" (1. 7) and his ability to disappear may cause awed admiration, Macavity is "a fiend in feline shape, a monster of depravity" (1. 18). As a matter of fact, the narrator reports the opinion of many that Macavity is the worst criminal of them all; that, in fact, the others are his subordinates:

> And they say that all the Cats whose wicked deeds are
>   widely known
> (I might mention Mungojerrie, I might mention Griddlebone)
> Are nothing more than agents for the Cat who all the time
> Just controls their operations: the Napoleon of Crime!
>
> (11. 39-42)

Like Growltiger and Mungojerrie, Macavity is a thief and destroyer, and like Growltiger again, he is a murderer:

> And when the larder's looted, or the jewel-case is rifled,
> Or when the milk is missing, or another Peke's been
>   stifled,
> Or the greenhouse glass is broken, and the trellis past
>   repair—
> Ay, there's the wonder of the thing! *Macavity's not there!*
>
> (11. 23-26)

The activity that separates Macavity from his criminal colleagues is his taking of state and military secrets:

> And when the Foreign Office find a Treaty's gone astray,
> Or the Admiralty lose some plans and drawings by the way,
> There may be a scrap of paper in the hall or on the stair—
> But it's useless to investigate—*Macavity's not there!*
>
> (11. 27-30)

Macavity is different from the ferocious, physically battered Growltiger in that he is "outwardly respectable" (1. 21). Whereas Growltiger "scowled upon a hostile world," returning the hatred society feels for him, Macavity is debonair, preferring to dupe society rather than to confront it:

> He sways his head from side to side, with movements
>   like a snake;
> And when you think he's half asleep, he's always wide
>   awake. . .
> Macavity, Macavity, there's no one like Macavity,
> There never was a Cat of such deceitfulness and
>   suavity.
> He always has an alibi, and one or two to spare:
> At whatever time the deed took place—MACAVITY
> WASN'T THERE!
>
>   (11. 15-16, 35-38)

Macavity possesses all the attributes of the urbane cat who can operate outside and against the social order successfully:

> Macavity's a Mystery Cat: he's called the Hidden Paw—
> For he's the master criminal who can defy the Law.
> He's the bafflement of Scotland Yard, the Flying
>   Squad's despair:
> For when they search the scene of crime—*Macavity's
> not there!*
>
>   (11. 1-4)

Up to this point, we have been looking at two important facets of *Old Possum's Book of Practical Cats:* Eliot's conviction that catkind/mankind is prone to crudity, cruelty, and violence, and is beyond reformation. The several examples reflect that conviction by the fact that criminals figure prominently in the poems. Now we will turn to a second important element, the quest for order.

For Eliot, order is an essential goal. In a famous little essay, "*Ulysses,* Order, and Myth," Eliot discusses order and his belief that literature can be an effective means of creating it. Joyce's "mythical method," his use of *The Odyssey* as a pattern for the structure of *Ulysses,* Eliot says, "is simply a way of controlling, of ordering, of giving a shape and a significance to the immense panorama of futility and anarchy which is contemporary history."[4] While Eliot was a staunch conservative, he was not a totalitarian, however. In a November, 1930, letter to Bonamy Dobrée, Eliot writes that

> . . . "Order" and "Authority" are more dangerous catchwords
> now, than "Liberty" and "Reform" were fifty or seventy-five

years ago. Order and Authority may point more directly to the yellow press and the crook capitalists than Liberty and Reform pointed to Socialism. I am terrified of the modern contempt of "democracy" . . . I am as scary of Order as of Disorder.[5]

In the same essay, Dobrée reports an incident that may further clarify Eliot's position concerning order:

I remember once meeting him [Eliot] accidentally in Piccadilly during the coming into prominence of Hitler, and saying, "I suppose one must have order," and his answering: "Yes, but there are different kinds of order" (p. 82).

We must not expect Eliot to be dogmatic in his desire for order. As we shall see, to Eliot "order" is not a synonym for repression, but rather the condition of love, justice, mercy, and harmony toward which catkind must always strive, but in which it will never find itself.

The majority of poems in *Practical Cats* show various types of disorder. From burglary to mob violence, disorder abounds among Eliot's cats. Only a few manage to overcome it. The disorder in the basement is one of the things that motivates the Old Gumbie Cat. The Rum Tum Tugger is an anarchist of sorts, loving nothing so much as a muddle. And the outlaws, Growltiger, Mungojerrie, Rumpelteazer, and Macavity, live disorderly, desperate lives and are responsible for disrupting the lives of their victims.

The theme of order is important even in the least serious poem in the series, "Mr. Mistoffelees." Mistoffelees is a superior magician, "The Original Conjuring Cat" (1. 2):

> At prestidigitation
>   And at legerdemain
> He'll defy examination
>   And deceive you again.
>   (11. 10-13)

The result of such deceit is some apparently harmless mystery and disorder:

> He holds all the patent monopolies
> For performing surprising illusions
> And creating eccentric confusions.
>   (11. 7-9)

Besides his slightly ominous-sounding ability to "creep through the tiniest crack" (1. 25), Mr. Mistoffelees does nothing to cause alarm.

Order is also a theme of the poems which describe the three most "practical" cats in the series: Gus, Bustopher Jones, and Skimbleshanks. For these three, order is respectively: a method of attaining superiority, a way of living a long life, and a way of achieving security.

The title character in "Gus: The Theatre Cat" is a retired actor, now forced to make his living by manning the theater door. When he gets together with his friends, Bus "loves to regale them, if someone else pays, / With anecdotes drawn from his palmiest days" (11. 13-14). These anecdotes consist of his own exploits on the stage and the characters he portrayed:

> He once played a Tiger—could do it again—
> Which an Indian Colonel pursued down a drain.
> And he thinks that he still can, much better than most,
> Produce blood-curdling noises to bring on the Ghost.
> And he once crossed the stage on a telegraph wire,
> To rescue a child when a house was on fire.
> (11. 39-44)

And when he gets a little smashed, Gus will remark on the relative merits of modern actors and the actors of his own time. Notice the emphasis he puts on order and discipline:

> And he says: "Now, these kittens, they do not get trained
> As we did in the days when Victoria reigned.
> They never get drilled in a regular troupe,
> And they think they are smart, just to jump through a hoop."
> And he'll say, as he scratches himself with his claws,
> "Well, the Theatre's certainly not what it was.
> These modern productions are all very well,
> But there's nothing to equal, from what I hear tell,
>   That moment of mystery
>   When I made history
> As Firefrorefiddle, the Fiend of the Fell."
> (11. 45-55)

When compared to the past, the present is usually chaotic. The perspective that age gives us is narrow. Memory fails. Events have passed; we have dealt with them, survived them; they are known.

And, of course, ego is involved. The individual associates his own vitality and talent with that of his age, and when his body fails him, he clings to his age. Back then we were strong; then we were triumphant. My father will not admit that Hank Aaron is a better hitter than Babe Ruth. Joe Louis, in his prime, he says, could take Muhammed Ali any day. For Gus, being "trained," being "drilled in a regular troupe" is the proper way to be educated, and the difference, he thinks, between the present and the past is that the past was a time of order while the present, by implication, is a time of disorder and disarray. Order and discipline, Gus feels, made him and his colleagues superior to the actors of the present generation. Opposed to his own versatility and creativity is the modern cat's cheap trick, merely a physical act of no importance.

In "Bustopher Jones: The Cat About Town," the orderly life accounts for physical well-being. Bustopher Jones does little all day except walk from one club to another enjoying the cuisine of each, and that is the reason that he is "remarkably fat" (1. 2). Bustopher dresses fashionably; this shows him to be superior to his fellows, and he enjoys their admiration:

> He's the Cat we all greet as he walks down the street
> In his coat of fastidious black:
> No commonplace mousers have such well-cut trousers
> Or such an impeccable back.
> In the whole of St. James's the smartest of names is
> The name of this Brummell of Cats:
> And we're all of us proud to be nodded to bowed to
> By Bustopher Jones in white spats!
> (11. 5-12)

His friends are aware of his increasing obesity, but Bustopher is unwilling to admit it. He is in good shape, he thinks, because he leads a well-ordered life:

> It can be no surprise that under our eyes
> He has grown unmistakably round.
> He's a twenty-five pounder, or I am a bounder,
> And he's putting on weight every day:
> But he's so well preserved because he's observed
> All his life a routine, so he'll say.
> (11. 31-36)

The narrator agrees. Bustopher leads the good life, founded solidly on routine, on order, and that is far more important than his size:

> It must and it shall be Spring in Pall Mall
> While Bustopher Jones wears white spats!
> (11. 39-40)

The theme of "Skimbleshanks: The Railway Cat" is that peace, satisfaction, and security derive from order. " 'The Night Mail just can't go' "(1. 8) unless Skimbleshanks is in control of the operation of the train, organizing services, protecting and pampering the passengers. When it seems that Skimbleshanks will not make the train on time, "The guards and all the porters and the stationmaster's daughters" (1. 5) panic.

After he has given the signal and the train has departed, Skimbleshanks sets to work to insure that things go smoothly. Like Bustopher Jones, Skimbleshanks is a cat who lives by routine:

> From the driver and the guards to the bagmen playing
> cards
> He will supervise them all, more or less,
> Down the corridor he paces and examines all the faces
> Of the travellers in the First and in the Third:
> He establishes control by a regular patrol
> And he'd know at once if anything occurred.
> (11. 19-24)

He is also prescient, dictatorial, and powerful. He does not allow any disorderly behavior:

> He will watch you without winking and he sees what
> you are thinking
> And it's certain that he doesn't approve
> Of hilarity and riot, so the folk are very quiet
> When Skimble is about and on the move.
> You can play no pranks with Skimbleshanks!
> He's a Cat that cannot be ignored;
> So nothing goes wrong on the Northern Mail
> When Skimbleshanks is aboard.
> (11. 25-32)

Skimbleshanks' control produces creature comforts and security. The passenger's berth is found to be "very pleasant" (1. 33) and "very neat with a newly folded sheet / And there's not a speck of dust on the floor" (11. 35-36). He even follows the attendants around to make sure they perform courteously and conscientiously:

> Then the guard looks in politely and will ask you very
> brightly
> "Do you like your morning tea weak or strong?"
> But Skimble's just behind him and was ready to remind
> him,
> For Skimble won't let anything go wrong.
>   (11. 41-44)

As the train rumbles through "the watches of the night" (1. 51), the passengers can rest peacefully, because Skimbleshanks is constantly "keeping on the watch" (1. 53). Skimbleshanks, like a father, protects the passengers so completely that they need not worry at all. He provides everything. He is the complete guardian.

Skimbleshanks appears to be the kind of cat who could maintain order in any situation, but the environment in which he works would seem to be well-regulated without him. Eliot creates a character called the "Great Rumpuscat" to take charge in an unusual circumstance, a riot, a scene of general violent disorder.

"Of the Awefull Battle of the Pekes and the Pollicles: Together With Some Account of the Participation of the Pugs and the Poms, and the Intervention of the Great Rumpuscat" describes a confrontation between two breeds of dog who "everyone knows, / Are proud and implacable passionate foes . . ." (11. 1-2). The Peke and the Pollicle, the narrator explains—and here we again encounter racial and nationalistic bigotry—are, on the one hand, "Heathen Chinese" (11. 26, 31) and, on the other, "a dour Yorkshire tyke" (1. 33) who are constantly fighting. Pugs and Poms are usually passive, but sometimes lend their voices to the terrible din of barking that precedes a battle.

The only thing that keeps the Pekes and Pollicles apart is the police. But now "the big Police Dog was away from his beat" (1.14). Just as the friends of Growltiger abandon him to pursue personal pleasures, so the Police Dog turns his back on his duty: "He'd slipped into the Wellington Arms for a drink" (1. 16). The Law no longer present, there is no obstacle in the way of the combatants.

It is a moment of great tension, and the observers are terrified:

> Now when these bold heroes together assembled,
> The traffic all stopped, and the Underground trembled,
> And some of the neighbours were so much afraid
> That they started to ring up the Fire Brigade.
>
> (11. 46-49)

But now the Great Rumpuscat appears, "suddenly, up from a small basement flat" (1. 50).

He displays a curious combination of vehemence and boredom:

> His eyes were like fireballs fearfully blazing,
> He gave a great yawn, and his jaws were amazing;
> And when he looked out through the bars of the area,
> You never saw anything fiercer or hairier.
> And what with the glare of his eyes and his yawning,
> The Pekes and Pollicles quickly took warning.
>
> (11. 52-57)

It is as if the Great Rumpuscat has been involved in such situations so many times that the only emotion associated with them is boredom and contempt for the parties so childishly embroiled.

He does not ignore the situation, as one without moral scruples might very well do. However, we are given no indication that he is particularly concerned with morality, or even with order. He seems contemptuously detached from it all even when he moves to disperse the opposing mobs:

> He looked at the sky and he gave a great leap—
> And they every last one of them scattered like sheep.
>
> (11. 58-59)

That's all. The Great Rumpuscat is not challenged. His authority, based only on his physical superiority and his fierceness, is absolute. Order is restored, and "when the Police Dog returned to his beat, / There wasn't a single one left in the street" (11. 60-61)—not even the Great Rumpuscat. He has disappeared too, perhaps to return, to make another dramatic, surprising appearance when the Pekes and Pollicles again threaten violently to disrupt the peace.

Elizabeth Sewall thinks that "sly theological eddies wander through the Possum book" and she believes that "the GREAT RUMPUSCAT (Mr. Eliot's capitals) might represent God.[6] Only a highly speculative case can be built to support such a thesis, and even then it is necessary to ignore certain details. If the Great Rumpuscat is the vengeful Old Testament God, for instance, what does one make of the fact that he appears "up from a small basement flat"? We are on much firmer ground if we say that he is a formidable and mysterious character who imposes order and so, like Skimbleshanks, is a hero.

Sewall's observations on "The Song of the Jellicles," the only poem in the series which celebrates harmony and joy, are more to the point. Sewall says that

> there is set moving in "The Song of the Jellicles," at long last and in despite of all impediments and far beyond any of the supposedly more poetic works, a dance so free and loving and joyful, yet quiet and half secret, that is a clear image of heaven, and an invitation thither (pp. 71-72).

Most of this description is accurate, but the sense of anticipation and preparedness clearly demonstrates that Sewall is wrong when she says the poem is an image of heaven. Heaven, according to traditional concepts, is the ultimate consummation, and so it would be unlikely that there the Jellicles would "practice their airs and graces / And wait for the Jellicle Moon to rise" (11. 11-12). This contentment, this waiting for the right moment, appears in each stanza:

> Until the Jellicle Moon appears
> They make their toilette and take their repose. . . .
> They're quiet enough in the morning hours,
> They're quiet enough in the afternoon,
> Reserving their terpsichorean powers
> To dance by the light of the Jellicle Moon. . . .
> They are resting and saving themselves to be right
> For the Jellicle Moon and the Jellicle Ball.
>   (11. 17-18, 25-28, 35-36)

The Jellicles, fully confident that the time for the ball will eventually arrive, possess none of the vulgar impatience, none of the nervousness that characterizes those who have little faith in the future.

Size is an important element in the Jellicle cats' personality. They are described somewhat inconsistently as being "rather small" (1. 2), "not too big" (1. 14), "of moderate size" (1. 22), and "small" (1. 30). Their smallness might be concomitant with a lack of sophistication, for certainly they cannot be said to be world-weary, as are most of the cats in these poems. They "develop slowly" (1.13) we are told, and in this case at least, such immaturity is a positive trait. As a matter of fact, except for their patience, the Jellicles are rather like children. They are embodiments of potential. They are physically active. They lack sophistry. They are "merry and bright" (1. 7), "pleasant to hear when they caterwaul" (1. 8), and they have "cheerful faces" (1. 9) with eyes that are "bright black" (1. 10) and "moonlit" (1. 24).

"The Song of the Jellicles" might be a depiction of heaven, but it is as much of a heaven as catkind/mankind can create for itself on earth. It is a heaven of "repose" (1. 18) and of dancing "a gavotte and a jig" (1. 16), of innocence and harmony, of happiness and satisfaction. It is a heaven of the best kind of order—inherent and welling up from the spirit and expressed in the movement of the body. In *Ash-Wednesday,* Eliot prays that God will "teach us to sit still"; but here the goal is not stasis but movement, a dance in the half light of the future:

> *Jellicle Cats come out tonight,*
> *Jellicle Cats come one and all,*
> *The Jellicle Moon is shining bright—*
> *Jellicles come to the Jellicle Ball.*
>
> (11. 1-4)

Wherever Eliot looks in the world he sees aspects of "the immense panorama of futility and anarchy"; he sees violence, licentiousness, and disorder. It follows from such a vision that the criminal's act may be seen as a type of the moral and ethical crimes and failings that beset us but for which we are not considered dangerous, and that order is a positive ideal. It is a vision that does not exclude the possibility of finding joy and harmony, or of creating it, as the dancer and the poet do. Eliot says much the same things to children in *Old Possum's Book of Practical Cats* as he says to adults in his other work.

NOTES

1. *The Complete Poems and Plays: 1909-1950* (New York: Harcourt, Brace, and World, 1952), p. 152. All quotations of the poems are from this edition.

2. 3rd ed. (Chicago: Swallow Press, 1947), p. 487.
3. *Great Tom: Notes Towards the Definition of T. S. Eliot* (New York: Harper and Row, 1974), p. 191, note.
4. M. H. Abrams and others, eds., *The Norton Anthology of English Literature*, v. 2 rev. (New York: Norton, 1968), p. 1824.
5. Bonamy Dobrée, "T. S. Eliot: A Personal Reminiscence," *Sewanee Review*, 74 (Jan. 1966), rpt. in Allen Tate, ed., *T. S. Eliot: The Man and His Work* (New York: Dell, 1966), p. 79.
6. "Lewis Carroll and T. S. Eliot as Nonsense Poets," *T. S. Eliot: A Symposium for His Seventieth Birthday*, Neville Braybrooke, ed. (London: Hart-Davis, 1959), rpt. in Hugh Kenner, ed., *T. S. Eliot: A Collection of Critical Essays*, Twentieth-Century Views (Englewood Cliffs, N. J.: Prentice-Hall, 1962), p. 71.

CHARLES DICKENS, MARCEL PROUST AND GÜNTER GRASS ON CHILDHOOD

Jane Missner Barstow

Three major novelists, Charles Dickens, Marcel Proust and Günter Grass, each associated with a different culture and a different period, have written quasi-autobiographical novels based on the importance of childhood. At first glance such a simplistic common denominator would seem too general to offer much significance. In fact, the combination of first person subjective narration and an emphasis on the specific nature of a child's perspective is quite rare.[1] Moreover, the vastness of *David Copperfield, A la recherche du temps perdu* and *Die Blechtrommel,* the narrative complexity in terms of varying points of view, and the interesting blend of confession and social satire grant these works comparable status in their respective national literatures. A comparison of the three would be meaningful on many levels and, in particular, offers fascinating insights about the development of the literary "cult of the child" from the 1800's to the present. The way a child acts and reacts, how he evolves from one way of seeing the world to a more adult way, and how the adult recaptures some of the qualities of the child to aid him in becoming an artist, are the themes which form much of the content of each of these novels.[2] These themes also typify many of the literary attitudes towards the child prevalent at the time each author was writing.

In Dickens, we find an essentially romantic view of the child as innocent and pure, the symbol of a harmonious dream-like world in conflict with reality. Several decades later, with Proust and other turn-of-the-century writers, the focus shifts to the child as natural artist — given the privileged quality of his perceptions and his apparent spontaneity and freedom from the constraints of adult rationality. Finally, with Günter Grass as representative of post-war writers, the child becomes a product or projection of the evil forces at work beneath the surface of civilization.

Even such a brief summary illustrates the immense distance traversed by the motif of the child over the last hundred years and its relationship to changes in philosophic and literary attitudes. Using Dickens as the base from which to examine the "cult" of the child, we find several important areas common to all three works and periods which allow for a closer examination of the implications of the above categories. The quality of a child's perception is central to all literature dealing with children and childhood and often relates to issues of narrative technique. Some degree of conflict between adults and children also seems a necessary aspect of these works; even older characters can often be evaluated with respect to their "child-like" personalities. And finally, the structures of these works usually follow the archetypal pattern of paradise lost and (sometimes) regained. The nature of that paradise and the way in which the child is banished from it offers particularly illuminating insights about the evolution of the literary child.

   David Copperfield illustrates all three basic components, each of which is dominated by an overriding moral concern presented as an on-going struggle between good and evil. The helplessness of the child, the vulnerability which is the by-product of his innocence, bears witness against man's inhumanity and cruelty. The resulting morbidity and, at times, sentimentality — though clearly a product of Dickens' own personal obsessions with an unhappy childhood — do reflect eighteenth century philosophic concerns about the meaning and value of childhood and nineteenth century social concerns about the industrial exploitation of children.[3]

   Much of the power of the world created by Dickens derives from his use of David's youthful perspective. As seen through the child's eyes, this world is grotesque, magnified out of proportion both physically and emotionally. The ugliness of Salem House, "the damp about the house, the green cracked flagstones, an old leaky water-butt and the discoloured trunks"[4] contrasts with the charm of Yarmouth and its "Aladdin's palace" (DC, 30) creating a veritable fantasy land of ogres and good fairies. This contrast forcefully conveys both the moral sense of Dickens' art and the fundamental subjectivity of the child's naive vision. The child finds Peggotty beautiful, though the comparison he makes between the roughness of her complexion and the smoothness of a footstool (DC, 17) suggests that the "beauty" of which she is a "perfect specimen" may be a very private one. The gentleman caller, on the other hand, because he threatens David's sole possessorship of his mother's heart, appears reduced to a pair of 'ill-omened black eyes' (DC, 19), though we learn later that he is actually quite handsome and looks on Clara with affection (DC, 21-22). When secure and happy, David sees Yarmouth as an enchanted place where "all was made snug" (DC, 32); but when he visits it after his mother's death, he feels rather disappointed (DC, 140). Even the air of the church can be altered by the fact that David is sitting next to Miss Murdstone, and not to the beloved Peggotty (DC, 52).

All of these indications of the child's rich and creative imagination primarily serve to emphasize his exceptional helplessness and loneliness once "trapped between the world of innocent awareness and the world of man's insensitivity to man."[5] In *David Copperfield* the theme of the child-as-victim crystallizes in a Rousseauistic concern for a proper education dependent on the child's nature rather than on adult misconceptions. Several forms of "learning" appear in the novel. There is the gentleness of the mother, Clara, and the crocodile book with its "flat black letters . . . the novelty of their shapes, and the easy good nature of O and Q and S" (DC, 53); there is the firmness of Mr. Murdstone and his cane; there is the brutality of Salem House and the kindness of Dr. Strong's academy. Dickens' views on education line up along the antithesis of good and evil and the issue of knowledge almost disappears from consideration.

The various individuals who guide David's development also reveal Dickens' feelings on the proper atmosphere for learning. From the first, David rejects the imprisonment of the Murdstone religion, instinctively recognizing in it a denial of life. Ironically, by biting Mr. Murdstone, he behaves exactly like the little savage they believe him and all children to be. After rejecting the Murdstones, David turns to Steerforth as a father-substitute, thus going from one extreme to another. Steerforth brings out the worst romantic qualities in David. The "story-telling" in the dark encourages his dreaminess and his admiration for the irresponsible Byronic charm that Steerforth embodies. Still, it is due to Steerforth's patronage that David actually learns something while at Salem House (DC, 34). Affectionate protectiveness seems to provide a better environment for education than firmness, despite the difference in the moral worth of these attitudes.

David goes from Steerforth's shadow to the Micawbers, that is, to no supervision at all. Dickens, however, is not interested in exploring how such an innocent would fare if left on his own. As soon as he has finished the portrait of the Micawbers and of the wine factory, (giving both a humorous and self-pitying expression to some of his most oppressive memories), Dickens has David run off to find Aunt Betsy and his proper birthright. It is in this good and reasonable — and slightly eccentric — environment that David grows up in the most "normal" of boyhoods. Evil is still lurking nearby in the person of Uriah, but this hardly seems a threat to David. From this point on, David's own history ceases to be of dramatic interest and Dickens finds other "innocents" to worry about.

In spite of this variety of moral influences, we find that it is man's basic inhumanity, rather than the economic condition which is the primary source of child abuse and exploitation. The industrial revolution may have been responsible for the existence of factories which subsequently hired innocent and frail children, but certainly the Murdstones of the world bear responsibility for forcing children to work. David, we note, did not need to work. Had his mother been alive, he would still have been at school. This "poor" child is not only oppressed by the Murdstones: he also suffers humiliation in the presence of Mr. Quinion and Littimer; he is taken advantage of by waiters and pawnbrokers and even by Mrs. Crupp and his own servants; he is squashed and literally sat upon in a coach; he is totally at the mercy of those arch-victimizers Heep and his mother. "A tender young cork . . . would have had no more chance against a par of corkscrews . . ." (DC, 255).

Dickens does not idealize innocence, he rather blames the world for placing it in constant jeopardy. David "survives" because he is protected first by Peggotty, then by Steerforth and his Aunt Betsy, and finally by Agnes. Other Dickensian "children," though full grown, fall in the same category. Mr. Dick survives because of Miss Betsy just as Dr. Strong survives because of the innate goodness of his wife. As Jane Stedman points out in her essay on the "child-wives" of Dickens, most of these frail creatures seem unprepared for the trials of existence. Innocence is equated with impracticality, emotional immaturity and frivolous curls.[6] Annie, unlike Dora and Clara, can mature with the help of her father-teacher-husband. By extension, Wickfield avoids damnation because of the faith and love of his daughter-wife Agnes. All of these "children" need protection in order to stand up against the forces of evil; goodness of heart is not enough. Yarmouth itself embodies Dickens' somewhat simplistic notion of Paradise: life by the seaside supervised by the loving care of an adoring adopted father is a very obvious wish-fulfillment. And yet, even Yarmouth is not immune from evil, not secure enough to withstand its onslaught. Moreover, because it may be easier for a melodramatic artist like Dickens to portray disaster than to convey goodness, the Yarmouth of David's youthful dreams fades in comparison to the violent tempest which marks its final appearance in the novel.

The problem here is that Dickens also romanticizes innocence; he sees childhood as a privileged time of life and innocence as a privileged form of existence. Paradise is thus persistently defined as an incredible fantasy world in which "difficulties and dangers disappear like mist."[7] David escapes from the wine firm to a comfortable life and good education; Dora's father dies, thus removing the block to their marriage, and then Dora herself dies so that David may fulfill his destiny by marrying Agnes; Micawber ends up working for Heep, which leads to the salvation of Mr. Wickfield, and all the characters left over are sent off to Australia where fortune miraculously awaits them.

As a novelist, Dickens can easily be accused of simply disposing of the problematic and of escaping from the pressures of a realistic rendering. There is, however, imaginative truth to such a fanciful and illogical depiction of life. Rather than following a pattern of cause and effect, Dickens creates the rhythm of drama in which happiness and disaster alternate with the speed of a daydream. Moreover, there is an intensity to his characterizations which derives from their symbolic nature and which corresponds to the powerful distortions of a child's vision. The child divides his life into zones of happiness and sadness, of security and fear, and transforms the actors who partake in it according to his highly subjective evaluation of their roles. This imaginative world continues to hang "like a mist of fancy over well-remembered facts" (DC, 169), offering a substitute for the reality which both Dickens and his narrator would like to dispel.

In *David Copperfield,* the element of the fairy-tale persists throughout, in spite of Dickens' concern to emphasize his hero's moral development. Because of the seriousness of the later chapters, the fruits of Dickens' exuberant imagination seem less integrated into the fabric of the narrative. Mr. Peggotty, a representative of one of the child's happiest fantasies, returns, but his presence is less colorful when dissociated from the fairy-land of Yarmouth. The Murdstones' continued cruelty is reported, but the evil they symbolize no longer carries a threat. Dickens is clearly attempting to illustrate that David's life has come full circle, that he has gained maturity without relinquishing the imaginative richness of his earlier experience. Unfortunately, the concluding portrait of David's newly acquired rationality and sanity proves too dry to support such fantasies. And so Dickens transfers this type of vision to Traddles and his wife, whose efforts to camouflage drab reality with images of their own invention form a contrast with David's comfortable and unimaginative security.

The difficulty for Dickens was to show his protagonist as ultimately successful in his struggle with life and yet retain the imaginative power of his childhood. His Paradise Regained, because reduced to a tranquil picture of parents and children gathered around the hearth, rings false, given the more powerful negative images of exploitation. And yet there is consistency here; such an idyllic existence does represent the womb-like security of the romantic concept of childhood exemplified by Yarmouth. The fact that Dickens glorifies David's sufferings does not destroy the myth, for one must lose paradise and obtain consciousness of evil before it can be regained. Unfortunately, the new found world pales in comparison with what it replaces. Not until the turn of the century does the symbolic balance seem restored, when the world of "art" replaces that of the hearth as the realm of a childhood regained.

The cult of the child took two very distinct directions after Dickens: one includes the work of Proust, and the other continues to exist today in the work of Grass. Both derive from the fundamental contrast of the child's perception and the adult's rationality, explored most often in Romantic poets such as Blake and Coleridge. Both Proust and Grass replaced the Dickensian emphasis on innocence with spontaneity and imagination as the treasured virtue of the young. One resolved the child-adult antithesis in the name of art, the other accented the necessity of revolt in the name of freedom. We find examples of each stream at the turn of the century: Hesse's, Cocteau's and Gide's young rebels turning their backs on adult morality, Anatole France's and Rilke's young artists searching for a "baguette de magicien" which will enable them to recapture their childhood sense of beauty.

Proust, perhaps more than any other novelist, depicts childhood as a privileged state of existence. Combray becomes the symbol of a harmonious world, a time of life rendered marvelous by the magic of belief. The adult world, by contrast, appears petty and lacking in imagination, but it is not threatening in the same way that the Murdstones' world is. Proust emphasizes the spontaneity and freshness of the child's vision and the beauty of his world. The richness of the child's innate love, whether for his mother and grandmother, or for "les aubépines," his belief in the uniqueness of even "un bouton de porte," calls attention to the lack of imagination and the inability to love "sans la réserve d'une arrière pensée"[8] on the part of most adults.

Though Proust is more concerned with the child's imagination than with his innocence, he does recognize the need for security on the part of all child-like human beings. The recurring image of the nest is particularly significant here, for perfect tranquillity involves the construction of a private world totally one's own. The "chambres" that have marked the protagonist's life resemble the traditional womb/tomb image found in both *David Copperfield* and *Die Blechtrommel;* they represent moments of pure harmony similar to death in that they are devoid of all change and movement. When the child is sent to his room at night, "il fallut boucher toutes les issues" and "creuser mon propre tombeau" (RTP, I, 28), he writes, in order to prevent the penetration of the odor of the hated "escalier" which separates him from his mother. When, during the day, he reads in his bedroom, the "chambre" itself is seen to protect "en tremblant se fraîcheur transparente et fragile contre le soleil de l'après-midi" (RTP, I, 83). In both cases the image is that of an enclosure where the child is safe from outside intrusions.

This desire for the "influence anesthésiante" of that which is comfortably well-known characterizes all levels of life in Combray. The family believes in a version of society "comme composée de castes fermées" (RTP, I, 10), just as they cling to a notion of an individual which does not allow much room for deviation. When an unknown individual appears in Combray, the whole family, indeed the whole town (an extension of the family), becomes involved in "des recherches bien conduites" intended to "réduire le personnage fabuleux aux proportions d'une personne qu'on connaissait" (RTP, I, 58). Tante Léonie would send out Françoise to investigate the appearance of even "un chien . . . qu'elle ne connaissait point" (RTP, I, 58).

The child's superiority derives from his ability to grapple more flexibly with the little mysteries of his life, and to notice the novelty and freshness of things when seen in a new light.[9] The magic lantern may at first seem an unwelcome intruder into the room Marcel has so painstakingly made his own, but he cannot help but be fascinated by the beauty and iridescence of its disturbing projections. The superiority of the child's perceptions shows up in a variety of observations. He is aware, for example, of "les nuances changeantes" of Gilbert le Mauvais depending on what hour he arrives at church (RTP, I, 171) and he picks up a very slight physical movement which awakens the possibility "d'un Legrandin tout différent de celui que nous connaissons" (RTP, I, 125) long before the family discovers this character's other self. Presumably, the outside of their house will always look the same to the adults whose vision is clouded over by habit. The child, however, like the impressionists, catches the differences caused by the angle in which the light strikes its windows (RTP, I, 133).

Perhaps the most important distinction between the child's vision and the adult's is the more unified sensuality of the former. Children demonstrate a primitive form of synesthesia in which the senses, instead of being isolated by the intelligence, participate together in perception. Thus, the "I" speaks of the "couleur de temps" and of "l'air saturé de la fine fleur d'un silence...succulent" (RTP, I, 49). Some of this imagery must be attributed to conscious symbolism.[10] Nonetheless, the child does see the world as composed of organic unities in which every part appears intrinsically related to every other, and the adult narrator must recover this mode of vision if he is to become a "true" artist.

Combray itself, which is in a way as fanciful a Paradise as Yarmouth, resembles a Dickensian daydream divided into gigantic pieces of good and evil; Françoise is a saint one minute and a murderess the next. Misfortune falls in the child's lap the night his grandfather, for no apparent reason, has him dismissed from the table without his goodnight kiss, and is as quickly transformed into its opposite when his father miraculously permits his mother to spend the night with him. There is also a similarity between the child's fascination for Mme de Guermantes and the traditional fairy-tale quest for the unattainable princess. Here, the child's fantasies are reinforced by the convergence of history, art, and reality; Mme de Guermantes belongs to the past of Combray (her ancestors are depicted on the Church tapestry), and she is a descendant of the same Geneviève de Brabant who appears on the child's magic lantern. That "les Guermantes" live a life apart from that of the middle-class inhabitants of Combray adds to their mystery and charm.

Mme de Guermantes is only one of the objects of the child's rich imagination. In effect, almost everything associated with the Combray epoch of the protagonist's life (the peasants of Roussainville, the "aubépines," "l'église" and both "côtés,") is instilled with the magic of belief. Loss of childhood, of this sensual paradise, coincides with loss of belief in the truth of this vision. The fundamental harmony of Combray becomes suspect with the growing recognition of the discord "entre nos impressions et leur expression habituelle" (RTP, I, 155). Françoise, for example, reveals a savagery which cannot be accounted for in the child's notion of her. More important is the discovery of duplicity in himself, of the "démon" that pushes him to irritate Françoise by deliberately contradicting her belief in family loyalty (RTP, I, 154). Paradise is lost most dramatically the night that the child succeeds in disobeying his parents, and in so doing, realizes the pain that he causes them. Later, this same consciousness of guilt is reiterated when his parents agree against their basic principles to allow Marcel to attend the performance of "la Berma": "après avoir détesté leur cruauté, leur consentement me les rendait si chers que l'idée de leur faire de la peine m'en causait à moi-même une . . ." (RTP, I, 443).

This form of self-awareness is also accompanied by a growing awareness of time. The static quality of the child's life relates to Combray's security and harmony. Because "sa vie" seems "une création artificielle" of his father (RTP, I, 173), because things and people offer the child the image of himself, his vision remains essentially undisturbed throughout childhood. Discovery of an "indice de réfraction" (RTP, I, 716) suggesting the possibility of a "moi-inconnu" (RTP, I, 723) takes him by surprise, as does his father's remark "de n'est plus un enfant." All of a sudden he sees himself "dans le temps" (RTP, I, 482-483) and his life becomes a "voiture" taking him further and further away from his "enfance" (RTP, I, 719). A profound unhappiness marks the entire post-Combray—pre-Revelation span of the protagonist's life as one deception follows another and the young man begins to learn that "on ne trouve jamais aussi hauts qu'on avait espéré une cathédrale, une vague dans la tempête, le bond d'un danseur" (RTP, I, 528).

Recovery of paradise lost is rendered all the more dramatic by the narrator's persistent fear of wasting time and of his life's futility. Like Dickens, Proust must use fairy tale images to convey the magical nature of such a recovery. When the "I" unexpectedly comes across a long forgotten phrase of Albertine's in a letter from someone else, the words "firent jouer comme une Sésame les gonds de cachot" (RTP, III, 641). Similarly, the name Guermantes on an invitation brings back, at least for a moment, "le charme et la signification" that it had for the child in Combray (RTP, III, 856). As the protagonist rides towards the Guermantes' new "hotel," he thinks about his childhood belief "que les Guermantes habitaient tel palais en vertu d'un droit hereditaire" and that "pénétrer dans le palais du sorcier ou de la fée, faire s'ouvrir devant (lui) les portes qui ne cèdent pas tant qu'on n'a pas prononcé la formule magique, (lui) semblait aussi malaisé que d'obtenir un entretien du sorcier ou de la fée eux-mêmes" (RTP, III, 857). By moving from his "palais," the Prince de Guermantes has himself. destroyed the basis of the child's vision, or so the protagonist mocks his own fantasies. However, the "I" will later discover that this fantasy contains the secret to the truth. In effect, he must accidentally discover the magic formula which will open the gates to his past, not to the material reality of the Guermantes residence, but to its spiritual reality within his own imagination. The revelations of "la petite madeleine" and of the multiple sensations experienced outside the Guermantes "salon" offer precisely such keys.

The basic circularity of the novel (in contrast to *David Copperfield,* where the protagonist moves in a linear progression from innocence to maturity), raises the question of how paradise regained differs from paradise lost. The answer is that a "souvenir," unlike the original impression, "peut être sinon approfondi, du moins précisé, grâce à un repérage de circonstances qui expliquent pourquoi une certaine saveur a pu vous rappeler des sensations lumineuses" (RTP, III, 375). In other words, these memories, because they join together the past and present, exhibit the precision of metaphor. In order to grasp the "sensations vagues" obtained from a work of art, "il aurait fallu trouver, de la fragrance de géranium de sa (Vinteuil's) musique, non une explication matérielle, mais l'équivalent profond . . ." (RTP, III, 375). It is only by the "miracle d'une analogie" that the essence of an impression can be captured. Without this, it will be subject to the laws of change and its secret will remain invisible. Paradise regained, a recaptured sensation, is superior to that which has been lost precisely because it combines the spiritual and the material. Reality always proves deceiving since it cannot be seen with the imagination the "seul organe pour jouir de la beauté" (one can only imagine that which is absent, according to Proust). In paradise regained the sensation is mirrored "à la fois dans le passé, ce qui permettait à (son) imagination de la goûter, et dans le présent où l'ébranlement effectif de (ses) sens . . . avait ajouté aux rêves de l'imagination . . . l'idée d'existence (RTP, III, 872). The child's world itself was divided between ideal and reality; by receiving "la céleste nourriture" of an accidental encounter with "un peu de temps à l'état pur," the narrator liberates "l'essence permanente et habituellement cachée des choses" (RTP, III, 873) and thus overcomes that division. Like Scheherazade, he saves himself and his past through the act of narrating, thereby miraculously transforming life into art.[11]

The philosophic bent and intricate symbolic structure of Proust's work distinguishes it from other depictions of childhood. His emphasis on the innate creativity and on the spontaneity of the child does form a clear contrast with the sterility and rigidity of the adult world (the rules of the Verdurins appear as ridiculous as those of the Queen of Hearts or of the Murdstones). The focus, however, remains on the privileged communication between the two ideal realms (art and childhood) rather than on adult exploitation or youthful rebellion. Life naturally takes Marcel away from dependence on his family and the security of childhood. (For Gide's, Hesse's and Joyce's potential artists, some sort of violence against authority seems necessary for the assertion of self and the discovery of a creative vocation.)

The violence against the pillars of bourgeois life which every individual must supposedly destroy before he can become himself — though a characteristic of much literature at the turn of the century — does not reach its peak until after World War II. What distinguishes Günter Grass's Oskar from other rebellious children of earlier decades is the degree of insanity and perverse destructiveness that dominates his response to even the least threatening of objects. In order to understand Grass's use of the child-motif, we must recognize the transformation of the rebellion theme in recent years. We have already suggested that a continued emphasis on the need for security and protection accompanied the transfer of focus from innocence to spontaneity. The world, whether seen as evil or merely repressive, offered a clearly defined enemy. By Grass's time, however, the child or primitive was no longer viewed as the potential victim of civilization, but rather as the symbol of the perversity that made civilization necessary.[12]

The protagonist of *Die Blechtrommel* symbolizes both the innately evil child (as for example, in Golding's *Lord of the Flies*) and the perversity of the world as reflected through the eyes of a child who is its product (as for example, in Kosinski's *The Painted Bird*). Actually, the grotesqueness of the narrator's perspective as handled by Grass recalls Dodgson's *Alice in Wonderland* written one hundred years earlier where the child's fantasies are seen to possess the psychic truth of nightmare. Moreover, Oskar is a compound of many elements — both affirmative and negative — of the literary children of the nineteenth and twentieth centuries. He rebels against the authority of a father who wants to determine his identity from the day he is born, as does Hesse's Emil Sinclair; he exhibits an appreciation of sensuality which draws him to women, as does Joyce's Stephen; and has a death wish to return to the perfect security of the womb, as does Proust's Marcel. He is immoral and spontaneous, a natural artist, as are the children of Salinger's Glass family; he is also capricious and cruel, ambiguous and complex, as are Golding's schoolboys. He is a skeptical observer of adult activities, like "le petit prince," and also the product of human stupidity and the horrors of war like Koskinski's six-year-old orphan. Finally, despite his refusal to grow (which belongs to the escapist tradition of *Peter Pan*) he proves unable to avoid the assumption of guilt in a nightmare world such as one finds in Moravia's "Agostino."

Grass's interest in childhood is as pervasive as that of Dickens, but his concern for perspective (as emphasized by Oskar's three foot high point of view) resembles Proust's focus on the child's mode of vision. Grass looks to childhood as a source of rich imagery unhampered by the "distinctions which adult rationality imposes on the objects of perception."[13] He also uses the child's natural immorality to comment on the basic naiveté of adults. Most importantly, Grass is fascinated by the behavior of children when placed in an adult context. In an interview quoted by W. J. Schwarz, he tells about a three year old he once observed in the home of friends: "Händchen sollte er geben und guten Tag sagen. Er aber übersah die Erwachsenen, wollte den Tag keinen guten Tag nennen und hielt nur auf seine Trommel."[14] The willfullness of such a child can lead to evil; it is also the mark of a basic humanity. In *Die Blechtrommel* Grass defines being human as "kindlich, vielschichtig, unmoralisch"[15] and most of his most sympathetic characters do fit this category. One thinks of the two women giggling like schoolgirls over Rasputin's obscenities or even of Meyn brutally murdering his cats out of loneliness and grief. Like Dickens, Grass makes a pronounced value judgment in favor of the childlike. The uncontrollable emotions and immorality of his "children" may be far removed from the simplicity and innocence of a Mr. Dick or a Dr. Strong, but they are seen as equally natural.

Oskar himself is only part child; he is born with a fully developed adult consciousness. This means that he not only absorbs what is happening all around him rather dispassionately, but that he also understands it. As in the case of Proust, we must distinguish between the ideal world of childhood, here reduced to the womb-like space beneath the grandmother's four skirts, and the very human and therefore less-than-perfect child. Oskar's lack of moral principles, rather than demonstrating his innocence, represents a form of evil consciously pursued. On the other hand, his extreme vulnerability results from his inability or refusal to play adult games. Here we find the Dickensian antithesis of good-versus-evil or of innocence-versus-exploitation maintained, but without the correlative contrast between adults and children; age seems almost an irrelevant concern. The cruelty of other children may lie hidden behind the façade of game playing as they force Oskar to eat the awful soup they have concocted (DB, 109); he himself never plays.

Grass's analysis of protection against vulnerability takes the form of a modern psychological examination of the games people play. Skat-playing, for example, offers the only counter to Jan's terror during the attack on the Polish Post Office and the only possible camouflage for the tension between Agnes' lover and husband. Though Oskar states: "ich spielte nie, ich arbeitete auf meiner Trommel" (DB, 69), his drum does serve the same purpose as most games, protecting him from himself and from others. His tantrums when a drum is taken away from him, the very intensity of the manner in which he clings to it, suggests comparison with the traditional security blanket. Without his drum, he explains, he is the "Blossgestellte" (DB, 334).

Since in Grass's highly ambiguous universe nothing is ever exactly what it seems, we must also consider the drum as a "primitive" and child-like form of art. Oskar, like Marcel, demonstrates the apparent correspondence between child and artist. Grass also seems aware that more sophisticated art forms, unlike Francoise's cooking, depend on intellectual as well as sensual endeavours. The other side to Oskar's art, his screaming, begins as self-defense but develops into something much more complex: "Aus blossem Spieltrieb, dem Manierismus einer Spätepoche verfallend, dem 'l'art pour l'art' ergeben, sang Oskar sich dem Glas ins Gefüge und wurde älter dabei" (DB, 78). The comparison with the succession of artistic styles is particularly appropriate here in that a change in technique does not necessarily indicate improvement. "Alter" refers to the literal passage of time; Oskar is older in age, but he is not more mature. Ironically, the last stage in this development proves the most playful. Decadence coincides with the childishness of a late epoque in life. Oskar uses his voice to tempt potential thieves and to aid the Dusters in their nihilistic raids. His more primitive drum, on the other hand, frees the people from the spell of Nazi rhythms, replacing military marches with the more human waltzes and fox-trots. Screaming enables Oskar to play the role of Satan, drumming enables him to recapture his own childhood and to protect himself from his own anxieties.

It would be easy to juxtapose children and adults based on the nature of their art forms. Grass, however, uses images which suggest associations without quite fitting. He teases the reader into looking for explanations in a world in which there are none. Oskar himself exhibits so many contradictions that his nature can only be described as a series of mutually exclusive paradoxes. He likens himself to both Jesus and Satan, Goethe and Rasputin, Odysseus and the Prodigal Son. The most profound duality is between the inhumanity and obscenities perpetrated by his mind, and the compassion and self-pity expressed by the tears in his eyes (DB, 581).

Chronological movement takes place in this context. The first book concludes with the death of Oskar's mother, which, like the death of David's mother, marks the end of childhood security and the loss of paradise; the second book concludes with the end of adolescence, with the freedom and responsibility which comes with the death of both fathers; and the third ends with the musings of a man of thirty looking back from the threshold of maturity. Moreover, Oskar's life has followed the traditional path of novels-of-development. He revolts against the middle class ideal, refusing to fashion a future for himself as storekeeper, and plays an active Freudian role in the killing of his two presumptive fathers "weil er es satt hatte, sein Leben lang einen Vater mit sich herumschleppen zu müssen" (DB, 485).

After the death of his second father, Oskar is totally free. And with this freedom comes responsibility and physical growth. This is described as an active decision on Oskar's part; he places his drum in the grave and much like David Copperfield expresses his wish to take his place in society, to work, get married and lead a good, peaceful Burger life. Most of all he desires happiness (DB, 530). Maria, however, unlike Agnes, refuses to marry him: "so wurde aus Yorick kein Bürger, sondern ein Hamlet, ein Narr" (DB, 552). Oskar must continue his quest for the meaning of life outside this bourgeois context. He does eventually achieve a degree of success and fame as a drummer, but he is still stricken by a fundamental need for something more, for a human warmth which he associates with the "Frühzeit" which means so much to him (DB, 676). Friends and family offer the only possible deterrents to human alienation and loneliness, but even they continue to elude Oskar as he remains trapped between the need for communication and the threat of intimacy, between the desire for love and the fear of suffocation. Apparently, the paradise Oskar seeks cannot exist in the real world; it can only be expressed as a dream in which the grandmother sends out invitations and the whole family meets beneath her skirts (DB, 709). Such a fantasy does offer emotional truth. Throughout the novel history and legend, religion and superstition, literature and mythology mix freely as the boundaries between fact and fiction, subject and object are eliminated in a manner that seems better to approximate Oskar's vision of the world than a more logical representation possibly could.

One of the major themes of the novel is credibility as it relates to the fantastic. Oskar, by stating that one ending to the family legend surrounding his grandfather's disappearance sounds even more preposterous than another (DB, 35), implies that a point exists at which fantasy loses its tie to reality. That the statue of Jesus one day begins to drum is more fantastic than Oskar's own precocious talent.

It provides, in effect, a miraculous demonstration of a Freudian omnipotence of thought; to Oskar the action is frighteningly real. Rather than seeing in reality objects which conflict with the vision of his imagination, Oskar transforms reality to fit his conception of it. The process is dramatized through the use of daydreams: "Alte Frauen mit . . . Enkelkindern . . . Obelisken, sinnbildlich geborstene Säulen . . ." of cemetery paths modulate into an image of "Christus in Steinsandalen" blessing the elm trees (DB, 534). Even such positive and peaceful visions soon produce their antithesis and the desire for Maria or Sister Gertrude is replaced by the frightening presence of the "witch" Lucy.

The difference between Oskar and the protagonists of the other two novels is that he never develops beyond the stage of belief in his own highly subjective world. Throughout *Die Blechtrommel* the most fantastic incidents will be described with the most detailed realism and vice-versa. It is never clear where description stops and invention begins. The absurdity of death, for example, is given form with highly ironic (because so appropriate) images of the way in which people die. Greff the green grocer hangs himself from a weighing platform carefully balanced with bags of potatoes (DB, 377), and Matzerath, who had been one of the first to hop on the Nazi bandwagon, swallows his party pin (DB, 473). In each case, Oskar focuses on the trivial, the "Funfundsiebzig Kilo" reading on Greff's scale (DB, 378) and the "Ameisenstrasse" which builds a detour around Matzerath's body (DB, 474).

Oskar also thinks of himself in terms of images: with and without drum, dressed up as a little Rasputin, or as a baby with clenched fists awaiting his drum. Such images are necessarily contradictory because of Oskar's confusion about his sanity. The opening line of the novel: "Zugegeben, Ich bin Insasse einer Heil-und Pflegeanstalt" throws doubt on everything the narrator will write. Yet he immediately suggests that the world outside is insane and not he. And because he renders the subject matter of his fantasies in such a compelling manner, the reader tends to agree with him and to distrust the easy rational explanation. When reality remains unknown and the possibilities are infinite, Oskar teaches us through his fanciful constructions that only imagination can approach the truth. The "Feldgendarmen" chasing Kolijaiczek fail, precisely because they are unable to envisage more than two possibilities (DB, 20).

Finally, all of Oskar's daydreams and nightmares reduce to the overwhelming presence of the "Schwarze Köchin." The fairy tale element is never rejected, because it alone contains the truth. In *David Copperfield*, fantasy evolves into fate as David must relinquish his belief in fairy tale kingdoms of love in order to work out his own destiny. The princesses of his dreams, his mother and Dora, are replaced by the common sense angel-Agnes. In *A la recherche du temps perdu*, fantasy evolves into art. The mysterious rulers of the magic land of Guermantes who existed only in the child's imagination will be transformed into their aesthetic equivalents. Both of these novels end with the vision of a spiritual realm superior to both the dreams and realities that made up the protagonist's life. Oskar does not seek transcendence; he merely attempts to dispel the images of his nightmares by articulating their significance.

Perhaps the best way to determine Grass's position within the evolution of the literary child is by returning to our original categories and summarizing the depictions of imaginative vision, child-adult conflicts, and paradise lost and regained which dominate our three representative authors' handling of the subject.

It is, in effect, the child's rich imagination and the nature of the world as seen through his uneducated eyes which has fascinated artists since the early nineteenth century. In both *David Copperfield* and *Die Blechtrommel* the distortions of the child's vision, his tendency to magnify the pleasing and displeasing aspects of his world, result in a powerful blend of the lovely and the grotesque. The Murdstones and the Black Witch (not to mention the Hitlers of the world) contrast with the Peggottys and the Grandmother. As a more modern writer, Grass may avoid Dickens' sentimentality — but the morbidity and nightmares remain. In both cases, images of the ugly and frightening prove more compelling than those of security and tranquillity. Proust is also interested in the child's imaginative tendency to divide his world into zones of happiness and sadness, of peaceful beauty and threatening cruelty. He goes much further, however, in analyzing the particular components of such a vision. In particular, he emphasizes the primitive nature of the child's senses and the role of imagination in coloring his response to reality. Synesthesia and belief in the uniqueness of people and things dominate the child's perspective as well as the artist's. Finally, it is the correlation between child and artist which distinguishes Proust's work from Dickens' and Grass's and which introduces a more powerful affirmation of the child's privileged vision.

In all three novels the child's perspective does function as the antithesis of the adult's and sometimes of the adult narrator's. The freshness of his vision, the immediacy of his reactions, the innocence of his understanding — all of these factors determine the way a child sees. An adult, on the other hand, bases his observations on analysis, memory and the accumulation of experience. This is not to say that young David, Oskar and Marcel are totally immune to the optical illusions created by habit or overly rational expectations. On the contrary, Oskar is part adult throughout *Die Blechtrommel* as the result of his highly developed intelligence. And Marcel shares the family's false certainties as to the character of various of Combray's inhabitants. David alone is pure in his innocence and naiveté, but he too very early in the novel begins to grow up. Similarly, all three narrators retain or regain qualities of their youthful vision. Oskar still sees the Black Witch; his world remains magnified out of proportion because of his own small stature. And Marcel manages to make metaphors which abstract his images from the effects of time despite his adult awareness of temporality. Again it is only David whose vision as narrator can be termed totally adult. But here we seem to be dealing with an almost disembodied moral voice, a mouthpiece of maturity that speaks but does not see.

Our authors also contrast mature and immature responses to vulnerability and innocence. Dickens, who emphasizes the conflict in adult/child relationships insists on a basic inhumanity and cruelty which separates the exploiters from the exploited. All of his victims, no matter how old, are child-like and naive, whereas all of his victimizers seem self-aware and calculating. This polarity crystallizes in the theme of education which itself can depend on affection and protection from evil or dominance and the perverse desire to hurt. Proust is not sure that cruelty and love can be so easily isolated. Françoise's excessive love for her kin certainly does not preclude her sadistic exploitation of the kitchen maid's allergies. Nonetheless, Proust does recognize the child's need for security and his fear of the strange and the unknown. This desire for a womb-like world safe from intrusion characterizes all ages and all social classes. The difference between the children and adults is that the child is still fascinated enough by mystery to risk the unknown whereas the adult who has more carefully constructed a highly conventional and rigid world has stronger defenses. Thus, the

Proustian antithesis of adults and children crystallizes in the spatial contrast between the child alone in his room faced with the beauty and disturbance of his magic lantern versus the adults in their salon training a new guest to obey the rules of their little clan. With Grass it becomes still more difficult to distinguish between adults and children. Like Proust, he seems aware of the need for defenses and of the games people play to protect themselves against the unknown. And like Dickens, he seems aware that evil represents a constant threat to the most innocent of bystanders. Children, however, are just as cruel as adults, if not more so, and equally sophisticated in their building of protective walls. Guilt itself becomes problematic since it sometimes appears deserved and sometimes accidental. Oskar cannot really be blamed for his mother's death, yet he does seem guilty of exploiting the weak when he sings holes in jewelry store windows. The Dickensian melodrama between good and evil moves into the psyche of the individual. And, though Grassian adults do seem more prone than children to explain the inexplicable, they prove equally in need of security blankets and games. With respect to the moral implications of the child-theme, there is a clear progression in the direction of increasing ambiguity. The relationships between innocence/good and experience/evil become more and more complex as we move from 1860 to 1965.

The way in which the paradise/paradise lost drama is resolved most distinctly dates the three works. Still, the paradises themselves are all equally imaginative and fanciful worlds: Yarmouth, Combray, the enchanted space beneath the Grandmother's four skirts. All depend on belief, all offer security and a kind of unreal beauty. Mothers also play privileged roles in the creation of childhood paradises. The unquestioning love and affection offered by this special person takes its place beside the special place each child associates with love. It is therefore no coincidence that banishment from childhood accompanies the death of both David's and Oskar's mothers and the assumption of guilt (of having betrayed the mother) in both *A la recherche du temps perdu* and *Die Blechtrommel.* Moreover, both David and Oskar mistakenly equate adulthood with the choice of a wife/surrogate mother (Dora and Maria).

Though growing up and crossing the threshold into maturity is a concern of all three writers, the subject dearer to their hearts seems to be the way childhood or paradise can or cannot be regained once it is lost. For David, attempting to cope with the past through retreat and the writing of an autobiographical novel seems a necessary transition. And yet we sense that the recovery of paradise is less his own doing than the work of Agnes who is, after all, his special angel. Presumably Agnes is a wiser, more mature woman than either Dora or Clara. She enables David to regain his innocence by building a solid, tranquil and rather bland nest for him. The joyful paradise of his childhood may have been banished to Australia, where it remains a beautiful and somewhat frivolous promise. Dickens and his narrator, as socially concerned writers, have more serious business at hand.

On the other hand, Marcel's recovery of paradise is an elaborate and significant component of his life and work. Like David, Marcel must retreat from the world before he will be able to write about the past. But his vocation also depends on a series of accidental and gratuitous revelations in addition to the development of an aesthetic theory of metaphors and analogies. The final victory amounts to no less than a recovery of his childhood vision deepened by the distance traversed and rendered dramatic by the imminent approach of death. Finally, it is the artist's faith in the uniqueness of his vision which corresponds to the child's belief in the uniqueness of his world. His paradise remains a subjective reality dependent on introspection rather than on projection or wish-fulfillment.

Oskar, who first addresses us from the confinement of his insane asylum cell, has also retreated (more or less willingly) and now attempts to come to terms with the past through writing. He alone fails in his task. The more he writes, the less he understands, and the more difficult it becomes either to cross the threshold into the kind of mature adult existence which David seems about to lead or to transcend his schizophrenic state through faith and art. On the contrary, wherever he looks, Oskar sees only the Black Witch.

From innocence preserved, to art sanctified, to nightmares codified — have we come full circle? Or is Grass's child the antithesis of Dickens'? Are we faced with a new myth of evil replacing the old myths of helplessness and innate artistic genius? The above discussion suggests that Grass combines the ambivalence and richness of Proust's world with the moral, even didactic, concern of a Dickens, that he combines the psychological realism of Proust's neurotic protagonist with the melodramatic victimization of Dickens' exploited child. As for Oskar's demonic nature, we should remember that Oskar is born innocent; he does not become guilty until the day of this third birthday. Furthermore, the guilt he assumes is collective; he shares it with his family, and by extension, with all of society. We note a certain romantic morbidity in Grass's belief that the only place where one can remain safe from hurting others is in the womb or the tomb. We also note a modern sense of realism which opposes romantic escapism and nostalgia in insisting that once the umbilical cord is severed "es war nichts mehr zu machen" (DB, 49). On the one hand, Oskar serves as the mouthpiece for Grass's skepticism at the childish cruelty and destructiveness of men, exemplified by the scene of SS men playing with the toys in Markus' store after they have brutally murdered him (DB, 235). On the other hand, Oskar's own childishness symbolizes a basic archetypal humanity which brings together those who "ans Paradies glaübten" (DB, 192).

NOTES

1. The traditional development novel begins with the time at which the protagonist becomes a socially functioning individual facing the problems of adjustment and of finding a place in society. Those novels that do deal with pre-puberty focus on childhood only in terms of the psychological sources of temperament or personality. For a detailed discussion of this topic see Roy Pascal, *Design and Truth in Autobiography* (Cambridge: Harvard University Press, 1960), p. 84.
2. Actually *Die Blechtrommel* could be viewed as a negation of such an evolution from child to adult. Yet even viewing Oskar as an "anti-child" involves acceptance of the importance of childhood to this work as well as to the other two.
3. Angus Wilson, "Dickens on Children and Children", in *Dickens 1970: Centenary Essays,* ed. Michael Slater (New York: Stein & Day, 1970), p. 202.
4. Charles Dickens, *David Copperfield* (1850; rpt. London: Oxford Univ. Press, 1966), p. 79. Subsequent references to this edition will appear in the text.
5. Peter Coveney, *Poor Monkey: The Child in Literature* (London: Rockliff, 1957), p. 98.
6. Jane Stedman, "The Child Wives of Dickens", *Dickensian,* 59 (1963), 115-116.
7. See A. O. Cockshut — *The Imagination of Charles Dickens* (London: Collins, 1961), p. 121 — for discussion of such fairy tale elements.
8. Marcel Proust, *A la recherche du temps perdu* (Paris: La Pleiade, 1954), I, 10. Subsequent references to this edition will appear in the text.
9. Rosalie Taylor, "The Adult World and Childhood in Combray", *French Studies* 22, (1968), 27.
10. See Marcel Muller — *Les Voix narratives* (Geneve: Droz, 1965), pp. 60-61 — for a detailed examination of the role of "l'ecrivain" as well as "l'enfant" in this passage.

11. David also considers himself a modern day Scheherazade (DC, 93). For a detailed analysis of Proust's allusions to the *Arabian Nights*, see Allan A. Pasco, "Marcel, Albertine & Balbec" in "Proust's Allusive Complex." *The Romantic Review* 62 (1971), 113-126.

12. This view was incorporated into the work of many earlier novelists; Conrad, Gide and Thomas Mann, for example, as well as Freud himself, all recognized the need for civilization. Their emphasis, however, was on the more immediate need for self-exploration in the face of powerful social inhibitions.

13. Michael Hamburger, "Moralist and Jester: The Poetry of Günter Grass", *Dimension Special Issue 1970: Günter Grass*, p. 77.

14. Wilhelm Johannes Schwarz, *Der Erzähler Günter Grass* (Bern: Francke, 1969), p. 37.

15. Günter Grass, *Die Blechtrommel* (1959: rpt. Berlin: Luchterhand, 1971), DB, 103. Subsequent references to this edition will appear in the text.

THE CURRENT STATE OF CHILDREN'S LITERATURE IN ARGENTINA

Federica Dominguez Colavita

In Argentina we are only beginning to realize the existence of a literature for children. Interest in the subject is rather young, but it is also strong and general: editors, writers, journalists, teachers, and researchers seem to have discovered a new field.

Research trends:

Research trends indicate that in Argentina, children's literature is still conceived mainly as a teaching aid. Specialists are interested in the effects of certain texts on the developing child, but forget to study these texts as literary objects. This pedagogical approach results from the fact that the researchers are usually educators, and the subject of Children's Literature is taught not in the Language or Literature Departments, but in the Education Departments of the universities.

Seven national universities and two private universities offer a course in children's literature as part of their "preschool teachers training program":

1. Universidad Nacional de Cuyo. Profesorado de Jardín de Infantes. Centro Universitario Parque Gral. S. Martín. Mendoza. Argentina.
2. Universidad Nacional de La Pampa. Profesorado de Jardín de Infantes. 9 de Julio 149. Santa Rosa. La Pampa. Argentina.
3. Universidad Nacional de Río Cuarto. Profesorado de Educación Pre-Escolar. Campus Universitario. Enlace 84, Km. 603. Río Cuarto. Córdoba. Argentina.
4. Universidad Nacional de San Juan. Profesorado en Jardín de Infantes. Santa Fe 10, Este, 2°Piso. San Juan. Argentina.
5. Universidad Nacional de San Luis. Profesorado en Enseñanza Pre-Primaria. Calles Chacabuco y Pedernera. 5700 San Luis. Argentina.
6. Universidad Nacional del Centro de la Provincia de Buenos Aires. Profesorado en Jardín de Infantes. Pinto 399. Tandil. Buenos Aires. Argentina.
7. Universidad Nacional del Comahue. Profesorado en Jardín de Infantes. Buenos Aires 1400. Neuquén. Argentina.[1]

8. Pontifìcia Universidad Católica Argentina "Santa María de los Buenos Aires." Profesorado en Jardín de Infantes. Juncal 1912. Buenos Aires. Argentina.
9. Universidad del Salvador. Profesorado de Jardín de Infantes. Alberti 158. Buenos Aires. Argentina.

The higher institutes for the training of kindergarten teachers also offer courses in children's literature. Of these two of the best known are:

1. Instituto Nacional de Profesorado en Jardín de Infantes "Sara C. de Eccleston." Calles Figueroa Aloorta y Dorrego. Capital Federal. Argentina.
2. "Belgrano Day's School." Profesorado de Educación Pre-Escolar. Calles Juramento y Conesa. Capital Federal. Argentina.

There is one exception to this general trend of considering the subject only as part of programs for training kindergarten teachers—the Instituto SUMMA (Yerbal 65, Buenos Aires, Argentina), which trains Literature Professors who wish to specialize in Juvenile Literature.

In our University—the Universidad Nacional de San Luis—children's literature is taught by the Education Department, and it is part of a three year program for the preparation of future "preschool teachers." In their first year, the students take a course on preschoolers' language; in the second year they have a course in literature for children up to seven years of age; the course plan includes:

a) some general notions about literature;
b) the study of children's short stories: their analysis, evaluation, selection, and in some cases re-elaboration; the student also learns narration techniques, and practices them in kindergartens of the area;
c) the study of poems for children: their analysis, evaluation and selection; the student also learns and practices methods for teaching poetry to pre-school children;
d) the study of drama for children: the students create short puppet plays, and, as part of another course—the art workshop course—they stage one of these plays at a kindergarten;
e) some general notions on the exterior presentation of literature for children: illustrations, size and materials of children's books; the correct way of organizing a kindergarten library.

Our University also has a research program funded by the Secretary of Science and Technology of the National Ministry of Education. Its objective is to establish what linguistic, structural and thematic conditions children's short stories must fulfill in order to be comprehensible and enjoyable for children of four and five years. The outstanding children's literature specialists in our country are:

Ione Artigas de Sierra: Professor of kindergarten teachers. Author of an essay on the history and current state of children's literature in Spanish-America ("La literatura infantil y juvenil en Hispanoamérica," *Revista del Instituto de Investigaciones Educativas,* I, N°2, July 1975, pp. 35-49); and of *Aproximación del niño a la obra literaria* (Introducing the child to a literary text, Bs. Aires: Plus Ultra, 1974), an introduction to a series of work books that offer literary selections for children of 5, 6 and 7 years of age.

Mane Bernardo: Puppet player and Professor at the Universidad Nacional de Buenos Aires. She has written several books on the art of puppetry, among them: *Títeres=Educación* (Puppets=Education, Bs. Aires: Estrada, 1970); and *Títeres* (Puppets, Bs. Aires: Latina, 1972).

Elsa Isabel Bornemann: Author of a book on children's poetry: *Poesía infantil, estudio y antología,* (Bs. Aires: Latina, 1976).

Beatriz Capizzano de Capalbo: Professor of kindergarten teachers at the Instituto Nacional de Profesorado en Jardín de Infantes "Sara C. de Eccleston." Author of the volume on children's literature of the *Enciclopedia Práctica Preescolar* (Practical Pre-School Encyclopedia, Bs. Aires: Latina).

Nelly Cattarossi Arana: Author of the essay "Juvenile literature in Argentina: an encouraging reality" (*Bookbird,* vol. XIV, N°4, 1976, pp. 25-30).

Marta Gómez de Rodríguez Britos: Professor of kindergarten teachers at the Universidad Nacional de Cuyo, author of *Investigación literaria: Juegos infantiles tradicionales en la Provincia de Mendoza* (Literary research: Traditional children's games in the Province of Mendoza, in print by Fondo Nacional de las Artes).

Juan Carlos Merlo: Author of several essays on literary criticism and on the sociology of literature. He has studied the effects of television on children, and the possibility and advantages of a relationship between television and children's literature. His book *La literatura infantil y su problemática* (Children's literature and its problems, Bs. Aires: El Ateneo, 1976) analyzes some of the "problems" of children's literature: the existence of massive reading materials for children, the lack of knowledge that some writers show about today's child, and the problem of language and style in children's books.

Dora Pastoriza de Etchebarne: Professor and co-director of the Instituto SUMMA. Author of two basic texts on children's literature: *El cuento en la literatura infantil* (The short story in children's literature, Bs. Aires: Kapelusz, 1962), an analysis of the short story in general and in Argentinian children's literature; and *El oficio olvidado: el arte de narrar* (A forgotten trade: the art of story telling, Bs. Aires: Guadalupe, 1973), a book on narration techniques.

Fryda Schultz de Mantovani: Pedagogue specialized in children's literature. Author of *El mundo poético infantil* (The poetic world of children, Bs. Aires: El Ateneo, 1944); *Nuevas corrientes de la literatura infantil* (New trends of children's literature, Bs. Aires: Estrada, 1970); and *Sobre las hadas* (About the fairies, Bs. Aires: Nova, 1974).

María del Carmen Villaverde de Nessier: IBBY representative to Santa Fe, Argentina. Co-author with Clelio Pedro Villaverde of *Literatura infantil y juvenil de base folklórica* (Juvenile literature of folkloric roots, Rosario: Ed. Biblioteca, 1974), an attempt to nationalize and regionalize childrens' and adolescents' literature through the revaluation of folk themes.

Professional organizations:

CAPLI, or Centro de Asesoramiento y Promoción para la Literatura Infantil-Juvenil (Córdoba 1558, Buenos Aires, Argentina), was founded in October 1969, and its membership includes writers, illustrators, editors, show organizers, teachers and researchers in the field of children's and adolescent's literature. At present, Professor Ione Artigas de Sierra is the president. Various events have been organized by the association, among them, the First Iberoamerican Convention on Children's and Adolescent's Literature, which took place in April 1976 in Buenos Aires, with the endorsement of UNESCO and the National Ministry of Education.

IBBY is such a well known international organization that we need not speak about it. The address of the Argentinian Section is Yerbal 65, Bs. Aires. Its president is a teacher and author, Mrs. Martha Salotti.

OMEP, or Organización Mundial para la Enseñanza Pre-Escolar (World Organization on Preschool Education); among other activities *OMEP* organizes courses, conferences, and seminars on literature for kindergarten children. Its address is Figueroa Alcorta y Dorrego, Capital Federal, Argentina.

Writers:

A list of our writers must necessarily be incomplete. We can only select a few and hope that, for different reasons, they are representative of today's literature for children in Argentina.

Elsa Isabel Bornemann: Author of poems and short stories of intense lyricism. Two of her best stories are *Cuento con caricia* (Short story with a caress, Bs. Aires: Latina, 1972); and *El cazador de aromas* (The perfume hunter, Bs. Aircs: Latina, 1972). *Cuento con caricia* shows the power of tenderness in overcoming fear, ugliness and loneliness, as well as in breaking the barriers between man and animal. *El cazador de aromas* emphasizes a forgotten sense, the sense of smell, as a means of knowing the world; and it also criticizes our materialistic society for rejecting and ignoring the "poetic" trades.

Aaron Cupit: Author of short stories. Winner of the "Lazarillo Prize" 1973. He has said that he is "against children's literature done by adults . . . short stories should be done by the children themselves, in their own language; we can only correct their syntax and give them some form."[2] Among his works we will mention: *Cuentos del año 2100 y otras obras para niños en edad escolar* (Short stories of the year 2100 and other stories for school-age children); and *Amigo Chum* (My friend Chum, Bs. Aires: Plus Ultra, 1975).

Laura Devetach: Her best known book is *La torre de cubos*

(The tower of blocks, Bs. Aires: Luis Fariña, 1969), a collection of short stories. Even though these stories are aimed at very young children, the author does not shun the negative aspects of our society like poverty or social inequality: mothers are angry when their children complete their notebooks, because notebooks are expensive; a young boy needs to work and cannot find a job; another little girl has to cook and clean the house because both her parents need to work . . .

Beatriz Doumerc: Author of adult and children's stories. Her children's book *El pueblo que no quería ser gris* (The town that did not want to be gray, Bs. Aires: Rompan Filas, 1975) won the international prize "Casa de las Américas"; and *Un cuento muy blanco* (A very white short story, Bs. Aires: Latina, 1974) won a contest of stories for kindergartens organized by Editorial Latina. In this last story, a white sheet of paper playfully changes once and again its shape and color, in bright and imaginative combinations.

Berta Finkel: Puppet player, poet, and writer of short stories. While many authors write for children as if they suffered from a limited intelligence and an underdeveloped emotional life, Berta Finkel conceives of the child as a rich creature, capable of understanding and experiencing complex feelings like the anguish of solitude, guilt, shame, love or friendship. *Mientras voy creciendo* (As I grow up, Bs. Aires: Plus Ultra, 1976) is an excellent, lyrical book.

Martha Giménez Pastor: Author of poems and stories. She has recently published *La pancita del gato* (The kitten's "tummy," Bs. Aires: Plus Ultra, 1975).

María Hortensia Lacau: Author of stories and poems. *Yo y Hornerín* (Hornerín and I, Bs. Aires: Plus Ultra, 1974) is one of her best known stories; it tells the adventures of a seven year old girl in rural Buenos Aires, and at the same time depicts the local flora and fauna. *País de Silvia* (Silvia's country, Bs. Aires: Kapelusz, 1962); and *El arbolito Serafín* (Serafín, the little tree, Bs. Aires: Plus Ultra, 1975) are two collections of poems.

Susana López de Gomara: Winner of the literary competition

From *El caballo alado* (The winged horse), by Silvina Ocampo, ill. by Juan Marchesi. (Editorial La Flor)

From *La torre de cubos* (The tower of blocks), by Laura Devetach, ill. by Víctor Viano. (Editorial Huemul)

of Acme Publishers, 1975. Her novel *Las lunas de Juan Luna* (John Moon's moons, Bs. Aires: Plus Ultra, 1975) is aimed at the rather forgotten adolescent public.

Inés Malinow: Author of about one hundred children's short stories, aimed only at amusing her readers, without any didactic intention. She has created a tender and comic character, a little bear called "Inosito" (or the Anti-Bear), who reappears in many of her books. One of the most recent stories about "Inosito" is *Buena suerte Inosito ¡* (Good luck Inosito ¡, Bs. Aires: Plus Ultra, 1975).

Syria Poletti: Author and journalist. Her book *Reportajes supersónicos* (Supersonic interviews, Bs. Aires: Sigmar, 1972) is built around an interesting idea: a little girl receives a tape recorder as a present and starts a series of interviews. The book conveys much information, and shows a clear didactic purpose, but while some writers address themselves to an imaginary being—an unreal, almost nineteenth century child—, Syria Poletti's reader is a very contemporary child, a child that goes to school, watches television, and knows about moon trips and modern science.

Martha Salotti: Author of short stories. Her book *El patito Coletón* ("Taily" Duck, Bs. Aires: Guadalupe, 1973) presents fifty stories for kindergarten children which consciously avoid the world of elves and fairies: Martha Salotti considers that young children do not need these forms of the extraordinary since to them plain reality is already filled with magical moments.[3]

Javier Villafañe: Famous, almost legendary, puppet master, who for years travelled through Argentina with his puppet theatre, mounting plays and getting acquainted with his young public. He has written short stories: *Libro de cuentos y leyendas* (Book of stories and legends); poems: *El gallo pinto* (The spotted rooster, Bs. Aires: Hachette, 1965); and puppet plays: *Títeres* (Puppets, Bs. Aires: Hachette, 1967).

María Elena Walsh: Author of stories and poems, and composer of songs. She is non-conventional in her themes and style, mainly because she has emphasized an aspect of chil-

Covers of *El espejito de la montaña* (The little mirror on the mountain), by Lucila Maderal, ill. by Julia Díaz; *Los príncipes verdes* (The green princes), by Ester Picos, ill. by Clara Urquijo; and *Tutú Marambá,* by María Elena Walsh, ill. by Vilar.

dren's personalities frequently overlooked in our literature: children's capacity to enjoy humor and the absurd. According to María Elena Walsh, in children's literature "magic is related to language, humor and rhythm."[4] Her literary works absolutely avoid didactism: "I only want to entertain, and to feed the imagination, that poor victim of elementary school and of a world stultified by a solemn and false common sense."[5] Among her main works are: *Dailan Kifki* (Bs. Aires: Sudamericana, 1974), a narration; *Cuentopos de Gulubú* (Bs. Aires: Sudamericana, 1975), a collection of short stories; *El reino del revés* (The kingdom of upside down, Bs. Aires: Sudamericana, 1974), a collection of poems; and *Versos tradicionales para cebollitas* (Traditional poems for "kids," Bs. Aires: Sudamericana, 1974), an anthology of popular Spanish and Argentinian folk themes.

Publishers:

Argentina is a country of readers, with a powerful publishing industry. Children's books of Argentinian and Spanish authors, as well as many translations, are published by fifty or so different houses. Here is a list of the most important ones.

Atlántida. Florida 643, Buenos Aires, Argentina.

Biblioteca Popular Constancio C. Vigil. Alem 3078, Rosario, Santa Fe, Argentina.

Brughera. Hipólito Yrigoyan 646, Buenos Aires, Argentina.

Centro Editor de América Latina (Junín 981, Buenos Aires, Argentina) is currently publishing a weekly series of illustrated short stories for very young children: "Los cuentos del Chiribitil."

Codex. Doblas 954, Buenos Aires, Argentina.

Crespillo. Defensa 485, Buenos Aires, Argentina.

Crisol. Rivadavia 1255, 4°Piso, Buenos Aires, Argentina.

El Ateneo. Florida 340, Buenos Aires, Argentina.

Estrada (Bolívar 462, Casilla de Correo 789, Buenos Aires, Argentina) includes well known writers in its collection "Cuentos para seguir contando" (or "Short stories to go on telling"), with an emphasis on Argentinian authors and themes.

Eudeba. Florida 656, Buenos Aires, Argentina.

Guadalupe. Mansilla 3865, Buenos Aires, Argentina.

Hachette. Rivadavia 739, Buenos Aires, Argentina.

Huemul. Santa Fe 2237, Buenos Aires, Argentina.

Kapelusz (Corrientes 999, 1043 Buenos Aires, Argentina) offers several collections for ages ranging from four to sixteen.

La Flor (Uruguay 252, Buenos Aires, Argentina) has created a special collection called "La Florcita" which presents stories for young children from very famous Argentinian and foreign adult writers, like Eugene Ionesco, Italo Calvino, Ray Bradbury, Umberto Eco, Fernando Alegría, Griselda Gambaro, Silvina Ocampo, Augusto Roa Bastos, Clarice Lispector, Michel Butor, and others.

La Obra. Independencia 3124, Buenos Aires, Argentina.

Latina (Avda. de Mayo 953, Piso 11, Buenos Aires, Argentina) specializes in the preschool level, and has published an excellent collection of fourteen titles: "Cuentos del jardín" (or "Short stories for the kindergarten"), a successful co-operation between writers, illustrators and printers.

Librería del Colegio. Bolívar y Alsina, Buenos Aires, Argentina.

Plus Ultra (Viamonte 1755, Buenos Aires, Argentina) has published two interesting series: "Serie para escuchar y para hablar" (or "Series for listening and talking") for children of 5, 6 and 7 years; and "Serie para leer y comentar" (or "Series for reading and commenting"), for older children. Books from both series include special activities related to the literary texts: while younger children can paint, draw, cut, and answer simple questions on the stories and poems, the older ones are urged both to answer comprehensive questions and to give a critical opinion.

Quillet. Uruguay 1037, 4°Piso, Buenos Aires, Argentina.

Sigmar. Chile 945, Buenos Aires, Argentina.

Sudamericana. Humberto 1° 545, Buenos Aires, Argentina.

Information to the general public:

The Argentinian press gives much information on children's literature. Two of our main newspapers, *La Nación* and *Clarín,* have regular special sections on the subject: Syria Poletti, the well known writer and journalist, is in charge of the one in *La Nación;* and Selva Echagüe, a journalist, writes for *Clarín.*

Besides these and other newspapers, many women's and parents' magazines, as well as some television talk-shows, frequently ask children's literature specialists, psychologists, or pedagogues to write or speak about different problems in the field.

Finally, information on children's literature also reaches the public through the special efforts of some universities, of the National or Provincial Educational Boards, or of some local Town Halls. These institutions sometimes offer conferences or short courses on the subject, aimed either at local teachers or to the general public.

In Argentina there are some excellent authors, an intense publishing rhythm, and a press that reflects and understands the interest of the general public in the field of children's literature.

The main problem seems to be a tendency to consider this specialty as a research field associated almost exclusively with the preparation of the kindergarten teacher. The Language and Literature Departments of all the important universities should give to children's literature the relevance that it deserves. We have yet to understand that while this is an area of literature with laws of its own, it has aesthetic value in its own right, just as every other literary area.

NOTES

1. At the Universidad Nacional del Comahue, children's literature is also taught as part of the "elementary teachers training program" (literature for children from 6 to 12 years of age).
2. Interview with five of the participants in the International Seminar on Children's Literature, Bs. Aires, March 1974, "Un pàjaro es un helicóptero que canta," *Siete días ilustrados,* N°364, 13-19 marzo, 1974, p. 40.
3. Martha Salotti, *El patito Coletón: Cincuenta cuentos para el jardín de infantes,* (Bs. Aires: Guadalupe, 1973), p. 9.
4. Lydia P. de Bosch, "El problema de la literatura infantil: Testimonios a través de una encuesta," *Estudios e investigaciones I,* (Instituto de Ciencias de la Educación, Facultad de Filosofía y Letras de la Universidad Nacional de Buenos Aires, 1965), p. 33.
5. ibid., p. 34.

FLOWERS IN FULL BLOOM: *THE VARIETY OF CHINESE CHILDREN'S LITERATURE*

Thomas A. Zaniello

In the 1974 volume of *Children's Literature: The Great Excluded* I analyzed a number of Chinese children's books as representative of two periods in recent Chinese culture: pre-Cultural Revolution tales (early 1960's) and tales of the Cultural Revolution itself (mid-1960's). The former employed supernatural events and superheroes engaged in class struggle, emphasizing personal triumphs in the end, while the latter were about "ordinary" people who acted heroically for the collective. The Cultural Revolution tales were usually more didactic, with overt ideological messages. Since that article appeared, we have learned more about the underlying conflicts in Chinese society in the 1960's: my division into pre-Cultural Revolution and Cultural Revolution *periods* now seems a bit too neat. There were instead two major *trends* or contradictory *theories* of art and literature embodied in the political and cultural struggles of the 1960's and, like all activities in Chinese culture, children's book publishing was clearly affected by the tension between the trends.

What I regard as the primary Cultural Revolution trend of the mid-1960's might be called the "Red Guard" (or even "ultra-left") trend; but there was another, more "liberal" trend, which has become dominant in the 1970's, displacing but also absorbing some of the features of the "Red Guard" trend. This "liberal" trend encouraged the interaction or merger of aspects of foreign and traditional Chinese elite culture with themes from contemporary life. The result has been to create a mass popular culture in the 1970's in which communist politics need not be explicit and in which varieties of cultural expression are preserved.

Our view of the Cultural Revolution as an orgy of political militancy has some validity. Mao certainly encouraged the political leftism of the Red Guards, although he apparently withdrew some of that support in the end. But it seems that in matters of art and literature he was less of an absolutist than they: the more extreme units of the Red Guard did not accept his slogans "Make the Past Serve the Present" or "Let Foreign Things Serve China."

Chris Milton, an American who became an active Red Guard, com-
mented in 1967 on the activities of his peers when matters of
"apolitical" designs arose: "For about two weeks they went around
smashing what they considered to be capitalist hangovers. . . .Like
they would go into a store and see a glass that didn't have a revolutionary slogan or design. They would decide it was a bourgeois
glass and take it off the market or break it. They did this in all the
stores."[1] Other visitors to China have indicated that classical monuments, tombs, and even traditional paintings were damaged during
the Red Guard days.

In the earlier article I discussed *I Am on Duty Today* (1966),
a book which is typical of the Red Guard trend: a child at nursery
school during drawing-time very pointedly gives up the themes of
traditional Chinese painting ("flowers and birds / Or high mountains and streams") to draw instead "a little soldier hero." But
while the Red Guard trend was in temporary ascendency, other
materials were still being produced. *Flowers in Full Bloom* (written
by Huang Ching-yun, illustrated by Lin Wan-tsui, and edited by the
Kwangtung People's Publishing House) also appeared in 1966
(according to the information on the book's cover). It is a collection of poems with an illustration for each set of verses. This
is "Embroidering Seedling":

> The pillow cloth,
> Two feet long,
> Two clever girls in one family.
> The elder sister embroiders seedlings on the cloth;
> The younger one plants them in the fields.[2]

It is not likely that this poem, with its emphasis on traditional
and non-political craft-work or, for that matter, this entire collection—neither aggressively didactic nor political—would stand up
to a Red Guard critique. But its publication date of 1966 indicates
that there were varied opinions about what was suitable reading
matter for children. (As far as I can tell, this collection was not
available for import until 1971 or 1972, that is, until *after* the
Cultural Revolution.)

Flowers in Full Bloom fits quite easily into the post-Cultural
Revolution period, because its poems have an easy domesticity.
The poems focus on the lives of everyday people who are not
involved in direct political struggle; in fact, there is no heavy em-

phasis on politics at all. For example, the title poem, "Flowers in Full Bloom," certainly applauds the collective harvest, but its presentation is charming and casual:

> This little girl,
> Can arrange her hair,
> Decorating her ebony plaits with red silk bands.
> She dances at the harvest gathering,
> Like a butterfly fluttering among the flowers.
> With a carrying-pole she shoulders two baskets which touch
>   the ground;
> She carries a hoe taller than herself.
> She sings a song about pineapples and bananas,
> Which makes our mouths water.
> The audience clap her.
> And she nods back to them.

More recently a similar children's song, written by Li Hsing in 1975, appeared in *Chinese Literature* (No. 10, 1975,) China's English-language magazine. The song, "Golden Bamboo," celebrates traditional Chinese musical instruments, self-reliance, *and* Chairman Mao:

> Golden bamboo, closely jointed,
> We cut one to make flutes:
> One for elder sister, one for little sister,
> And the biggest one of all for little brother.
> We've formed a small orchestra
> And file in now to perform:
> Loud fluting, tuneful singing,
> Every note voicing our love for Chairman Mao.

The lyric celebrates normalcy throughout; its paean at the end may be obligatory, but it does not make the scene overtly political in the Red Guard sense.

A number of stories published *after* the Cultural Revolution do not differ, in terms of character and plotting, from the Cultural Revolution tales. *Little Ching and Hu Tzu Guard the Cornfield* (edited and illustrated by Ku Yu-tseng, Chang Chih, and Li Jui-sheng, 1974,) *In a Rainstorm* (illustrated by Wei Chiang-fan, Wu Yen-hsiu, and Chen Szu-tsung, 1974), and *Three Sweaters* (by Wang Sen and Illustrated by Ho Yen-jung, 1975) are all somewhat overly didactic tales, emphasizing, in the case of the first and third stories, the necessity of learning from experience and cooperating with others, and, in the case of the second, the unity of army and peasantry.

Similarly, tales of heroism by adults or children, typical of the Cultural Revolution, continue to be published. In *Billows Ferry* (edited and illustrated by the Cultural Center of Chitung County, Kiangsu Province, 1975) a People's Liberation Army man journeys to an island in the East China Sea. Here he recalls (and retells) an incident of twenty years past, when a courageous local fisher-woman (with a baby strapped to her back) helped him to cross "Billows Ferry" in the face of enemy fire. His reunion with this mother and child is the emotional climax of the book, but the practice manuevers in which he participates with the child (now grown up) is the political climax, paralleling the earlier crossing with the child's mother. In a similar tone, *Landing the Giant Sturgeon* (written and illustrated by Tu Wei, 1974) deals with the heroism of two children as they protect their collective's fish-hooks and nets from an intruding, sixteen-foot sturgeon whom they eventually capture.

Some recent books emphasize not only the Cultural Revolution themes of service to others but also encourage the development of logical analysis in the youngsters in the stories and, presumably, in the readers. One episodic book, Miao Yin-tang's *Good Children* (1974), contains a series of comic-strip-illustrations which, develop various slogans or mottoes. "Learning from Life," for example, begins with the frustrations of two children, trying to balance a see-saw. They go to a worker's stall (perhaps at a market) and observe the weighing of fruit on a balance. As a result of this direct experience of life, the older and heavier child realizes that he must decrease his distance from the center post (the fulcrum of the see-saw). Clearly this is a lesson in logic and science; but it also has "political" (in the broad sense of the word, popularized by the Chinese themselves) lessons as well. (Learning from workers, cooperation, and perhaps learning theory *from* experience, and then applying the theory to change life—these are common themes of contemporary Chinese philosophy). Peng Kuo-liang's *Stories of Little Red Guards* (1975) is a similar book of episodes, drawing lessons in selflessness and logic from the daily activities of primary school children. The episodes, like *Good Children,* does not have the political didacticism of the Red Guard trend despite the title of one of the books. The "story lines" in both of these books are quite ingenious and can be appreciated on various levels by children of different cultures.

Most of the books which I have discussed so far are realistic; fantasy was oddly missing from my earlier survey. Its omission, as usual, was more a matter of politics than taste, for books with fantastic themes did, and do, exist. A well-known adult fantasy is Wu Cheng-en's *Pilgrimage to the West* (also known as *Monkey* in Arthur Waley's translation), a sixteenth century romantic "novel" of connecting tales, many of which concern the supernatural magic of Monkey (also known as the Monkey King). A children's book, *Monkey Subdues the White-Bone Demon* (1964; 1973), excerpts one of the main lines of the original, the trek to the West by the Buddhist monk Hsuan-tsang and his disciples, Monkey, Pig, and Sandy (a man). Monkey offers a critique of Buddhism as the group travels, for Hsuan-tsang, true to his faith, trusts people who, unfortunately, always turn out to be demonic incarnations of the super-demon herself, the White-Bone demon. Monkey always knows better, but he is able (for a time) to kill only the *bodily* forms but not the spiritual forces behind them. The Monk can never understand Monkey's violence, since killing is always wrong: "A Buddhist disciple must be compassionate. Even if he's a demon you should persuade him to mend his ways, not kill him." Monkey's lesson-in-reply is the resolution of the plot; he finishes off the White-Bone Demon with a blow of his magic staff: "You can't take pity on a demon."

In addition to the wonderful plot line, *Monkey Subdues the White-Bone Demon* has line drawings in the traditional Chinese style somewhat rare today in Chinese children's books. (Most illustrations tend to be quite realistic and sometimes socialist/realistic—that is, heroic images of peasants, soldiers, and children). The preface tells us that the characters appear in "operatic costumes" to "add to the legendary atmosphere of the story." While pleasing aesthetically, these costumes raise a political issue as well, and their presence is a comment on the two trends I outlined above. These costumes are actually pre-Cultural Revolution Peking opera costumes; that is, they imitate the style of the old, "unreformed" Peking opera which had been criticized by Mao and Chiang Ching (Madame Mao) as the refuge of "emperors, princes, generals, ministers, scholars and beauties, and, on top of these, ghosts and monsters." The new Peking opera characters are, as a rule, workers, peasants, soldiers, and various villains from the Chinese upper classes or the Japanese invaders. It is precisely those "ghosts and monsters" that we see in *Monkey Subdues the White-Bone Demon;* they reappear, in classical dress and context, as if they had not temporarily vanished from Peking in the 1960's during a period of intense ideological struggle in the cultural realm. (Perhaps the dates of the two editions of this children's book are revealing: the first edition is 1964, pre-Cultural Revolution; the second is 1973, or post-Cultural Revolution.)

In fact the role of the classics and various derivative forms occupy an ambiguous position in official Chinese aesthetics.[3] Generally the policy is to *use* the works of the past to illustrate the decadence of the feudal lords and the incipient or abortive rebellions of the peasants. Even some Red Guard groups, during the Cultural Revolution, called upon themselves as the representatives of the Monkey King's power:

> Revolutionaries are Monkey Kings, their golden rods are powerful, their supernatural powers far-reaching and their magic omnipotent, for they possess Mao Tse-tung's great invincible thought. We wield our golden rods, display our supernatural powers and use our magic to turn the old world upside down, smash it to pieces, pulverize it, create chaos and make a tremendous mess, the bigger the better![4]

Although the "ultraleft" Red Guards apparently went so far as to destroy classical monuments, tombs, and paintings in an attempt to start a "new world" from scratch, a more typical use of the classics was Mao's poem, "Watching the Opera *The Monkey King Thrice Fights the White-Bone Demon*" (1961). The poem uses the Monkey King and the Demon as allegorical representations of China or Marxism-Leninism on the one hand and Russia or "revisionism" (counter-revolutionary backsliding) on the other:

> Since the thunderstorm has broken out over this earth
> A spirit has emerged from a heap of skeletons.
> The Monk, though stupid, is capable of correction,
> But the evil spirit will bring disasters.
> The Monkey King raises his mighty staff
> To disperse the spectral dust that fills the world.
> Let us hail him today,
> For the noxious fog is returning once again.[5]

(I suspect that the re-publication of *Monkey Subdues the White-Bone Demon* owes a great deal to the popularity of Mao's poem.)

A similar allegorical use of fantasy occurs in Chen Wei's and Peng Hua's *Two Peacocks* (adapted by Liu Chi and others; color wood-cuts by Chiang Tieh-feng, Chia Kuo-chung, and Wan Chiang-lin, 1975). *Two Peacocks* resembles a number of the post-Cultural Revolution tales I have discussed in its emphases on service to the people and respect for the Army; but its use of the Tai nationality of Yunnan Province adds a special dimension to the story. The Tai children (a "Little Red Guard" and his younger brother) in the book raise two peacocks from eggs they have found; a local "Grandpa" tells the children that peacocks are "birds of good fortune for us Tai people." He explains the Tai legend of the arrival of a flock of golden peacocks from the sun: "This legend expresses the hopes of the Tai people who were oppressed and exploited by landlords and bullies in the old days. They struggled on, always looking for the sunrise." The children then resolve to give the birds to the People's Liberation Army for its help in the revolution. The political lesson of the unity of people and army is thus carefully joined to a colorful mythical tale.

The only other "fantasy" book I have seen is the pre-Cultural Revolution *Adventures of a Lead Pencil,* written by Ho Yi (illustrated by Liu Wang-pin, 1958; 4th edition, 1964); it is no longer available from the American firm that imports Chinese books. A lead pencil, with arms and face, has a series of misadventures when his little mistress neglects to put him away. Although care of one's pencil (and the razor which the child uses to sharpen it) seems to be the theme of the book, there is little explicit development of that theme. The 1970 catalogue of the American import firm has some titles which seem to be "fantasy": *Duckling Goes A-Sailing with his Friends* (1962), *How the Monkeys Fished for the Moon* (3rd edition, 1963), and *How Yu King Moved the Mountains* (1965). Unfortunately I have not seen these three books as they are no longer available.

The task of studying Chinese children's literature is formidable: not only are some books available one year and then not the next, but the changes in political and cultural trends make very different kinds of children's books available in any given year. In 1975, just four months before *Chinese Literature* published "Golden Bamboo," which I characterized as being fairly apolitical, the magazine printed "Every Wall is a Battlefield," a song written by a Peking primary school pupil, Cheng Chun-ping:

Red brick walls,
And grey brick walls,
A field of battle each and all.

We Little Red Soldiers fight,
With vim and punch and pep,
Writing posters is a free-for-all.

Political cartoons we love to draw,
And little stories we write as well,
Both are our guns and ammunition.

We know Lin Piao was rotten,
Confucius and Mencius we debunk,
Our revolutionary fires burn bright.

Red brick walls,
And grey ones too,
Every wall is a battlefield.

This song might easily have come from the Red Guard period of the 1960's and yet it was published in 1975. This diversity should make it clear that although Chinese children's literature remains political in most of its forms, the political situation is rarely as monolithic as it is so often represented in the West. "Politics" can be defined broadly as "living one's life in a socialist country" ("liberal" definition) or narrowly as "active political struggle" ("Red Guard" definition). The "liberalism" of the Hundred Flowers Movement of the 1950's may be blossoming once more in Chinese children's literature: we should be aware, at the very least, of its varieties.

NOTES

1. Interview with Chris Milton, *The Movement* (San Francisco), Feb., 1969.
2. *Flowers in Full Bloom* and all other Chinese books mentioned in this essay are available (with exceptions as noted in the text) from China Books and Periodicals, the American import firm, located at the following addresses: 2929 24th St., San Francisco, Calif. 94110; 210 W. Madison Ave., Chicago, Ill. 60606; 125 Fifth Ave., NYC, NY 10003. All are in English translation and are published by the Foreign Languages Press in Peking. None of the translators' names are included in the texts.
3. My "Ten Propositions of Contemporary Chinese Aesthetics," *Minnesota Review*, N.S., No. 5 (Fall, 1975), 145-163, goes into some detail on these and

other matters of contemporary aesthetics in China.

4. Red Guards of Tsinghua University Middle School, in *Peking Review*, Sept. 9, 1966, quoted from *People's China* (Vol. 4): *Social Experimentation, Politics, Entry onto the World Scene, 1966 through 1972*, ed. David Milton, Nancy Milton, and Franz Schurman (New York: Vintage Books, 1974), p. 285.

5. Mao's poem translated by Jerome Ch'en and Michael Bullock, in Jerome Ch'en, *Mao and the Chinese Revolution* (Oxford: Oxford University Press, 1965), p. 355.

TRADITION AND THE INDIVIDUAL TALENT OF FRANCES HODGSON BURNETT:
A GENERIC ANALYSIS OF LITTLE LORD FAUNTLEROY, A LITTLE PRINCESS, AND THE SECRET GARDEN

Phyllis Bixler Koppes

Frances Hodgson Burnett's lasting contribution to children's literature consists of three books, *Little Lord Fauntleroy* (1886), *A Little Princess* (1905), and her best work, *The Secret Garden* (1911). This was Marghanita Laski's assessment in 1951, and subsequent critical opinion has usually agreed with her.[1] Burnett's individual achievement in these books can be described by placing them within the appropriate literary traditions. In *Little Lord Fauntleroy* and *A Little Princess* Burnett combined two genres she knew as a child: the fairy tale and the exemplum. In *The Secret Garden* she continued to use themes and motifs from these genres, but she gave symbolic enrichment and mythic enlargement to her poetic vision by adding tropes from pastoral tradition at least as old as Virgil's *Georgics*. Previous descriptions of development in Burnett's three best known works have focused on the increasing depth and subtlety in the portrayal of her main child characters.[2] While this approach highlights a special strength of *The Secret Garden,* it fails to explain why *A Little Princess* and especially *Little Lord Fauntleroy* remain "curiously compelling"[3] now that beautiful, innocent children are not as fashionable as when Burnett was writing. The following analysis of Burnett's earlier works as fairy tale-exempla, on the other hand, avoids using standards of psychological credibility in characterization more appropriate to realistic novels of child life. Moreover, a discussion of Burnett's use of mythic and pastoral traditions in *The Secret Garden,* shows this work to be her masterpiece not just because its main child characters are multi-faceted but because the work as a whole is richer than its predecessors in thematic development and symbolic resonance.

Both the exemplum and the fairy tale made a deep impression on Burnett as a child. In *The One I Knew Best of All: A Memory of the Mind of a Child* (1893) Burnett was highly critical of the exempla she had read. She described them as "horrible little books"

given by "religious aunts," books "containing memoirs of dreadful
children who died early of complicated diseases, whose lingering
developments they enlivened by giving unlimited moral advice and
instruction to their parents and immediate relatives."[4] In "Little
Saint Elizabeth" (1890), the story of a child whose good instincts
are warped by her aunt's religiosity and by the many "legends of
saints and stories of martyrs" she has read, Burnett similarly
scorned the excesses of the religious exempla as well as the attempts
to imitate them too literally and self-consciously.[5] Despite such
harsh criticism, however, Burnett returned to this genre repeatedly
in her memoir; like Little Saint Elizabeth, she had been much
affected by the religious stories she read. "There was nothing she
would have been so thankful for as to find that she might attain
being an Example," Burnett said of herself as a child; but self-
examination had told her that she could not match the fictional
children in their high standards of conduct or in their ability to
effect instant conversions in others (*The One I Knew Best*, pp. 188-
189). Fairy tales, on the hand, provided Burnett with more
affectionate memories. As an adult, she had friends on two
continents scouring old bookstores for a particular collection of
tales which she had owned, memorized, and then lost when she was
seven or eight years old. She was retelling the stories to children and
was about to publish them when someone found her "Lost Fairy
Book." In 1904 she wrote an appreciative preface to a new edition
of this work, *Granny's Wonderful Chair* (1856) by Frances Browne.[6]

Browne's fairy tales — which are at the same time parables
against greed and pride — could well have pointed Burnett toward
the combination of fairy tale and exemplum she achieved in *Little
Lord Fauntleroy* and *A Little Princess.*[7] From the religious
exemplum she took the child paragon who has a beneficial influence on those around him; her narratives are secularizations of the
story about a saintly child who converts others.[8] Cedric Fauntleroy
and Sara Crewe become the agents of secular conversions or rebirths
by bringing the socially alienated or insecure into the human
family. Cedric effects this marvelous change in his irascible,
misanthropic grandfather. Sara befriends two misfits and a servant
in Miss Minchin's school, and she gives the wealthy recluse next
door a reason to live. Burnett's exempla are secularized also in that
her main child characters do not need to be converted themselves
before they convert others — they are innocent. Cedric Fauntleroy

especially typifies what Burnett called "the innocent friend of the whole world," the child "born without sense of the existence of any barrier between his own innocent heart and any other."[9] Cedric's innocence plays a key role in the "conversion" of his grandfather; the child brings out the good in the selfish old man simply by assuming that his grandfather is good.

Despite the absence of supernatural trappings beyond a series of marvelous coincidences, Burnett's stories are fairy tales as well as exempla. Most obviously, they are versions of the tale which also underlies much of Burnett's popular adult fiction about women, the Cinderella tale.[10] An examination of that tale's many variants reveals that Cinderella is not only worthy to be a princess but also a princess by nature. When she is a scullery-maid, she is enchanted, under a spell; at the end of the story she simply returns to her natural, disenchanted state as a princess.[11] Sara Crewe undergoes a parallel pattern of enchantment and disenchantment. When her wealthy father brings her to school, she is recognized as a princess by all because of her fine clothes and regal bearing. After word arrives that her father died penniless, she is treated as a servant by the "wicked stepmother," Miss Minchin, and some of the older "stepsisters" in the school. Sara's real identity is at last discovered by the recluse next door, who restores to her the vast fortune which her father mistakenly thought he had lost. Cedric Fauntleroy's case is similar; by receiving the title of "Lord" he is merely being restored to his rightful inheritance. Like the Cinderella tale, Burnett's stories do not emphasize a change within the main character but rather in the recognition of that character's true nature. Cedric is "every inch a lord" and Sara is a "princess"[12] even when the world does not recognize them as such. The change comes within others, those who are influenced by the child's true nature.

In her portrayal of Cedric and Sara, therefore, Burnett's primary concern is not character change or development as might be expected in more realistic works, but rather character revelation. She reveals the true nature of her main characters in a manner peculiarly appropriate both to the fairy tale and exemplum: she presents Cedric and Sara with a series of tests. These tests are designed to demonstrate whether the children's conspicuous beauty, like Cinderella's, is a reliable sign of their nature, whether they are as inwardly noble and virtuous as their outward appearance would suggest. Cedric Fauntleroy, for example, must not allow his

affections to be bought by his grandfather's wealth; he must not be
sullen and angry because he is separated from his mother, his
"Dearest"; he must face the threat of an impostor heir with grace
and equanimity. Sara Crewe's test is to maintain the charitable
nature and even temper of a princess while she is treated as a
servant and beggar, and unlike Cedric she knows she is being tested.
Before she loses her vast wealth, for example, Sara suggests that she
may be "good tempered" simply because she has everything she
wants and everyone is kind to her. She wonders how she will ever
find out if she is "really a nice child or a horrid one": "Perhaps I'm
a *hideous* child," she says, "and no one will ever know, just because
I never have any trials."[13]

In *A Little Princess* Burnett's central themes of the testing of
virtue and the relationship between appearance and reality are
effectively amplified by the fact that recognition of Sara's true
nature becomes a test for other characters in the story. Most of
those we get to know well do pass this test — the pupils who visit
Sara in her attic room, the servant Becky, the Indian servant of the
recluse next door, and even Miss Minchin's sister, Miss Amelia. Like
a family of children in the neighborhood, these characters recognize
that Sara "is not a beggar, however shabby she looks" (p. 130). The
headmistress, Miss Minchin, of course fails this test and therefore,
unlike most of the adults in Burnett's stories, she is not "converted"
by the exemplary child. Miss Minchin does not recognize Sara's true
nature because there is a basic flaw in her vision: she judges only by
superficial appearances. She thinks that Sara can be changed from a
princess into a beggar simply by changing from a pink silk gauze
dress to a tight black frock (pp. 85-86). To Miss Minchin scullery-
maids are "not little girls" but rather "machines" for carrying
coal-scuttles and making fires (p. 74). She looks at an old table,
a soap dish, and colored tissue paper which Sara and her friends
are using to make their attic snack a magic feast, and she sees
only "rubbish" (p. 205).

The importance of a person's point of view is underscored also
by Burnett's symbolic use of fairy tale magic, a concept she will
develop further in *The Secret Garden*. In *A Little Princess* magic
becomes a metaphor for the ability to see with the imagination, for
example, Sara's ability to see her attic room as a dungeon or
banquet hall in a romantic story and to see herself as a princess in a
fairy tale. Like magic, this ability to see with the imagination is also

a power — it helps Sara to endure her physical hardships and to maintain her sense of self-worth in the presence of Miss Minchin's insults. And finally, magic becomes a way of explaining the marvelous changes that come about in Sara's life as her true nature and identity are rediscovered by the world. This is "the Magic that won't let those worst things *ever* quite happen" (p. 212). It is the larger "Magic" which works throughout the kind of story Sara finds herself living in (pp. 218, 221). *A Little Princess* is a modern version of a familiar fairy tale, and it has gained thematic and symbolic richness in Burnett's retelling.

The frequent references to fairy tales and magic make it difficult to mistake *A Little Princess* for a realistic novel of child life. The clues in *Little Lord Fauntleroy* are less obvious, but they are there. The story does contain a few explicit comparisons to the world of the fairy tale; the Earl's castle is "like the palace in a fairy story" for example, and Little Lord Fauntleroy is "rather like a small copy of the fairy prince."[14] But the primary clue to the kind of story Burnett offers is precisely that characteristic which makes it a failure as a piece of realistic fiction: its exaggeration. Cedric's change in station, like Sara's, is exaggerated to fairy tale proportions. He moves from considerable poverty in a New York City apartment to untold wealth in one of the most beautiful country estates in England. The main figures in Cedric's life are painted in broad strokes just as he is. His mother is a paragon of sacrificial parenthood, willing to deny herself her son's companionship for what she considers to be his good; like Fauntleroy, she is being tested, and the purity of her motives eventually becomes obvious even to the suspicious Earl. The Earl himself becomes a moral monster as Burnett increasingly darkens his outline; no one besides Cedric has been able to find anything good in this "cynical, worldly old man" (p. 110), a man who had neglected his own wife and had been indifferent to his own children (p. 147).

In the center of such a story, a hero of conspicuous beauty and incorruptible virtue is entirely appropriate. As a contemporary reviewer put it, Little Lord Fauntleroy is a "paladin in knicker-bockers."[15] His nobility shines forth in any environment, in a tiny corner grocery store as in a vast banquet hall. As he rides forth he extends the arm of charity to the less fortunate; he sets up his boot-black friend in business and provides special physical comforts for an old apple woman who had been kind to him. Armed only with

"WILKINS WAS CARRYING HIS HAT FOR HIM, AND HIS HAIR WAS FLYING, BUT HE CAME BACK AT A BRISK CANTER."

One of Reginald Birch's illustrations for the first edition of *Little Lord Fauntleroy* (1886) portrayed Frances Hodgson Burnett's exemplary child much as a contemporary reviewer described him, a "paladin in knickerbockers." (Reproduced by permission of The Huntington Library, San Marino, California) his innocence and goodness Fauntleroy tames the ogre in his castle — he changes a selfish old man into an affectionate grandfather and responsible landlord.

As is well known, this "paladin in knickerbockers" was not so successful in winning the affection of a generation of boys whose parents apparently believed, like Miss Minchin, that a change in children's clothes would effect a marvelous change in their nature. A justifiable sympathy for these real-life victims probably played a significant role in the unjustifiably negative criticism and reputation Burnett's book has sometimes received.[16] To defend Burnett's achievement in *Little Lord Fauntleroy,* however, critics need not just recite evidence that the fictional Cedric "is not really a sissy";[17] more important, it is necessary to recognize the kind of tale in which he figures. It is a combination of fairy tale and exemplum as is another story which has suffered from too-literal interpretations, the Clerk's Tale in Chaucer's *Canterbury Tales.* The Patient Griselda, like Little Lord Fauntleroy, has been deplored by readers as a monster of virtue despite the Clerk's declaration that he meant his tale to be taken not as an example of wifely behavior but as an inspiration to steadfastness in the tests which God sends us. The Clerk's Tale also uses exaggeration to state its symbolic theme; in comparing Chaucer's version of the tale with his sources, scholars have found that he intensified rather than softened the contrasts between the tyrannical husband and the patient wife.[18] In Griselda, as one critic put it, Chaucer "conjures up" "the spirit of heroic patience."[19] In *Little Lord Fauntleroy,* Burnett uses some of the same techniques of exaggerated characterization and plot to conjure up the spirit of heroic innocence. Both tales appropriately elicit our wonder: they have an evocative power precisely because their main characters as well as their situations are out of the ordinary — "too good to be true."[20]

Little Lord Fauntleroy, therefore, like Chaucer's Clerk's Tale and *A Little Princess,* is a *märchen,* a "wonder tale." But it is also an exemplum. Its purpose, however, is not that of the religious exempla about dying child saints, that is, to frighten readers into an early conversion. Nor is its purpose that of so many secular exempla in children's literature, to demonstrate or inculcate specific modes of behavior. *Little Lord Fauntleroy* survives changing fashions because Burnett returned to an earlier and more enduring use of the exemplum form to make a symbolic statement about the testing and the power of virtue.

In *The Secret Garden* Burnett built on her earlier works by continuing to use themes and motifs from the exemplum and the fairy tale, but, as I indicated earlier, she gave symbolic enrichment and mythic enlargement to her poetic vision by adding tropes from a literary pastoral tradition at least as old as Virgil's *Georgics*. *The Secret Garden*, like *Little Lord Fauntleroy*, is an exemplum about power, the power to bring to human life the marvelous change of physical healing and psychological rebirth. As in *A Little Princess*, Burnett uses the concept of magic to describe the workings of this power, and as in both of her earlier works, she shows the saving effect of this power on a reclusive adult. In the climax of *The Secret Garden*, the embittered widower Archibald Craven embraces the son he has avoided and joins the human family again. In contrast to her earlier works, however, Burnett now dramatizes a marvelous change not just within adults but also within her main child characters. Much of her story depicts the gradual physical and psychological rebirth of the orphaned Mary Lennox and her hypochondriac cousin, Colin Craven. In this story marvelous change has its source not so much in the nature of a child as in nature itself. The magic power which brings change in human lives is the same divine power which is evidenced by the seasonal cycle and the earth's fertility. By choosing a garden rather than an innocent child as the symbolic center of her story, Burnett drew on an ancient pastoral tradition and made the transition from fairy tale to myth.

Burnett's mythic imagination and her use of a more modern pastoral tradition are illustrated in the childhood memoir she wrote eighteen years before *The Secret Garden* (1911). In *The One I Knew Best of All* (1893), which might well be subtitled "A Portrait of the Artist as a Child," Burnett discusses the books and magazines which shaped her imagination. But she also assigns a large role in her development to nature; she describes an "enchanted" garden she played in as a very young child (pp. 29-43). Later, in an episode which foreshadows her famous fictional garden, she depicts her delight in imagining a profusion of flowers and green shoots in a long-locked and abandoned garden she discovered near her home in Manchester, England (pp. 254-260).[21] She devotes a long chapter to the formative effect the forests and mountains of Tennessee had on her as an adolescent, just before she sold her first story (pp. 251-285). Burnett's memoir as well as *The Secret Garden* thus belong to a modern pastoral tradition which suggests that there is a special affinity between the child and nature and that the child can be beneficially educated by nature. This tradition was established primarily by Rousseau's *Emile* (1762) and Wordsworth's *Prelude* (1805, 1850), was continued in nineteenth-century classics such as Mark Twain's *Tom Sawyer* (1876) and *Huckleberry Finn* (1885), and was restated in Kenneth Grahame's *Golden Age* (1895), which had a significant influence on the portrayal of childhood in children's literature during the early decades of the twentieth century.[22]

The pastoral episodes in Burnett's memoir also provide a preview of the mythic imagination at work later in *The Secret Garden*. She describes the "enchanted" garden she played in as the "Garden of Eden" because it was the scene of "the first Crime of her infancy" (p. 31). In this episode Burnett uses a Judeo-Christian myth to enhance her poignant portrayal of an impressionable child's exaggerated sense of guilt for a small misdemeanor. In contrast Burnett evokes a Pagan mythological tradition to express her unalloyed pleasure in nature as an adolescent. These days in the Tennessee mountains and forests she calls her "Dryad Days." She speculates that she felt so much a part of nature "because ages before — dim, far-off beautiful ages before, she had been a little Faun or Dryad — or perhaps a swaying thing of boughs and leaves herself" (p. 264). Later, she compares her revels with those of the "Bacchantes of old" (p. 280). In any case, she feels that she has been "reincarnated" from the age "when there had been fair pagan gods and goddesses who found the fair earth beautiful enough for deity itself" (pp. 264-265).

The Secret Garden is consistent with the Edenic myth in that Burnett portrays a garden fallen from former glory and main child characters who are not innocent, especially as compared with those in her earlier works. More explicitly, however, *The Secret Garden* evokes the pagan mythological tradition, particularly through two of the Yorkshire folk who help initiate Mary and Colin into nature's mysteries. The first is Mother Sowerby who works largely behind the scenes on behalf of her adopted children in the garden. This "comfortable wonderful mother creature," who has twelve children of her own she has fattened on "th' air of th' moor" and "th' grass same as th' wild ponies," has the aura of that archetypical God Mother, the Earth Mother.[23] In addition Mother Sowerby's twelve-year-old son Dickon, an un-self-conscious nature child, is obviously meant to suggest Pan. When Mary first sees Dickon, he is sitting under a tree and playing a rude pipe for some attending animals. The children call him an "animal charmer" who can charm the "boy animal" Colin (p. 192). As a more local nature deity than Mother Sowerby, Dickon participates in the garden ceremonies instituted to make Colin well. Despite her evocation of these pagan nature deities, however, Burnett stops short of a deification of nature itself: the "Magic" which the children summon is the creative life force that works *through* nature as well as through themselves (pp. 300-301, 349-350). Moreover, Burnett means to be non-sectarian in her description of this power and its appropriate worship.[24] Her "Pan" sings the "Doxology" (p. 344), and Mother Sowerby tells Colin that "th' Magic listened . . . It would ha' listened to anything tha'd sung. It was the joy that mattered. Eh! lad, lad — what's names to th' Joy Maker" (p. 350).

In dramatizing the workings of this magic power, Burnett draws on an ancient literary as well as mythic tradition. Much of the symbolic richness and formal integrity of *The Secret Garden* can be explicated by demonstrating its place within the georgic pastoral tradition (so called because this tradition is typified by Virgil's *Georgics* which describe the farmer's life rather than his bucolic *Eclogues,* which depict shepherd life). One of the most important characteristics of the georgic pastoral is an emphasis on time and change, especially as these are experienced through nature's diurnal and seasonal cycles. The bucolic shepherd usually enjoys a suspension of time and change, an eternal summer afternoon under the trees. The life of the farmer, on the other hand, is determined by the seasonal cycle.[25] Like georgic pastoralists before her, Burnett found that the seasonal cycle, especially the new life spring brings after the death of winter, provides a mythic metaphor for human change, growth, rebirth. Like Thoreau in *Walden,* Burnett uses the seasonal cycle to give form to her work as well as to symbolically underscore the marvelous change within her characters. Mary arrives on the moors during a late-winter rain storm; it is early spring when she and Colin enter the secret garden; during the summer the garden and the two children fully recover from their various ills; and this harvest of health is ready when Colin's father returns in the fall.

The georgic emphasis on the seasonal cycle tends to present nature as ever changing, ever new; most often, Burnett's children are interested in the new changes which springtime brings moment by moment to the garden. But the realization that nature's diurnal and seasonal cycles are themselves unchanging can also bring a glimpse of what Spenser called the "eterne in mutabilitie" (*Faerie Queene,* III, vi. 4.5). There are moments when "one's heart stands still at the strange unchanging majesty of the rising sun — which has been happening every morning for thousands and thousands and thousands of years" (p. 268). It is thus that Burnett describes Colin's feelings when he first learned that he could walk, when his first experience of the changes of springtime in the garden elicited his cry, "I shall live forever and ever and ever!" (p. 267).

A second distinguishing characteristic of the georgic pastoral tradition is its emphasis on work. In bucolic poetry the shepherd's life is admired for its leisure, idleness, *otium.* The georgic farmer, on the other hand, is praised for his work. Nature may sometimes cause him to contemplate its beauty, but it also invites him to participate in its wonders, to assist through his own work in nature's ceaseless creation; the farmer thus has almost a demiurgic role. In Burnett's novel, Mary and Colin experience this georgic cooperation between man and nature most obviously through their work in the garden. They search for green shoots under the dead brown, they pull weeds and plant seeds, and they rejoice as spring brings the garden into bloom. Perhaps less obviously, Burnett underscores this georgic theme through her use of the children's magic experiments to make Colin well. By incanting, by sitting and processing in a "mystic circle" (p. 322), the children become participants in nature's song and dance;[26] they practice magic as they work in the garden. As Colin says, "The Magic works best when you work yourself" (p. 341). But the children are aware that the magic cannot be controlled entirely by their own acts; that is why they call it "Magic." The power that makes Colin well must also come from outside him: it is like the spring which is needed if their own work in the garden is to be rewarded with bloom. The children's magic experiments (like their work in the garden) are examples of the georgic reciprocity between man and nature which Wordsworth described as being both "willing to work and to be wrought upon," of being "creator and receiver both" (1805, XIII.100, II.271). This georgic combination creates the conditions under which human rebirth can occur even as the seasonal cycle gives form to the experience of rebirth.

The georgic reciprocity between man and nature is reflected in two stylistic characteristics of Burnett's narrative which help account for some of its literary power. The book is both lyrical and incantational; its language is thus both an expression of being and a tool for doing. The members of the secret garden community are constantly describing nature's beauty in paeans which seem involuntary expressions of joy. From the beginning Ben Weatherstaff, the gardener, and Dickon, the boy from the moors — the folk who have long been close to "the good rich earth" — are the songsters of nature. But Mary and Colin also find themselves singing as they discover that the spring in the garden is moving inside of them too. These descriptions become incantatory even before Colin establishes incantations as a formal part of his magic experiment; before Colin first enters the garden, Mary soothes him to sleep after one of his tantrums with a soft, droning description of spring's beginnings in the garden (pp. 227-228). The children's imitation of the folk dialect of Yorkshire as they work in the garden can also be seen as the incantatory use of an especially potent language. Moreover, the novel as a whole has an incantatory as well as lyrical quality not only because of the liberal use of dialect but also because key words such as "brown," "green," "Spring," "Magic," "awakening," "growing," and "alive" are repeated over and over. Language becomes a tool for doing in Burnett's story also through the proverbial wisdom which Hesiod and Virgil established as part of the georgic tradition. Language is a repository and transmitter of lore which can guide man in his work. In *The Secret Garden* Mary and Colin are guided by the lore of Ben Weatherstaff, Dickon, and especially Mother Sowerby, whose proverbial wisdom is quoted as authoritative by many characters throughout the narrative.

The inclusion of that social creation, proverbial wisdom, points to another important characteristic of the georgic pastoral tradition: it emphasizes cooperation not only between nature and man but also between man and man. Unlike Virgil's bucolic *Eclogues,* his *Georgics* give an important role to family and community life. In Burnett's story human cooperation is demonstrated through the secret garden society formed to make Colin well. The magic rituals in the garden suggest the importance of human effort, but they are also expressions of social identity — the ceremonies give form to the garden community. Finally, as in *Little Lord Fauntleroy,* family reconciliation provides the climax to *The Secret Garden.* Communities as well as individuals can experience the marvelous change of rebirth.

Tradition and the Individual Talent of Frances Hodgson Burnett 203

The secret garden is the central georgic trope, the unifying symbol of rebirth in Burnett's novel. A closer examination of her use of the garden demonstrates how well she was able to meld themes and motifs from fairy tale, exemplum, and pastoral tradition into a coherent mythic statement. First, the garden is the place where the children work and observe the magic of change and new life which the seasons bring in nature and in themselves. But the garden's symbolic meaning is intensified in a number of other ways. For example, the garden represents that which is dead or apparently dead in the past. The sickness of the garden clearly suggests the illness and ill-temper which the children put behind them. The garden is also associated with Colin's dead mother: it was her favorite place and the occasion of her death; Colin's father, Archibald Craven, had the garden locked up because it reminds him of the past. But the garden also represents the redemptive magic which can infuse the present and future. According to Mother Sowerby, Colin's mother is still watching over him, especially in the garden. It was Colin's mother who magically initiated the plan to bring him to the garden by sending the robin to show Mary the hidden key and door (pp. 273-274). Like Burnett's earlier works, *The Secred Garden* suggests motifs from the Cinderella story. In some of that tale's variants, the supernatural agency which helps Cinderella is associated with her dead mother. Perrault's fairy godmother, for example, can be seen as the spirit of Cinderella's dead mother. Other variants express the mother's magical help more clearly as Burnett does, through animals, birds, plants. Cinderella is helped by a calf her mother had given her or by a bird which perches in a hazel tree Cinderella had planted on her mother's grave.[27]

Burnett's garden becomes representative of redemptive forces in the present and future also because she identifies it with the children as well as with Colin's mother. Like Mary, the garden has suffered neglect because nobody wanted it — it too is an "orphan." Also, both children are ten years old, and the garden has been locked ten years, since Colin's mother died shortly after he was born. The children, like the garden, are gifts which the dead mother has given to the present and future. Archibald Craven must accept all of these gifts if he is to live joyfully in the present and future.

Finally, Burnett connects the garden with human rebirth by making it a georgic "landscape of the mind."[28] One character says that being inside the garden is like being in a dream (p. 127). A recurring metaphor for what happens to the garden as well as to the characters is "waking up" or "awakening." Details such as the garden's secrecy and its "wild" rather than "tidy" appearance (p. 134) further suggest the unconscious mind. Unfortunately, Burnett sometimes allows this part of her symbolism to become too conscious, especially in a chapter in which she describes the power of the mind, the dangers of locking it up, and the necessity of replacing the weeds of bad thoughts with the plants of beautiful thoughts (pp. 353-355). More often, however, Burnett allows her fictional garden to speak for itself so that in its apparent artlessness it seems less a "gardener's garden" than "a wilderness of growing things" (p. 208).

Because Burnett has invested the secret garden with so much symbolic meaning, she can use it to make the family reunion at the end of her exemplum about power something more than just a sentimental cliché. The garden gives her not only a setting for this scene but also a vivid image for what her story suggests about rebirth. As Archibald Craven gets near the walled garden in search of his son, he hears "the laughter of young things, the uncontrollable laughter of children who were trying not to be heard but who in a moment or so — as their excitement mounted — would burst forth." And the garden's secret does "burst forth" in the person of a healthy Colin followed by his playmates; through the door now "flung wide open," Colin makes an "unseeing dash" "full speed" toward his father (pp. 369-370). Throughout the novel, Burnett has stressed that the garden can come back to life not because of its secrecy, but because of that which can somehow find a way inside its locked walls: the powers of nature and the helpful work of human beings. Now Burnett uses the walled garden to show that the marvelous change of rebirth is a secret that cannot be kept, that a community of the reborn has the ability — indeed, the inner necessity — to expand and include the world outside.

Because it taps some of the oldest of folktale motifs, pastoral tropes, and mythic themes, Burnett's exemplum about power has a resonant complexity; but it also has an integrity, especially because of its unifying symbolic image, the secret garden. In *Little Lord Fauntleroy* and *A Little Princess* Frances Hodgson Burnett had made her own poetic contribution to two genres within the tradition of children's literature, the exemplum and the fairy tale. In *The Secret Garden* she used a variety of literary traditions to create a work of thematic and symbolic richness which well deserves to be regarded as a juvenile masterpiece.

NOTES

1. Marghanita Laski, *Mrs. Ewing, Mrs. Molesworth, and Mrs. Hodgson Burnett* (New York: Oxford Univ. Press, 1951), pp. 81-91. For similar estimates of Burnett's achievement see, e.g., John Rowe Townsend, *Written for Children: An Outline of English-Language Children's Literature*, rev. ed. (Philadelphia: Lippincott, 1965, 1974), pp. 86-89; and Roger Lancelyn·Green, "The Golden Age of Children's Books," *Only Connect: Readings on Children's Literature*, ed. Sheila Egoff et al. (Toronto: Oxford Univ. Press, 1969), pp. 10-11. Although it does not merit a place with Burnett's three best known books for children, *The Lost Prince* (1915) deserves more critical attention than it has received. This longer work is Burnett's contribution to the adventure romance, a popular children's genre not discussed in this article. Especially interesting is the fact that Burnett anticipated some of the main themes and plot interests of J. R. R. Tolkien's *Lord of the Rings:* the use of two apparently insignificant creatures, in Burnett's case children, to help bring about the return of a king in exile.
2. See, e.g., Laski, pp. 81-91; Townsend, pp. 86-89; Gillian Avery with the assistance of Augusta Bull, *Nineteenth Century Children: Heroes and Heroines in English Children's Stories 1790-1900* (London: Hodder and Stoughton, 1965), pp. 177-179; and Ann Thwaite, *Waiting for the Party: The Life of Frances Hodgson Burnett 1849-1924* (New York: Scribner's, 1974), pp. 220-222.
3. Gillian Avery discusses *Little Lord Fauntleroy* as an example of the cult of the innocent child in children's literature during the last decades of the nineteenth century. "In spite of the clouds of sentimentality, *Little Lord Fauntleroy* (1886) is curiously compelling," Avery declares, p. 178.
4. Illus. Reginald B. Birch (New York: Scribner's, 1893), p. 111; hereafter, references to this memoir will be made in the text.
5. *Little Saint Elizabeth and Other Stories*, illus. Reginald B. Birch (New York: Scribner's, 1890), pp. 15-55.
6. Vivian Burnett, *The Romantick Lady (Frances Hodgson Burnett): The Life Story of an Imagination* (New York: Scribner's, 1927), pp. 10-11; Ann Thwaite, *Waiting for the Party*, pp. 12, 256.
7. Browne's "Story of Childe Charity," in fact, has many of the fairy tale and exemplum themes which this article discusses as central in Burnett's fiction; *Granny's Wonderful Chair* (rpt. New York: Macmillan, 1961), pp. 109-127.
8. See Avery, pp. 81-93, 170-174, for a comparison of the saintly child in evangelistic fiction with the secular innocent in late-nineteenth-century children's literature.
9. Burnett used these words to describe her son Vivian in "How Fauntleroy Occurred and a Very Real Little Boy Became an Ideal One," *Piccino and Other Child Stories* (New York: Scribner's, 1894), pp. 203, 163.
10. Burnett began her career by writing formula fiction for women's magazines.

Her early stories and novels often contain the familiar love match between the beautiful or talented young woman and a man who is socially or intellectually her superior. Sometimes, as in "A Quiet Life" (1878), the love match ends tragically. Often, however, the young woman marries her "Prince Charming." See, e.g., "Pretty Polly Pemberton" (1877) and *Louisiana* (1880). In a 1901 version of this formula, *The Making of a Marchioness*, Burnett made explicit references to the Cinderella tale.

11. Iona and Peter Opie, *The Classic Fairy Tales* (London: Oxford Univ. Press, 1974), pp. 12-14.

12. In *Sara Crewe* (1888) Burnett's main character was somewhat spoiled and ill-tempered at the beginning of the story; in *A Little Princess* (1905) Burnett brought her story more in line with the Cinderella tale by immediately establishing Sara's noble nature.

13. *A Little Princess: Being the Whole Story of Sara Crewe Now Told for the First Time* (rpt. New York: Scribner's, 1938), p. 35; hereafter, references will be made in the text.

14. *Little Lord Fauntleroy*, illus. Reginald Birch (New York: Scribner's, 1886), p. 71; hereafter, references will be made in the text.

15. William Archer, London *World*, 23 May 1888; Archer's review of the play Burnett wrote based on her popular novel is quoted by Vivian Burnett, *Romantick Lady*, p. 168.

16. In 1932, e.g., F. J. Harvey Darton lamented that *Little Lord Fauntleroy* "ran through England like a sickly fever. Nine editions were published in as many months, and the odious little prig in the lace collar is not dead yet," *Children's Books in England: Five Centuries of Social Life* (Cambridge: University Press, 1932, 1966), p. 239; in this survey, Darton does not mention any of Burnett's other books.

17. As she is dressing up Fauntleroy in paperback for readers in the 1970's, Ann Thwaite says that Cedric got his reputation as "a prig and a sissy . . . partly because of the original illustrations by Reginald Birch" which "did the book a disservice, pretty and skilful as they were." The fictional Fauntleroy, Thwaite argues, "is not really a sissy. He is brave, thoughtful, enterprising, unaffected; he is, in fact, a likeable boy. Perhaps he is rather too good to be true," Introduction, *Little Lord Fauntleroy* (rpt. London: Collins, 1974), pp. 8-9.

18. See, e.g., J. Burke Severs, *The Literary Relationships of Chaucer's Clerkes Tale* (New Haven: Yale Univ. Press, 1942), pp. 231-237.

19. Ian Robinson, *Chaucer and the English Tradition* (Cambridge: University Press, 1972), p. 170.

20. Ann Thwaite, Introduction, *Little Lord Fauntleroy*, p. 8.

21. In *My Robin* (1912) Burnett described a robin and garden in Kent which also provided models for *The Secret Garden*. Near the end of her life she wrote *In the Garden* (1925) describing her years of experience as a gardener and exhorting her readers to have gardens. From 1898 until she died in 1924, according to her son (*Romantick Lady*, pp. 286-287), she was "the Passionate Gardener." Much of Burnett's portrayal of nature in *The Secret Garden*, therefore, was based on her own observations. It was Burnett's lifelong habit, however, to transform her experience into the conventional forms of a story.

"This has been my way of looking at life as it went by me," she said in the Preface to *Giovanni and the Other: Children Who Have Made Stories* (1892). Just as she earlier found a fairy tale in her love for her son Vivian, she now saw mythic significance in her experience as a gardener.

22. On the significance of Kenneth Grahame's *Golden Age*, see Roger Lancelyn Green, "The Golden Age of Children's Books," pp. 11-13. For a fuller discussion of this modern pastoral tradition and its expression in children's literature, see Phyllis Bixler Koppes, "The Child in Pastoral Myth: A Study in Rousseau and Wordsworth, Children's Literature and Literary Fantasy," Diss. Univ. of Kansas 1976, chs. III-VII.

23. *The Secret Garden* (New York: Frederick A. Stokes, 1911), pp. 316, 38; hereafter, references will be made in the text. Some of Mother Sowerby's folk wisdom is archetypically appropriate — it is a global wisdom:

> "When I was at school my jography told as th' world was shaped like a orange an' I found out before I was ten that th' whole orange doesn't belong to nobody. No one owns more than his bit of a quarter an' there's times it seems like there's not enow quarters to go around.
> "But don't you — none o' you — think as you own th' whole orange or you'll find out you're mistaken . . . there's no sense in grabbin' at th' whole orange — peel an' all. If you do you'll likely not get even the pips, an' them's too bitter to eat" (pp. 244-245).

24. According to Vivian Burnett (*Romantick Lady*, pp. 376-377), Burnett was alternately interested in Theosophy, Spiritualism, Christian Science, and other forms of mind- or faith-healing. Except possibly in a discourse on the powers of the mind near the end of *The Secret Garden*, Burnett does not urge these sectarian ideas on her reader. They are more obviously on display in *The Lost Prince* (1915) and especially in *The Closed Room* (1904) and *The White People* (1917), both of which dramatize the belief that dead loved ones often stay close to one in some kind of afterlife.

25. As Virgil says in his *Georgics*, "The farmer's toil returns moving in a circle, as the year rolls back upon itself over its own footsteps," *Virgil, With an English Translation by H. Rushton Fairclough in Two Volumes*, rev. ed. (Cambridge: Harvard Univ. Press, 1957), Book II, p. 145. The distinctions between the bucolic and georgic pastoral traditions used in this article are developed more fully in Bixler Koppes, "The Child in Pastoral Myth," ch. I.

26. In the first book of his *Georgics*, p. 105, Virgil prescribes that country folk process around their fields calling on Ceres to bring fertility.

27. Iona and Peter Opie, *The Classic Fairy Tales*, pp. 117-121.

28. A number of critics have noted the tendency for a pastoral landscape to become a picture of the mind. See, e.g., Bruno Snell, "Arcadia: The Discovery of a Spiritual Landscape," in *The Discovery of Mind: The Greek Origins of European Thought*, trans. T. G. Rosenmeyer (1953; rpt. New York: Harper, 1960), pp. 281-309; and Richard Cody, *The Landscape of the Mind: Pastoralism and Platonic Theory in Tasso's Aminta and Shakespeare's Early Comedies* (Oxford: Clarendon, 1969).

ROGER SALE PUTS IN A WORD
FOR CHILDREN'S LITERATURE

K. Narayan Kutty

A large majority of the writers of children's books in the world live and work in America. Consequently, no other country in the world has produced so much literature for children—not all of it is trash—as America. Yet few subjects have suffered so much from critical neglect in America as children's literature. Contempt for children's literature among critics and professors of literature in this country contrasts strikingly with scholarly interest in and fascination with it in Europe and in England.[1]

The first writer in the West to give children a book they could call their own was Charles Perrault who, in 1697, published *Histoires ou contes du temps passé,* the first ever collection of fairy tales to appear in print. And Perrault was a member of the French Academy. The Brothers Grimm, who spent a lifetime collecting, editing, and publishing German fairy tales, were literary scholars and philologists, not anthropologists. The critical and creative writings of G. K. Chesterton, C. S. Lewis, and J. R. R. Tolkien, to name only three scholars from England, contain ample evidence that they did not consider fascination with children's literature beneath the dignity of their profession or calling in life.

Paul Hazard, who was the first European critic to write a full-length book on children's literature,[2] did not believe that books for children are less important than books for adults. He, too, was a member of the French Academy. Walter Benjamin, one of the original German critics of our time, not only read and collected books for children, but also was deeply impressed with the wisdom of oral literature.[3] Simone Weil, one of the most extraordinary human beings of this century, wrote a brilliant little essay on "The Six Swans," a Grimm's fairy tale.[4] Michel Butor, the noted contemporary French novelist, has written a penetrating essay on the classic French fairy tales.[5]

Children's literature has fared well—has it not?—with eminent scholars and writers on the other side of the Atlantic. Here, in America, its critical fate has been dismal. It has met with only contempt and ridicule in scholarly circles.

American professors of literature and non-academic critics do not dabble in such plebeian subjects as children's literature.[6] They will not, if they can help it. There are some, of course, who more than dabble in it; but being "guilty" of having betrayed the high and noble cause of LITERATURE, their literary sensibility becomes suspect and their intelligence dubious in the eyes of the academy. Most English Departments in the country scorn the subject openly; those that allow it to be taught tolerate it as an evil necessary to keep enrollments up.

The foregoing facts make Roger Sale's *Fairy Tales and After: From Snow White to E. B. White*[7] an unusual and courageous book. Sale is a professor of English (University of Washington) who has published critical essays in book form and in journals, such as *The Hudson Review, The New York Review of Books,* and *The New York Times Book Review.* Undeterred by the mindless snobbery and small-mindedness of his profession and prompted by a fascination with children's literature, which he has kept alive through his childhood and youth, Sale has written a serious book about some of the outstanding and not so outstanding works of children's literature.

There is no evidence that God has a Ph.D. in English or that he has taught English at an Ivy League school in America. So He will forgive Sale his sin. After all, hasn't His son said: "A little child shall lead them"?

Fairy Tales and After (the subtitle is misleading; the book is no survey) is a collection of literary commentaries on certain features of fairy tales, animal tales, and of the works of Andersen, Lewis Carroll, Beatrix Potter, L. Frank Baum, Kenneth Grahame, A. A. Milne, Rudyard Kipling, E. B. White, Jean de Brunhoff, Dr. Seuss, and some others.

Sale's commentaries are useful. They shed light on some important features of the works he deals with. Again, the book is useful in that it says emphatically what needed to be said a long time ago: that we should read children's literature seriously, slowly, patiently, and with respect, so that we experience the many delights it has to offer as well as become aware of its range and depth.

Among the more thought-provoking discoveries that Sale has made from a close study of his texts are:

Two of the finest works of Dr. Seuss are among his earliest: *The 500 Hats of Bartholemew Cubbins* (discussed over-enthusiastically but engagingly) and *The King's Stilts.* The best of early Seuss affords the adult reader the same intense pleasure as it does the child. The late Jean de Brunhoff, author of the Babar stories, has a unique gift for dealing with the unpleasant and even evil experiences of life, which few writers of children's books dare deal with, in a matter of fact and effortless manner. De Brunhoff offers more to the adult reader than to the child. It is possible that fairy tales depict the deepest fears and wishes of the communities that produced them. Fairy tales are not necessarily about the maturing process of young children, as Bruno Bettelheim would have us believe in his *Uses of Enchantment.*[8] Adults are likely to find the Pooh stories of A. A. Milne, which they enjoyed as youngsters, tiresome because of their priggishness and snobbery. Kenneth Grahame's world in *The Wind in The Willows,* though snug and cozy, is happily free from the smugness of the Pooh stories or Tolkien's *The Hobbit.* Lewis Carroll exposes Alice to the same kind of hardships as he himself had suffered as a child. In her ageless works, Beatrix Potter (Sale is particularly good on Potter), one of the toughest writers of children's literature, has created a small, enclosed world precisely, artistically, and completely. Animals are a source of power in the best of children's literature, and understanding why the best writers of children's fiction use animals is more important than whether they like or understand children. Andersen was clearly retarded in his mental growth as Lewis Carroll was, but in Carroll arrested growth was a source of strength; in Andersen, it was not.

Not all these discoveries are acceptable, but they provide a platform for debate; they force us to reexamine our views about these writers.

It is clear from what has already been said in this essay that Sale writes about children's literature with enthusiasm and without condescension. He makes us alert to the many subtleties in it; he persuades us to pay attention to usually neglected details; and he writes cautiously, avoiding controversial statements. However, in spite of its many strengths, *Fairy Tales and After* cannot be called an unqualified critical success. It does not make a serious case for the study of children's literature, which anyone with more than casual interest in the subject will expect it to, considering the negative attitude toward it among teachers of literature and the need to legitimize it as a field for scholarly study and research. Sale, of course, would counter this criticism by saying that making such a case was not one of his intentions in writing this book. But if a book about children's literature does not try to persuade its skeptical readers of the need to take the study of the subject seriously, then it is little more than a well-meant attempt to say generous things about it. Sale admits that criticism of children's literature is still in its infancy. But if it is to grow, a much grittier approach to it than is evidenced in *Fairy Tales and After* is required.

Is it smallness of aim then (or is it unseemly haste to have the book published) that has prevented Sale from accomplishing anything more than an invitation to the members of his profession to read children's literature with what he calls "profit and delight"? The point about Sale's not aiming high enough can be strengthened by listening to what appears to be a statement of purpose and method at the beginning of *Fairy Tales and After:*

> I write as an adult and for other adults; inevitably, and often
> regardless of any experience any of us had as children, I will
> look at these books in a way that some may find not just
> different from theirs, but alien as well. Here are these books, I
> want to say, good books, and we read them essentially as we
> read any book, left to right, top to bottom of the page, front
> to back. After reading them, we say what we have seen, felt,
> understood. But of course we don't see, feel, or understand
> the same things, and when we are dealing with good books
> about which little has ever been written, we will diverge in
> method and disagree concerning emphasis and tone perhaps
> more than we would if the subject were, say, Shakespeare.[9]

This is a critical cop out. The statement is so diffidently made that it makes one sense a certain conceptual penury on Sale's part in regard to children's literature that one seldom sees in his treatment of literature for grown-ups. In fact, what Sale says in the passage hardly amounts to a thesis statement or an announcement of method. As either, it is much too general, too wide open to demand critical rigor in analysis and discussion, and it permits meanderings without destination. However, if Sale were to do at least what he said he would in the passage, *Fairy Tales and After* would still draw praise from its readers, if not delighted applause.

Seldom does Sale speak of what he has "seen," or "felt," or "understood" in ways that make us see the books he has discussed as complete artistic structures. Sale is an attractive salesman of parts, not wholes. He interprets parts of Carroll's *Alice in Wonder-*

land, Jarrell's *Animal Family,* Potter's stories, the Oz books of Baum, and of Kipling's *Kim* with penetrating insight, but rarely does he put the parts together.

In Sale's discussion of "Snow White," there is little about Snow White who, after all, is the protagonist of the story. Unwittingly, as it were, he makes the antagonist, the Queen, the protagonist. As if to prove that this misplaced emphasis was no accident, he devotes all his attention to the titular tree and the stepmother in his discussion of "The Juniper Tree," a fairy tale from the Brothers Grimm. The story is clearly about the children in the story, but Sale ignores them completely. Because Sale has decided that there is nothing more important than the literal in literature, he makes nothing of the metaphorical and mythical elements in fairy tales and in the Mowgli stories of Kipling's *The Jungle Books.* Again, the picture we get of Kipling's eponymous Kim is a partial one, since Sale does not deal with the oedipal nature of his relationship with the lama or with the efforts of Reverends Victor and Vincent and General Creighton to transform him into what they want him to be. Although he is undoubtedly right about Milne's snobbery, Sale is wrong in suggesting that the only thing worth looking into in the Pooh stories is the nature of the friendship between Christopher Robin and Pooh. His discussion of Kenneth Grahame's *The Wind in the Willows* is incomplete in that he says nothing about the patriarchal Badger. (A good look at Grahame's utopia would have convinced Sale that it is not only male-dominated but also class-ridden.) He correctly points out the flaws in Andersen's art—his preachiness, his irrelevant social satire, his sentimentality, and his inability to detach himself from his material—but he fails to respond to Andersen's great ability to evoke the world of little people and things. (Andersen was not small in size, as Sale says; in fact, he was tall, lean, and gawky in an ungainly way.)

Children's literature embodies the essence of childhood; its proper subject is children. Although written by adults, it is about children, though not for children alone. The best in this trash-ridden field reminds us most powerfully of our beginnings. Like Wordsworth's rainbow in "My Heart Leaps Up," the characters, images, and metaphors in children's literature can provide us with a link with our past. It is this link from which the finest writers of children's fiction and poetry draw their inspiration that Sale talks least about.

The trouble with Sale is that he undermines the role of the child in children's literature. For him, how children's literature recreates childhood and how it recovers for us a certain important period in our lives that we have lost to time are matters of no consequence at all. He suggests that he is concerned only with what appeals to adults in children's literature. But how can this appeal be independent of the treatment of the material in it? And isn't the material the world of children? Doesn't children's literature provide us with a profound knowledge of children that issues from the intuitions of some adults in tune with the world of childhood? These questions compel us to consider a definition of children's literature. Sale has not only no use for a definition but he also assumes that his readers know what children's literature is.

How writers of children's books perceive children; how they individualize them in literature; how they explore the world of our beginnings; and how successful the writers discussed in *Fairy Tales and After* are in evoking that world are topics that have not attracted Sale's attention. One wishes they had. *Fairy Tales and After* would then be a substantial contribution to the study of children's literature.

Notwithstanding its limitations, *Fairy Tales and After* is a book lovers of children's literature would enjoy reading and profit from. Although it does not explore the range and depth of the literature written for children, it suggests them. The chapter on animal stories, which is recommended to anyone who cares for literature or animals, shows Sale at his critical best.

NOTES

1. If I do not allude to interest in children's literature in Asia, Africa, and Latin America, it is because in those parts of the world it is still a developing literary form. The reason for the slow growth of the form may lie in the strength of the oral tradition in literature in these countries. Wide-spread illiteracy may be another reason for the lack of interest in written children's literature. It must be emphasized, however, that in Asia, Africa, and Latin America, children grow up listening to stories—and these stories are inexhaustible—from their parents, grandparents, or relatives. The story hours satisfy two fundamental yearnings in children: fantasy and intimacy with adults. In the so-called underdeveloped parts of the world adults are very close to children. Luckily for the children growing up in these countries, civilization does not demand alienation of adults from children.

2. Paul Hazard, *Books Children & Men,* trans. Marguerite Mitchell (Boston: Horn Book, 1944). Despite its slightly sentimental attitude toward children and exclamatory style, Hazard's book is a pioneering work in the criticism of children's literature. Hazard is particularly perceptive about how children differ from adults in their perceptions of themselves and the world around them. He shows how adults oppress children and how they circumscribe their world.

3. See the second part of Charles Rosen's essay on Walter Benjamin's *The Origin of German Tragic Drama* in *The New York Review of Books,* XXV, 18 (November 1977), 36.

4. See Simone Pétrement's *Simone Weil: A Life* (New York: Pantheon Books, 1976), p. 36. Weil wrote the essay on "The Six Swans," which Pétrement paraphrases and quotes from, for her philosopher-teacher, Alain (Emile Auguste Chartier) in 1925 when she was a student at *Ecole Normale Supérieure.*

5. Michel Butor, "On Fairy Tales," in *Inventory,* trans. Richard Howard (New York: Alfred A. Knopf, 1961), pp. 211-224.

6. *Children's Literature* has for the last six years provided a unique opportunity for American scholars and critics to turn their attention to children's literature. But no prominent critic that I know of has yet contributed an essay to it on any aspect of the subject. The only major writer in America who has written seriously about an author of children's fiction is Gore Vidal. See Vidal's two-part essay on the Oz books of L. Frank Baum in *The New York Review of Books,* XXIV, 15 (September 1977), 10-15 and XXIV, 16 (October 1977), 38-43.

7. Roger Sale, *Fairy Tales and After: From Snow White to E. B. White* (Cambridge, Mass.: Harvard University Press, 1978). $11.00.

8. Bruno Bettelheim, *The Uses of Enchantment* (New York: Alfred A. Knopf, 1975).

9. *Fairy Tales and After,* p. 4.

LETTER ON THE CURRENT STATE OF CHILDREN'S LITERATURE

The following letter was sent by author Maia Wojciechowska to John R. Adams, a student at Concordia University in Montreal. It is reprinted here with the author's permission.

The present state of children's literature is appalling, horrifying, and possibly hopeless. I feel that there is a general conspiracy against excellence, that children's books reflect the common shoddiness and mediocrity of our culture. Adults can, and some actually do, withstand the assault on their minds (television, ericajongcrapandcompany in books) because they can turn off or dismiss the unimportant. But children fare less well because they are so receptive and trusting. The assault on *their* intelligence begins early (with picture books) and it is relentless.

The picture-book field is offensive in content if not in appearance; the illustrations seem to be designed to lull attention away from the vacuity of the words. Animals predominate in ninety percent or more of these books, pre-empting human beings as characters. Rodents are kings of this jungle of idiocy in which our children grow up, followed closely by alligators, rabbits and such. When an interesting animal makes a rare appearance, it is the victim of a castrating process which deprives it of all semblance to reality (remember Ferdinand, the bull?) Lions and tigers are portrayed as vegetarian; often they are engaged in imbecilic dialogue with Sambos and other stereotypes that have no capacity to act. If human beings appear, they do so as cutie-poo monsters that have nothing to do with 4000 years of Judaeo-Christian thinking, coping, or doing. Only about a dozen books don't offend the intelligence or the soul; the rest are the vomit of alcoholic old men, warty ladies, and editors who are physically and probably morally allergic to children. I exempt Sendak from all sins, and Bemelman is great. (*I've Got A Nightmare In My Closet* is one of those rare books that attack head on the juice that flows so freely and marvelously in young kids: fear.)

As we move from the sheer incompetence and insanity of the

picture-books to those books intended to be read by the kids themselves, we come to an area where the demolition of human beings assumes an awesome dimension. Here, animals give way to moral submidgets. "Humor" is dark, but certainly not funny. Idiots face problems that only idiots could face. The cookie molds are all the same and I can't recognize any human traits in these "creatures." Once in a while, an adult writes for other adults, but then the charm is mostly adult. One great book in this category is Seymour Leichman's *The Boy Who Could Sing Pictures.* It went to twelve publishers before Doubleday finally published it, ruining the great color of the original drawings. And then they let it go out of print.

In books for ages 12 and up (where I usually reside), there is a tendency to make the best of a dumb world. A few "hip" writers go bananas, and human beings slide away on the skin of an imbecile permissiveness. Maybe bad writing seems worse than it is because there is so much more of it in longer books. Of course, there are a few exceptions, probably because the editors were asleep: *A Wrinkle In Time,* (L'Engle), *My Enemy, My Friend* (Tunis), *Pigman,* (Zindel), Lipsyte's *The Contender,* and Hentoff's *Jazz Country* (but not his other abortions of propaganda disguised as juvenile novels).

The thing that is most horrendous about juvenile publishing is that the old it's-a-matter-of-taste routine applies where there is no question of taste — there is only pure mediocrity. And the evolutionary logistics take their toll: the more crap sells, the more crap will be published and the non-crap will appear less marketable to the publishers. (In one year, an experiment of weeding out the crap fails totally. Not one book in a catalog gets published, even though the agent is none other than Scott Meredith of Mrs. Exner's fame — not to mention Norman Mailer's $5 million contract.)

RE: my own *Christian.* Some of those who rejected it have written that although they always championed "controversial" books, God to them seems much too controversial a subject for children. (Give them perversion of one kind or another, but God forbid God!) The magnificent *I Wonder If I Should* . . . doesn't get published because "it doesn't solve anything at the end." Like life. The marvelously sensitive and incredibly funny *Inherit The Earth* doesn't make it because it is more adult than juvenile, and too juvenile to be adult. (As if the editors don't know that some kids read both juvenile and adult fiction, and that these kids don't stay for long with the juvenile stuff after they discover that books can be readable and meaningful.) The touching *Miracle* doesn't make it because "it's just one day in the life"; *Saving The Nation,* a satirical book, is "too thought provoking," and *The Crazy Old Lady And Me* is "too realistic"! Hell, what can you say except CENSORSHIP AGAINST QUALITY is a fact of life in juvenile publishing.

Maia Wojciechowska

Reviews

FOLK TALES: BEST OF ALL?

Margaret P. Esmonde

Cricket Boy, by Feenie Ziner. Illustrated by Ed Young. Garden City, New York: Doubleday & Company, Inc., 1977.

The Seeing Stick, by Jane Yolen. Illustrated by Remy Charlip and Demetra Maraslis. New York: Thomas Y. Crowell Company, 1977.

King of the Fish, by Marian Parry. Illustrated by the author. New York: Macmillan Publishing Company, 1977.

The Hundredth Dove and Other Tales, by Jane Yolen. Illustrated by David Palladini. New York: Thomas Y. Crowell Company, 1977.

Midsummer Magic, compiled by Ellin Greene. Illustrated by Barbara Cooney. New York: Lothrop, Lee & Shepard Company, 1977.

Masks of the World, designed by Deborah R. Horner. New York: Charles Scribner's Sons, 1977.

In *The Uses of Enchantment,* Bruno Bettelheim calls on literature not only to entertain and to arouse curiosity, but to enrich the child, stimulate his imagination, help him develop his intellect and clarify his emotions. His studies lead him to conclude that the best kind of literature to fulfill all of those needs is the folk-fairy tale. If this is true, then children are well-supplied with materials; numerous folk tales, singly and in collections, are published each year, some of them "retellings" and some newly-composed "literary" folk tales. But their quality varies greatly.

Cricket Boy, Feenie Ziner's retelling of a Chinese tale, is designated by the publisher for the 7-10 age group, but both the tale itself and the illustrations seem more suited to older tastes. Ed Young's lovely drawings, with colors carefully subdued by the dark brown backgrounds, reproduce the delicacy and subtlety of Chinese art. But the miniatures are an acquired taste, a taste which few if any 7-10 year olds have. For the young child, they are for the most part dull, dark, small pictures. The twenty-one pages of text are set in large type, easy for children to read, but more words than the young reader is accustomed to find in the 8½ by 11 inch picture book format. In addition, the large type seems aesthetically inappropriate alongside the delicacy of the miniatures.

The tale itself is unsuited to the young reader. Though the story is called *Cricket Boy,* the protagonist is the Scholar Hu, whose quest it is to win a government post. His son, Hu Sing, the Cricket Boy of the title, attempts suicide after accidently killing his father's fighting cricket. In the end, however, the boy saves the day through temporary reincarnation as a cricket, although this is not made clear to young readers, most of whom will be asking with the Scholar Hu, "What really happened?" Scholar Hu's search for knowledge may appeal to the mature reader, but Ziner has summed up the book's weakness in her description of the Cricket Boy: "But Hu Sing was a child. He was not interested in large questions."

Jane Yolen's *The Seeing Stick* is written in the style of a Chinese folk tale. It tells of the Emperor of China who offers rich rewards to anyone who can cure his little blind daughter. Many try and fail. Finally, a poor old man with a tall walking stick on which he carves pictures succeeds by teaching the princess to see with her fingers and to find joy in living.

The story lacks the vitality of the true folk tale, particularly in the characterization of the princess. Released from her self-centered existence, she teaches all the blind children of Peking to see as she has done, an action more characteristic of Goody Two-Shoes than the Emperor of China's daughter. The old man, who has received a fortune in jewels, gives them all away. The surprise ending which reveals the old man's blindness seems gratuitous. The story leaves the reader unsatisfied; the princess isn't really cured. She has only learned to make the best of her handicap, a conclusion which smacks of moralizing, as does the rest of the story.

Technically the book is appealing. Yolen's text is set in short lines varying from two to eight words with lots of white space. The two artists, using wax crayon and pencil on vellum, manage to capture the spirit of Chinese art without being as imitative as Ed Young. The use of the "Wizard of Oz" technique, opening with black and white illustrations and changing to delicately tinted four-color pastels when the princess begins to see via the stick, is quite effective.

Illustrator Marian Parry had adapted a Korean folk tale in her story, *King of the Fish,* though the story has nothing particularly Korean about it. The rabbit hero might just as easily have been Br'er Rabbit. The virtue of the story is the simplicity of the plot in which the "trickee" becomes the tricker in a turnabout which will amuse the young readers. The text is brief, with as little as two lines to a two-page spread.

Parry's three-color illustrations dominate each page. The bold watercolor pictures suggest hyperkinetic energy as the water churns and splashes in bold strokes sometimes reminiscent of finger painting. The pop-eyed fish twist and swirl. The king of the fish looks properly grumpy with the fish hook through his nose.

For older readers Jane Yolen has written a collection of short stories called *The Hundredth Dove,* illustrated with the striking charcoal drawings of David Palladini. The writing is lucid and deceptively simple, in the tradition of true folktales, but the stories themselves are of uneven quality. The title story is a tale of a huntsman who follows duty though it destroys what his master and he love most, and, according to the book jacket, is meant as a parable against blind obedience. But the story never indicates why the Lady Columba changed into a dove or why the huntsman was tested. His destruction of the white dove (though he hasn't killed the other ninety-nine) suggests he doesn't trust his emotions should he set the dove free. Practically speaking, the death seems the only resolution to the plot, for if he spares the Princess-dove, she has promised to be his love. But she is already betrothed to the huntsman's master. As a parable it may have a point, but as a folk tale, it lacks inner consistency. "The Maiden Made of Fire" and "The Lady and the Merman" are well-written and evoke the same feeling of sadness as some of Hans Christian Andersen's stories of lonely people who find love only in death. The religious parable, "Once a Good Man," seems somehow out of place in the collection. Perhaps the tale that comes closest to the folk-fairy tales Bettelheim speaks of is "The Wind Cap" in which a boy learns how to accommodate two aspects of his nature and learns in the bargain that "magic is magic and not for men."

Another entry in the field of the folk-fairy tale is Ellin Greene's *Midsummer Magic,* a compilation of tales, lore, charms and recipes connected with the Midsummer festivals celebrated in the British Isles and Northern Europe. The seven tales, all of them traditional, have as a general theme the magic that can occur on Midsummer's Eve. "Wee Meg Barnileg" is a grimly humorous warning to untidy, self-centered children but the story may appeal more to parent than child. "Maid Lena" and "The Golden Bird" are traditional "third son" tales. "The Girl Who Met the Witch of the Woods" incorporates a Red-Riding Hood theme but its best feature is the characterization of the witch. Most touching are the two tales of human/fairy marriage—"Diccon and Elfrida" and "Count Alaric's Lady." The former offers the bittersweet resolution of a deathbed reunion and the latter, a truly happy ending when Alaric discovers that "love is only perfect when it gives up even the thing which it loves, for that thing's sake." Interspersed between the tales are tempting recipes for cakes, cookies, and desserts as well as herb and flower lore, love charms and customs associated with the festival.

Technically the volume is well-produced. The bright white paper, the clean typeface, and Barbara Cooney's understated black and white illustrations and chapter ornaments contribute to the volume's quiet appeal.

The final entry in the round-up of folklore isn't really a book. *Masks of the World,* designed by Deborah R. Horner, is meant to be cut out by its readers. The masks in question are based on actual masks that have been used in dance festivals and ceremonial plays by people the world over, and represent gods, demons, and mythical animals. It is suggested by the artist that the masks, which are printed on heavy stock in vivid colors, can serve as a Halloween disguise or for a school project on folklore.

Each of the nine pages contains a brief explanation of the individual mask with directions for construction. One caution—the construction of the masks requires considerable skill in cutting out the different pieces and fitting them together. Most likely parental assistance will be required.

CHILDREN'S LITERATURE AND THE MEDIA

Francelia Butler

Children's Literature and Audio-Visual Materials in Africa. Ed. by
Nancy J. Schmidt. Buffalo, New York: Conch Magazine, Ltd.,
1977. $15.00 Trade Paperback.

Specialists in audio-visual materials tell me that it is still difficult
to find work in educational institutions because many professors of
literature and librarians do not know how to relate the media to
their discipline. Reaction to the media either is passive or negative.
It seems to me to be more constructive to find ways of enhancing
interest in literature through the media.

For African literature, this manual, edited by the Head of Tozzer
Library, Peabody Museum of Archaeology and Ethnology, Harvard,
serves as an exciting guide. It is many faceted. It contains, for
instance, critical analyses of films available on African culture
which can be used as a foil for the reading or telling of African
fiction and folktales. To complement this material, there are also
critical essays on picture books, stories, and folktales about Africa.

A bibliography of publications from the African countries and
from all parts of the world is included in this helpful book which
also attempts honest appraisals of available resources. Such a work
is particularly valuable because it helps scholars to interest children
in the rich African culture, which was neglected for so long. Of
course, it is equally educational for adults.

RECURRING PATTERNS IN THE NOVELS OF M. E. KERR

Marilyn Kaye

Dinky Hocker Shoots Smack! New York: Harper & Row, 1972.
Gentlehands. New York: Harper & Row, 1978.
If I Love You, Am I Trapped Forever? New York: Harper & Row, 1973.
Is That You, Miss Blue? New York: Harper & Row, 1975.
Love Is a Missing Person. New York: Harper & Row, 1975.
The Son of Someone Famous. New York: Harper & Row, 1974.

From the type of adolescent or junior novel which began to appear in the mid 1960s, certain patterns have emerged in structure and characterization. Among the character elements found in these novels are the troubled, alienated teen-age narrator, parents who are somewhat weak in terms of their ability to guide and counsel, and often an eccentric or unusual adult with whom the adolescent develops some sort of unique relationship. In terms of structure, the story tends to open with the adolescent reflecting on some recent situation which is bothering him, and which has somehow disrupted his life.

A series of incidents and meetings occur which either provokes or aggravates the original situation, or creates an environment for new or refined definitions of the situation. Eventually there is a climactic moment in which some sort of hostile, desperate, or highly emotional act of some sort is committed—usually by the protagonist, occasionally by some one else with the protagonist observing and reacting. Toward the end there is a semi-reconciliation, with the parties involved making movements toward a semblance of resolution. There is an open ending, with the original situation still existant, but with optimistic overtones suggesting that the situation will eventually be under control, if not actually resolved.

The novels of M. E. Kerr embody many of the formulaic elements found in the contemporary adolescent novel. Her adolescent protagonists are confused and apprehensive. They are symbols of a high-strung age where life has become a series of crises, and the objective is to survive rather than to succeed. Tucker Woolf, one of the two major characters in Kerr's first novel *Dinky Hocker Shoots Smack,* announces that he plans to become a librarian because he's a nervous person, and "libraries are filled with people who are nervous. You can blend in with them there . . . A library is a great place to hide" (p. 147).

More often, Kerr's characters imply their needs rather than announce them as Tucker does. Dinky Hocker, the other protagonist in this novel, is an unkempt, obese, and consciously disagreeable girl who suffers from the unintentional neglect of her busy parents. She keeps her needs for concern and attention behind a facade of sarcasm and disdain for sentimentality. Brenda Belle Blossom, in Kerr's *The Son of Someone Famous,* has a mother who nags at her for her lack of social grace. Adam Blessing, the 'son' of the title, suffers from his father's lack of attention. Both disguise their unhappiness with a mask of nonchalance. While Alan Bennett, the hero of *If I Love You, Am I Trapped Forever?,* exudes an inordinate amount of self-confidence as the novel begins, and proclaims himself the most popular boy in his high school, he reminds the reader that this story is being told in retrospect and that his fragile self-confidence would soon be crushed by a series of catastrophic blows.

Kerr emphasizes the alienation of her protagonists by making most of them 'only' children. The 'only' status of the adolescents makes them more vulnerable to the needs and attitudes of the parents. Flanders Brown, in *Is That You, Miss Blue?,* feels torn by her parents' recent divorce, and compelled to take sides. Although she takes no responsibility for the divorce, she is the only common link between them now and represents the single product of an unsuccessful relationship. The 'only' child in this type of situation has no one to talk to, since pride forbids the discussion of a family member with anyone outside the family.

Kerr takes pains to stress the conventionality of her protagonists; it is important that her main characters be perceived by the reader as ordinary and having a basically normal emotional make-up. The characters describe themselves as being 'average' and non-eccentric. Suzy Slade, in *Love Is a Missing Person,* refers to herself as being "not one of your snazzier Slades" (p. 2). Alan Bennett, in *If I Love You . . .* tells the reader of "a certain truth I had to admit—I was really mediocre, in the long run. I was small potatoes" (p. 40). By making her characters ordinary people, without unusual talents,

Kerr provides an avenue of identification for her readers. These novels are works designed as communications directed to a specific audience. If the work is to be recognized by the audience, the protagonist has to be portrayed as one of them.

Since Kerr's works deal heavily with emotional reactions, it is important that she maintain the essentially sound emotional make-up of her protagonists so that their reactions may be perceived as normal. In order to emphasize the normalcy of these protagonists, Kerr occasionally offers contrasts in order to show readers a direct comparison between the ordinary protagonist and an extraordinary, or somehow abnormal, peer. In *Dinky Hocker Shoots Smack*, Dinky has a visiting cousin, a diagnosed schizophrenic who talks in rhymes; in *Is That You, Miss Blue?*, Flanders has a deaf classmate who throws screaming tantrums when her garbled words are misunderstood. Alan Bennett, in *If I Love You . . .*, has a classmate who's a hypochondriac. These are characters with medically confirmed emotional or physical problems. By contrasting their problems with those of the protagonists, Kerr affirms the elemental normalcy of the protagonists, despite their intense emotional reactions.

While few of Kerr's parents are portrayed in a positive light, it is interesting to note that in the majority of her novels the fathers are weaker in temperament than the mothers. Often, there is the suggestion that the father, irresponsible and selfish, is at the root of the adolescent's troubles. In both *If I Love You . . .* and *The Son of Someone Famous*, a father deserted a mother during the early years of their marriage. When Alan Bennett encounters his father for the first time, sixteen years after his father's desertion, he finds that his father is an emotionally disturbed alcoholic who is verbally abusive to his second wife. In *The Son of Someone Famous*, Brenda Belle Blossom has never known her father—he died shortly after he deserted her mother—but her mother's insensitive treatment of Brenda appears to be the result of her shame at having been deserted. Flanders Brown's father is a 'pop' psychologist whose theories are publicly ridiculed. In *Love Is a Missing Person*, the divorced father remarries a vacuous, empty-headed girl half his age who utters inanities in front of his visiting daughter. Even in *Dinky Hocker Shoots Smack*, where Tucker Woolf's parents are portrayed as sensitive and intelligent people, the father fumbles about in his search for rewarding employment while the mother stoically copes with an unfulfilling job that is obviously beneath her intellectual capacities. Kerr's portrayals of fathers become another method of emphasizing the insecure world of the adolescent. No longer the wise, sane, tower of strength in the traditional model of the American family structure, the father has relinquished his role as head of the family, leaving the family without a figurehead. The suggestion that there has been a breakdown in the traditional, supportive nuclear family accentuates the solitary position of the adolescent, who is forced to make decisions without guidance.

In several novels, the only adult with whom the adolescent can relate in any way is an unusual or strange person, someone who, intentionally or not, has removed him/herself from the society of other adults. In *Love Is a Missing Person,* Suzy Slade is attracted to a middle-aged librarian who dresses in fashions of the 1940s, and talks about her love affair of thirty years earlier. Other adults regard her as bizarre. A strange schoolteacher in *Is That You, Miss Blue?* who claims to receive personal visits from Jesus has the loyalty of her students when they discover that she is to be fired because of her religious fanaticism. In *If I Love You . . . ,* the mysterious and unhappy mother of a classmate captures Alan Bennett's attention and affection. These adults have all in some way left the social order—they have either been rejected by or have intentionally removed themselves from the normal adult world as the adolescent sees it. Their unusual circumstances or behavior has set them apart and alienated them from adult society, just as the adolescent feels alienated and rejected by parents, and ignored by adults in general. The adolescent recognizes the strangeness of this particular adult, and feels sympathy and compassion.

The majority of Kerr's novels are narrated in the first person. As mentioned earlier, they are designed as communications between the protagonist and the reader. In each of the first-person novels, the protagonists introduce themselves and describe their families, their friends, and their situations. They all acknowledge the reader, who is addressed as 'you'; this sets up an immediate one-to-one relationship and establishes sympathy firmly with the protagonist.

The novels usually begin with a recent change in the protagonists' lives. In *Dinky Hocker Shoots Smack,* Tucker's father has lost his job. The recent divorce in *Is That You, Miss Blue?* has resulted in Flanders being sent away to boarding school. In *Love Is a Missing Person,* the protagonist's sister has left the divorced father she has been living with and comes back to live with the protagonist and her mother. Adam Blessing in *The Son of Someone Famous* has been kicked out of a boarding school and gone to live with his grandfather. The world of the adolescent has thus been established as an insecure one, subject to changes and major and minor calamities. By beginning each novel with a change, Kerr sets up a predicament which is as unfamiliar and new to the protagonist as it is to the reader. Reader and character are sharing the novelty of a new situation.

An uncomfortable family relationship is usually established at the beginning of the novel. Flanders Brown resents her mother for having an affair which Flanders believes initiated her parents' subsequent divorce. Suzy Slade feels unwanted by her father who chose her sister to live with him after her parents' divorce. Adam Blessing feels ignored and unwanted by his famous father. Because Alan Bennett's father deserted Alan's mother, the boy feels hostility towards the man, whom he has never met. Dinky Hocker resents her parents' preoccupation with their work. This immediate awareness of family difficulties sets up an atmosphere of tension.

In accordance with the elements of the formula presented earlier in this paper, a series of incidents and meetings occur which in some way affect the original situation and relationship. A major reason for Kerr's success in operating the basic formula is the clever manner in which the climactic moment is developed. By concentrating on indirect and symbolic reactions, rather than direct confrontations, the climactic act becomes a message that carries implications which are more powerful and more meaningful than a verbal argument could have been. Two examples will illustrate this. In *Is That You, Miss Blue?*, Flanders and her friends steal a valuable painting from their school in order to give it to a teacher who has been unjustly fired. Together, they are making a statement, reacting to what they see as the unfairness of a social order which allows an unsympathetic person (the headmistress) the power to make a defenseless person (the teacher) unhappy. The adolescents identify with that defenseless person, as they too are subject to and affected by adult whims and perceived injustice. Their vandalism is a cry against the society of people who make them unhappy. In *Dinky Hocker Shoots Smack*, Dinky paints the words of the title on the walls outside the building where her mother is receiving a community award for her drug rehabilitation work. Dinky's act is a cry for attention; she asks, must I be a drug addict in order to merit your concern? The author appears to be saying that the fashionable, contemporary concern for the obvious and apparent problems of youth and society has distracted attention from the implicit, common, emotional needs and problems of youth.

The formulaic element to which Kerr invariably adheres in her novels is the open, unresolved but basically optimistic ending. Tentative movements toward reconciliations are made. The protagonist acknowledges the beginning of an understanding. The adult begins to recognize the needs of the adolescent. In essence, Kerr's endings are beginnings for the characters involved. The implication is that the adolescents have survived these particular crises, and have gained some knowledge in the process. The ending of *The Son of Someone Famous* contains the expectant tone typical of Kerr's novels. Adam Blessing is preparing for a reunion with his father, with whom the overtures of a relationship have begun. Adam says: "We'll travel light—I like that. I'm not ready for anything heavy. I want to start out slow and easy while I get used to a few things . . . like being the son of someone famous. That's just a part of being me. But not the biggest part. I know that now" (p. 222). In the same fashion, Suzy Slade ends her story thinking of her sister who has left home, wondering where she is and what her disappearance means. Flanders Brown contemplates the events of the past year and remembers Miss Blue, the strange schoolteacher who has somehow affected her life. This type of reflective conclusion is ideally suited to the contemporary adolescent novel; each novel constitutes an experience, one of many which the typical adolescent might have, and with each experience comes a little more wisdom, a little more maturity. The emphasis is on the idea that the protagonist will continue to grow, and that the experiences will continue to happen. Therefore, there can be no real resolution in the novel, since few experiences in life are neatly resolved.

Kerr's most recent novel, *Gentlehands*, is a strange and disturbing work; as it poses special problems, it is mentioned separately here. The book deals with an adolescent boy's relationships: a romantic involvement with a wealthy, snobbish girl, and a warm relationship with his adored grandfather. The grandfather, who is portrayed as a sensitive and cultured gentleman, is discovered by a journalist to be a former Nazi SS officer noted for his brutality in the concentration camps. As the journalist is about to reveal the grandfather's identity, the grandfather flees the town, leaving the boy stunned and bewildered.

The work includes several of the character elements one has come to expect from Kerr: the troubled adolescent, weak parents who cannot communicate with their son, and the grandfather who certainly qualifies as an "unusual" adult. The structure of the story also tends to follow the basic pattern of her earlier works, particularly in regard to the unresolved ending. But Kerr falls short this time, and it is the characterization of the grandfather which prevents the novel from being a distinctive work. While Kerr's other "unusual" adults were capable of being understood without any real development of their personalities, the "eccentric" aspect of the grandfather is overwhelming. His past requires some explanation, some further discussion of the nature of this man and his perverse history. His situation distracts attention from the protagonist and leaves the novel without a focus. Kerr has attempted to incorporate a complex and horrifying element into her formula, and the incorporation becomes intrusive; her sensitive exploration of identity and relationships becomes buried under its impact.

In her other novels, however, Kerr has been remarkably successful in manipulating the formulaic elements within each work. By concentrating on individual feelings and reactions to a situation, rather than on the situation itself, Kerr avoids being labelled as a "problem" novel writer. She adapts the adolescent pattern to suit her purpose, which varies from novel to novel. For Kerr, the adolescent formula operates as a framework within which she creates unique and distinctive stories.

RECENT LITERATURE FOR CHILDREN BY AND ABOUT NATIVE AMERICANS

Priscilla A. Ord

Climbing to the Sun, by Jeffrey Carroll. New York: The Seabury Press, 1977. $6.95.

Frozen Fire: A Tale of Courage, by James Houston. New York: Atheneum, 1977. $6.95.

Malcolm Yucca Seed, by Lynne Gessner. Illustrated by William Sauts Bock. Irvington-on-Hudson: Harvey House, 1977. $5.99.

Bear's Heart, by Burton Supree, with Ann Ross. Philadelphia: J. B. Lippincott Company, 1977. $8.95.

Edward S. Curtis: Photographer of the North American Indian, by Victor Boesen and Florence Curtis Graybill. New York: Dood, Mead & Company. $6.95.

Eskimos: Growing Up in a Changing Culture, by Carolyn Meyer. New York: Atheneum, 1977. $7.95.

North American Indians, by Marie and Douglas Gorsline. New York: Random House, 1977. $.95.

Settlers and Strangers: Native Americans of the Desert Southwest and History as They Saw It, by Betty Baker. New York: Macmillan Publishing Company, 1977. $7.95.

The Art of the Southeastern Indians, by Shirley Glubok. Special Photography by Alfred Tamarin. New York: Macmillan Publishing Company, 1978. $7.95.

The Art of the Woodland Indians, by Shirley Glubok. Special Photography by Alfred Tamarin. New York: Macmillan Publishing Company, 1976. $7.95.

Children of the Yukon, by Ted Harrison. Montreal: Tundra Books, 1977. $7.95.

Hawk, I'm Your Brother, by Bird Baylor. Illustrated by Peter Parnall. New York: Charles Scribner's Sons, 1976. $6.95.

And It Is Still That Way, by Bird Baylor, as told by Arizona Indian Children. New York: Charles Scribner's Sons, 1976. $6.95.

Anpao: An American Indian Odyssey, by Jamake Highwater. Philadelphia: J. B. Lippincott, 1977. $8.95.

Coyote the Trickster, by Gail Robinson and Douglas Hill. New York: Crane, Russak & Company, 1976. $6.95.

The Girl Who Married a Ghost. Edited by John Bierhorst. Photographs by Edward S. Curtis. New York: Four Winds Press,
1978. $9.95.

The Loon's Necklace, retold by William Toye. Illustrated by
Elizabeth Cleaver. New York and Oxford University Press, 1977.

Mouse Woman and the Mischief-Makers, by Christie Harris. Illustrated by Douglas Tait. New York: Atheneum, 1977. $6.95.

The Summer Maker: An Ojibway Indian Myth, retold by Margery
Bernstein and Janet Korbrin. Illustrated by Anne Burgess. New
York: Charles Scribner's Sons, 1977. $5.95.

Recent works of fiction whose protagonists are Native Americans
vary in quality and treatment of their subject. *Climbing to the Sun*
concerns a herd or "tribe" of mountain goats, whose movements
are first observed on the rocky-ridged cirque of Koos Kroom by the
Tsimshian Indian boy, Kwayo, and his father, Noo Kwat, who live
in the Montana valley below. The story is told from the perspective
of the goats. On the night that the boy dreams that the mountains
have fallen around him, the tribe of goats is aroused from its sleep
by one of the early fall avalanches which sweeps the old leader,
Tum Lum, his son, Tum Tsoy, a doe, Seo, and her son, Tsa Kull,
down the mountain slope to the valley of strange smells. The story
that follows is the twenty-four hour chronicle of the goats' encounters with the world below their world. In the background, the
restless, inquisitive boy is taught the lessons of the wild under the
watchful tutelage of his father.

In *Frozen Fire,* thirteen year old Matthew Morgan whose mother
has been killed in an automobile accident, accompanies his father, a
geologist, to Frobisher Bay, a community on Baffin Island in the
Northwest Territory of Canada. Matthew is hurriedly placed in
school, and his father and his old friend Charlie, an Australian
helicopter pilot, fly off in Charlie's shiny red *Waltzing Matilda* in
the face of an oncoming storm, despite unsatisfactory weather
reports, to search for copper with the recklessness of strike-it-rich
prospectors instead of a calculating scientist and a seasoned pilot.

The two men, predicably, fail to return, and Matthew and his
new-found Inuit friend Kayak fly with the Royal Canadian
Mounted Police rescue plane for two days to search for them. When
the weather grounds the rescue teams, Kayak proposes a daring plan
to find the two men, and the boys head nearly one hundred miles
toward the mountains on a borrowed snowmobile. It is here that

the traditional training that the young Eskimo boy has learned from his father, grandfather, and nature prove more useful than the lessons that he is required to learn at school. Although they too become lost and have to be rescued, both boys exhibit courage, determination, and ingenuity in their fight for survival.

James Houston based his tale of courage, *Frozen Fire*, on the events surrounding a similar fight for survival and rescue of an Eskimo boy who was lost in the Canadian Arctic in the 1960's. It is regrettable that he did not decide to stick closer to the boy's story, championing the traditional Eskimo way of life, instead of enmeshing it with the rather weak "copper rush" plot involving Matthew's father.

Malcolm Yucca Seed is the story of a young Indian boy who returns home from the boarding school hoping that this summer he will be found worthy of being given an Indian name. On two occasions he attempts to impress his family with his bravery claiming to have killed a coyote or chased away a mountain lion that had threatened the flock of sheep entrusted to him, but neither story earns him a new name. Only later, as the result of a purely selfless act, is Malcolm rewarded. In the earlier situations he reflects that, ". . . they probably didn't believe his story about killing the coyote." His parents and the author, however, have done him a great disservice by not verbalizing it, for it tends to perpetuate the image of the "lying redskin," which is disturbing.

The detailed pen and ink illustrations which William Sauts Bock has drawn for this story are superb. The faces of the people, particularly the grandfather, the desert scenes, the hogan, the silver jewelry making—all are executed with care. It is regretable that they must accompany a story that is somewhat mediocre.

Works of non-fiction dealing with Native Americans includes *Bear's Heart*, which is subtitled "Scenes from the Life of a Cheyenne Artist of One Hundred Years Ago with Pictures by Himself," a sensitive account of a Plains Indian who, like many Cheyennes, Arapahoes, Kiowas, and Comanches, following their tribes' placement on reservations in Oklahoma, participated in hostile raids off the reservation. These Indians and others like them were hunted down and captured by the U. S. Army and, after a brief stay at Ft. Sill, Oklahoma, they were removed to a prison at Fort Marion, Florida.

This book reproduces the series of pictures that Bear's Heart drew with colored pencils in a school notebook to record the trip from Oklahoma to Florida and the subsequent three years imprisonment. Lieutenant Richard Henry Pratt, who was concerned about the Indians, requested that they be placed in his charge; he accompanied them to Fort Marion and remained with them. The captions on each of the original drawings are in his handwriting.

The Indians attended school at the prison, and at the end of the three year period, although many returned to their reservations, Bear's Heart and several others were admitted to the Hampton Institute in Virginia. Lt. Pratt went on to found the Indian School in Carlisle, Pennsylvania. Bear's Heart's notebook, which had been presented as a gift to General William Tecsmseh Sherman when he visited the prison on an inspection tour, has been preserved by the Heye Foundation of the Museum of the American Indian.

In *Edward S. Curtis: Photographer of the North American Indian,* Victor Boesen and Florence Curtis Graybill have produced an outstanding biography of the famous photographer by using his unfinished memoirs, the log of a trip to the Far North in 1927, notes from talks with his daughters, correspondence with his editor, and material from the twenty volumes of *The North American Indian* which he produced, as well as several magazine and newspaper articles about him and his work. It was Curtis' interest in the Native American which led him to devote his life's work to recording this "vanishing race," in settings as life-like as possible, for future generations. The book traces his life from his early yearnings for a camera as a boy to the exciting and rewarding trips to take the pictures for the last volume of *The North American Indian.* The photographs which have been included have been carefully selected from his collection and have been faithfully reproduced to show the work of this great artist to its best advantage. The book is a marvelous tribute to his vision.

Carolyn Meyer's *Eskimos* is a delightful, educational year long chronicle of the life of an archetypical, modern Eskimo family. It begins with the seal hunting at the advent of the spring break up of shelf ice in April and continues through the end of the winter freeze up the next March. Although the village, Chaputnuak, which was named for an ancient village that once occupied the site of modern Chefornak, is fictional, it is "real in the sense that this is what an Eskimo village in Southwestern Alaska is like." Similarly, Jim Koonak and his immediate and extended family are fictitious, but they too are "real in that same sense: this is how many Eskimos of this area live, and how they sometimes feel about themselves and about an outside world that is continually affecting their ancient culture, even when it cannot completely change or absorb it."

The inexpensive, "Please Read to Me" book, entitled *North American Indians,* is a decidedly simplistic but surprisingly accurate and informative book for younger children. A map at the beginning divides the U. S. into the five major regions of Native American habitation. Then, grouped within these divisions, the tribes and peoples of the Northeast, Southeast, Great Plains, Southwest, and Northwest are named and discussed with respect to their type of dwelling, hunting and/or farming techniques, foods, clothing, and pasttimes. Technical or foreign terms are not avoided but are carefully explained or translated, and detailed, realistic illustrations are provided to help maintain the interest of the read-me-a-story audience.

Writing about some of the tribes of Native Americans who live in the southwest desert of Arizona and New Mexico, Betty Baker's *Settlers and Strangers* is a forthright history from the Indian point of view. Even today few people fully comprehend what it must have been like to be invaded by strange-looking Europeans, given tribal designations which were unfamiliar, occasionally enslaved to search for cities of gold which they knew did not exist or build a church for a god which was so unlike their own, or forced to submit to political rulers from far away who were not of their tribe; and when they could no longer defend themselves and their land, they were rounded up and assigned to reservations, which were usually on less than desirable land. Who *could* understand that? The story is not told bitterly, but it is, regretably, told truthfully.

In the category of art and picture books, there have been a number of notable books published. Both *The Art of the Southeastern Indians* and *The Art of the Woodland Indians* follow the format of Shirley Glubok's other "Art of . . ." books. These two volumes are companions to three previously published volumes on the art of Native Americans of the Southwest, Northwest Coast, and Plains, respectively.

Each volume delineates a particular region of the United States and names the tribes who inhabit or once inhabited that area. Background information concerning such topics as settlement, dress, material culture, language, or customs is provided briefly, followed by detailed descriptions of a wide range of art objects produced by these people even into modern times.

The material for each text has been researched thoroughly, although it might be useful if a selected bibliography were appended for those who wish to study the art of a particular tribe or region further. Each pictured artifact or drawing has been carefully photographed by Alfred Tamarin or reproduced from the original in sufficient size and detail to aid easy identification from its description. A label for each artifact indicates the museum and/or collection to which it belongs. The text and vocabulary are relatively simple, which makes these books available to younger readers without compromising their appeal to anyone who would be interested in the art of our Native Americans.

Ted Harrison's *Children of the Yukon* is delightful. The simple, rainbow-colorful illustrations could be compared favorably to the drawings for the Beatles' movie, *The Yellow Submarine* and would easily appeal to the sit-on-your-lap/read-me-a-story set as well as school children who would like to know more about children who live in a land which is different from their own.

The topics which would interest children and those in which children participate are just those which have been included. It is a book about children for children. Their activities are described in the supporting text, and they are prominently portrayed in the illustrations.

The final page includes a fairly standard "About the Author" description, but it also includes a very unique, more useful abreviated encyclopedia-type entry which provides the vital statistics for the Yukon. Here one may note that, "Its population of 23,000 includes 5,000 school age children." This is probably the sort of thing a child using this as a source book instead of a picture book would actually like to know.

In *Hawk, I'm Your Brother* Rudy Soto yearns to fly like a bird. His wish is so desperate that he steals a baby redtail hawk from its nest before it learns to fly and imprisons it in a cage, allowing it freedom only at the end of a string tether tied to its leg. The young boy wants to please the hawk, for he is sure that the hawk will become content, and as his brother they will be able to fly together. Rudy soon realizes, however, that his wish cannot be fulfilled, and he gives the hawk its freedom. In doing so he gains the thrill of flying in observing the preparatory movements and actual flight of the young hawk.

The lyrical text is extremely compelling, easily carrying the tempo of the dreams and frustrations of an earthbound Indian boy. Peter Parnall's expressive pen and ink drawings are almost poetry in themselves. It is easy to see why not only *Hawk, I'm Your Brother* but also the previous book by this same distinguished author and illustrator, *The Desert Is Theirs,* were named Caldecott Honor Books in 1976 and 1975, respectively.

Caution must be exercised when the folklore of one culture is adopted or adapted as a form of literature for another culture. This is particularly true in the realm of children's literature, for here myths, legends, and folktales are frequently borrowed to amuse children. Aside from the usual problems one encounters with translation, there is the question of the significance that a tale might have had within the religious or ceremonial life of the people from which it originated. Its true meaning or impact may be lost, or its significance may not be revealed, without extensive scholarly research. Bible stories, for example, such as the account of the flood and Noah's Ark, are suitable for children, but they are not children's stories, nor are they completely comprehendable to adults in the form in which they are transmitted today. Similarly, although not translated, English nursery rhymes, such as "Sing a Song of Sixpence," or "Hey Diddle Diddle," which are now an established literary form, may have been once a kind of political satire for the amusement of adults. One cannot, therefore, read a translated, adapted, and/or retold Native American tale to a child and consider it an authentic representation of the literature of that culture.

In *And It Is Still That Way* Byrd Baylor has judiciously left the telling of the tales to the children of Arizona themselves. In this respect the stories should appeal to younger children, particularly in the context of the classroom. Although it is emphasized that these stories have not been made up but come from the oral tradition of the Indian children, it should be remembered that the significance or meaning of these tales is probably not clear to the children who tell them. They are being told in a place and time apart from that in which they would normally be told, and as children are not adept storytellers in the traditional sense, the stories are neither complete nor wholly representative of the tribes which they themselves represent.

Jamake Highwater's Newbery honor book *Anpao: An American*

Indian Odyssey, is a tapestry of Native American tales. Drawing from the oral tradition of the Great Plains and Southwest, he has woven a tale through which the ficticious Anpao travels. He has used the skills of a traditional storyteller which are a familiar part of his Blackfeet/Cherokee heritage to tell the story and has applied his knowledge of anthropology and literature to refine it. Sources and a bibliography are provided.

Coyote the Trickster is actually a collection of trickster tales featuring the raven as well as the coyote. The tales are drawn from the legends of several tribes, each being labeled according to its origin. Retold by Gail Robinson and Douglas Hill these tales remind us as they reminded the people from whom they originated that ". . . ordinary people as well as the People can be stupid and clever, cruel and kind, brave and foolish all at the same time." That is a useful lesson in any society.

The Girl Who Married A Ghost is a sample of the narratives which were collected by the famous photographer, writer, and explorer Edward S. Curtis during his travels along the Northwest Coast, in California, through the Plains, and in the North Woods, Southwest, and Alaska. Accompanying the tales are the even more spectacular photographs from Curtis's gravures in the collections of the University of Pennsylvania Museum and the Philadelphia Museum of Art, printed here with great care and sensitivity in warm, rich sepia tones. John Bierhorst, who edited the volume, should be congratulated for his outstanding achievement.

The retelling of a Tsimshian legend is the basis for William Toye's *The Loon's Necklace.* The illustrations, collages of torn paper, paper cutouts, and linocuts, are the result of artist Elizabeth Cleaver's interpretation of this tale. Popular as the subject of a short film which was released in 1950, this presentation of the tale appears flawed in its abbreviated form as captions under the unusual but colorful illustrations.

Using the lore of the Northwest Indians as her basis, Christie Harris has written a second book of stories involving the escapades of Mouse Woman—a narnauk or supernatural being. *Mouse Woman and the Mischief-Makers* and the former *Mouse Woman and the Vanished Princess* provide a collection of tales in which to observe this tiny woman's efforts to set the world right.

The artful yet simplified retelling of an Ojibway myth for *The Summer Maker* has been made even more appealing by Anne

Burgess's pen and ink drawings of the animals who seek to bring warmth to their world of ice and snow. The story could have easily carried itself, but the endearing caricatures of Ojeek, the fisher, Otter, Beaver, Lynx, and Wolverine provide added enjoyment for the reader.

THE ADVENTURE OF FANTASY AS STRUGGLE FOR SURVIVAL

Jack Zipes

The Borribles, by Michael de Larrabeiti. New York: Macmillan Publishing Company, 1976. $6.95.

Fantasy literature is enjoying a boom these days, but there is very little of the fantastic in this literature which seeks to stretch our minds and go beyond the market expectations of the publishing business and the consumer interests of readers. Most fantasy literature either tries to capitalize on the profits garnered by science-fiction writers of sensationalism forecasting our doom or endeavors to imitate those fairy tales which conceive more idyllic worlds to escape the envisioned technological catastrophes awaiting us around the corner. Certainly the trend toward fantasy is a reflection of how impoverished and dangerous the computerized routines of everyday life have become for us. And yet, the value of fantastic literature as presenting solid social commentary on the erosion of humanist values has rarely been demonstrated by contemporary authors. Instead, fantastic fiction generally estranges us to remain helpless and hopeless, unprepared to cope with the forces operating on us save for the escapist flight into the imagination. Rarely are we estranged positively to remain estranged, that is, to gain and retain critical distance through a fantastic narrative which makes us conscious of the need to reshape the reality of our situation. This is all the more reason why Michael de Larrabeiti's novel *The Borribles* should be recognized as one of the finest fantasy works in recent years: at a time when fantasy literature is being instrumentalized to divert us from dealing with crucial social problems, especially those confronting our youth, de Larrabeiti leads us on a fantastic adventure which can only move us to become more involved in the outcast state of young people and compel us to grasp the meaning of adventure as a struggle for survival.

The Borribles comes from the land most famous today for bringing us hobbits. And to a certain extent, de Larrabeiti's novel can be considered a more radical creative endeavor in the direction taken by Tolkien in *The Hobbit* and *Lord of the Rings* in order to use fantasy for social criticism. It is obvious and well-known that Tolkien's fairy-stories reflected his disenchantment with the progress of technological society and its devastation of nature and humanity. Progress in the name of profit and exploitation took the form of machine-minded dragons and goblins who parasitically undermined traditional morals and values. According to Tolkien, the only solution to such "progress" was to resist it through the moral stance and behavior of hobbits, those humble, basically conservative little people, who did not lack in courage and virtue when put to the test. Yet, this hoped-for resistance and fortitude of little people in Tolkien's fantastic world have not been realized in the contemporary world, and this may in part account for de Larrabeiti's more penetrating and radical use of fantasy to question the essence of human progress. Whereas Tolkien set his story in the past with older creatures like hobbits as his heroes, de Larrabeiti uses present-day London as his setting and focuses on young drop-outs named Borribles as his protagonists. Ironically, the magic of de Larrabeiti's narrative depends on his rendering these Borribles true-to-life so that their fantastic situation transcends fiction to serve as a kind of documentary of the inner and outer worlds of disfranchised youth in the London of today. Though there may be some difficulty at first for an American reader to grasp the complete meaning of de Larrabeiti's witty Cockney language and rhyming slang, the characters and their situations are drawn with such deft, narrative skill that they come alive and transcend cultural and age barriers. Both young and old alike can follow the adventures of the Borribles, those intriguing creatures of fantasy and fact.

Now what about these Borribles? Who are they exactly? What is their story? Well, Borribles can be found throughout the world. They are children who never grow up, are neglected by their parents, never have their ears clipped, survive by their wits, and adhere to a code of ethics which is essentially anti-authoritarian. The worst thing that can happen to a Borrible is to get caught by adults or police (woolies) and be reintegrated into society. "Normal kids are turned into Borribles very slowly, almost without being aware of it; but one day they wake up and there it is. It doesn't matter where they come from as long as they have what is called a 'bad start.' . . . So Borribles are outcasts but unlike most outcasts they enjoy themselves and wouldn't be anything else. They delight in feeling independent and free and it is this feeling that is most important to them. Consequently they have no real leaders, though someone may pop into prominence from time to time, perhaps because he has had a good idea and wants to carry it through. They manage without authority and they get on well enough together, though like everyone they quarrel." The worst enemies of the Borribles are actually not adults but Rumbles, who live in the outlying suburbs of London and represent spoiled youths known for their "riches, power, haughtiness, and possessions." They are depicted as rodent-like furry creatures with snouts and beady red eyes. They pronounce their "r's" as "w's" very much in the fashion of the middle class in England. The animosity of the marginal poor kids of London toward the privileged rich kids of the suburbs provides the material for de Larrabeiti's class-struggle story. Though it is difficult to do justice to de Larrabeiti's narrative which weaves the fantastic with reality so that inner and outer experiences are fused with unusual sensitivity and sensuality, let us briefly summarize the plot before discussing the overall significance of the novel.

One evening Knocker, the chief lookout of the Battersea Borribles, discovers that Rumbles are invading the London territory. An emergency session of Borribles is called by Spiff, the chief steward of the district, and it is decided that the Rumbles must be taught a lesson once and for all. Thus, Knocker is called upon to train eight unnamed Borribles from the eight tribes of London in guerilla warfare. Generally speaking, Borribles must earn their names, and these names indicate the degree of their prowess and talents. For example, the eight unnamed Borribles must win their names from those of the eight top leaders in the Rumble high command by outwitting and killing them. Without leadership, the Rumbles will no longer present a threat to the Borribles. After a strenuous training period, Knocker leads the eight highly trained Borribles (five white males, one black male, two white females) on the Great Rumble Hunt. They are joined by a remarkable Borrible from Hamburg, Germany, named Adolf Wolfgang Amadeus, who had heard about this great adventure and wants to earn another name (Winston) by participating in it. The merry crew proceeds on its way, and, before they even enter Rumbledom territory, they are caught by two adult Borrible Snatchers (shades of Charles Dickens) who use the youths to pilfer for them so they can amass a great fortune. After a long period of torture and maltreatment, the

Borribles find a way to kill their two tormentors. Now with the aid of Sam the horse, formerly in the employ of the Borrible Snatchers, they make their way to Rumbledom. Once there they survey the surroundings and eventually discover a way to enter the bunker of the Rumble high command. The encounters of the Borribles with their adversaries is described in great detail: the battles are vicious, bloody, and suspenseful. Though outnumbered, all the Borribles manage to escape, with the exception of Adolf, who is killed while helping Knocker save the Rumble money treasure which Knocker had been assigned to steal. This money turns out to be a curse for the Borrible guerillas, for on their way back to Battersea, they are betrayed by the Wendle Borribles, the most ferocious of the tribes, who seek to keep the treasure for themselves. Three of the Borrible guerillas including Knocker are killed by the Wendles while the others escape. The treasure itself is lost in the mud of the Wandle River. The story ends with the survivors reporting about their deeds in Battersea. Spiff, the master-mind of the Great Rumble Hunt, regrets that his friends were betrayed and the money, lost: "Shame about the money. I was never concerned about the Rumbles at all, really. Couldn't have given a monkey's. It was the money. I could have done with that."

A strange ending. It seems that the Borrible guerillas were actually manipulated by Spiff to think that the Rumbles were going to invade the London territory. He was primarily interested in gaining their money. Thus, the heroic adventures of the chosen Borrible guerillas are somewhat cast in a cloud. Their struggle was not really for the defense of all Borribles but for wealth. Nevertheless, we must remember that the Borrible guerillas did not know this, nor (with the exception of Knocker) did they have this as their goal. Consequently, the comradship, solidarity, and courage which they develop during their struggles cannot be diminished by our knowledge that they were manipulated. In fact the ending reminds us very much of the reality of marginal youths in the big city. The name of the games they play always comes down to money, and, though none of them fully realizes how much their lives depend on money (as Spiff himself says), they all need it and will remain governed by it directly or indirectly. Their violated lives are informed by the pursuit of money, and de Larrabeiti's novel does not shy from describing the social conditions which make the Borribles both deprived and cruel as they seek to justify their

meager existence with a Great Adventure. Nor does the novel shy
from viewing the Borribles with a critical eye, for their mettle is
determined by the manner they *choose* to respond to their
ontological situation. Ultimately the adventure of fantasy poses the
question of integrity and autonomy.

Some British reviews of *The Borribles* have objected to
de Larrabeiti's glorification of anti-authoritarianism and a petty
criminal subculture with the suggestion that the novel could incite
young readers from the lower classes to liquidate wealthier people.
Indeed, the book is problematic but only in a meritorious sense.
De Larrabeiti confronts problems which most writers of fantasy
want to escape, and these problems have to do with violence and
criminality. In fact, he leads us on an imaginative odyssey to show
us how the wishes, needs, and dreams which large groups of young
people are forced to repress can lead to violence and criminality.
In no way does de Larrabeiti celebrate criminality in this novel.
On the contrary, he has an uncanny eye for portraying the criminal
social conditions which lead children to become Borribles. Such a
state is not considered ideal, but it is preferable to the lives of
conformity which "normal" children lead. Borribles live in fear of
getting caught. They never say good-by or so long to each other.
Their traditional farewell expression is "don't get caught." A Borrible
learns to use his or her wits to remain free. "A Borrible's main
business is to stay alive. This is an occupation that takes up most of
his time; getting food from what is left about, finding stuff before it
is lost and knocking off barrows and out of the store-rooms of
supermarkets and the like." There is no real heroism in such a life
just as the heroism of the Great Adventure turns out to be futile.
The kids of the story are thrown upon their own resources to
escape the mismanagement of adults, and de Larrabeiti endeavors to
grasp the culture developed by these marginal types to retain their
sense of human dignity. And this is the achievement of his novel: he
sensitively explores the psychic drives of lower-class youths and
articulates their imaginative yearnings for autonomy while con-
cretely depicting the forces which threaten them with extinction.
In essence, de Larrabeiti's fantastic narrative defends the struggle of
rejected youths to cultivate their own identities with an acquired
sense of independence. The Borribles who undertake the Great
Adventure do not seek wealth but an identity and a place in society
which is earned through their own resourcefulness. The odds are

stacked against these "unmanageables," and they are even at each other's throats. However, they remain admirable figures, much more so than the hobbits of old, because they reject social integration and harmony which they view as repressive. At a time when fantasy literature seeks to serve as a palliative against our sense of alienation and manipulation, it is gratifying to read a novel which allows our minds to sharpen our disturbed sensibility and outrage about the forces which foster violence and criminality. After all is said and done, the struggle for survival by the Borribles is our own adventure which we, like them, must play out with courage, wit, and imagination.

THE NOVEL OF CRISIS:
CONTEMPORARY ADOLESCENT FICTION

Steve Roxborough

Forever, by Judy Blume. New York: Bradbury Press, 1976. $6.95.
I Am the Cheese, by Robert Cormier. New York: Pantheon, 1977. $6.95.
Year King, by Penelope Farmer. New York: Atheneum, 1977. $6.95.
Hitchhike, by Isabelle Holland. Philadelphia: J. P. Lippincott, 1977. $6.95.
Hiding, by Norma Klein. New York: Four Winds Press, 1976. $5.95.
Pardon Me, You're Stepping On My Eyeball, by Paul Zindel. New York: Harper & Row, 1976. $6.95.

In his landmark discussion of pornography in mid-Victorian England, Steven Marcus constructs an abstract paradigm of the form, based on Max Weber's assumptions concerning "ideal type." Marcus' "pornotopia" is a descriptive model—no actual example exists—derived from significant aspects of individual manifestations of the form, and its purpose is descriptive, rather than judgemental. A similar model can be imagined for one kind of contemporary adolescent literature.

Certain attributes are shared by much of the fiction written for young adults today. Most of it is, in the broad sense of the word, mimetic; that is, imitative, rather than fantastic. The setting is the contemporary world. The main characters are, in the ambiguous language of age groups, neither children nor adults, but, rather, adolescents. Situations arise out of home and school life, generally, and involve family and peers. We see the world through the eyes of the youthful protagonists. Perhaps the most significant aspect of contemporary adolescent fiction is its focus on the moments of crisis that are typical of the transitional stage between childhood and adulthood. This focus so informs the fiction that it can appropriately be called, following Marcus' lead, "crisotopia," the novel of crisis.

The crises that are the *raison d'être* of the form are, as mentioned above, typical, and they are traditional in literature written for youth. The confrontation between parent and child, peer relationships, and crises of identity are as apparent in the literature of the eighteenth century as they are in that of the twentieth century; only the treatment changes.

The "ideal type" of contemporary adolescent fiction focuses on two kinds of crisis, although many related crises are tied to those. The recognition by youth of the breakdown of the traditional values and institutions of the adult world, be it the family, marriage, or parenthood, translates itself into novels about divorce, runaways, and unwanted pregnancy. Related to this, but distinct from it, are novels that deal with growth and burgeoning self-awareness, specifically, consciousness of sexuality. Neither of these foci are new; Crusoe rejected his father's much-praised middle way and ran away to sea, while Pamela—not to mention Clarissa—suffered considerably from her forced awareness of her sexual nature. What *is* new is the radical resolutions that our culture allows and the explicit treatment of all aspects of the crisis.

As mentioned above, the most frequent setting for the adolescent novel of crisis is the home or the school. Louisa May Alcott's domestic stories and the school stories typified by Thomas Hughes' *Tom Brown's School Days* testify to the fact that the tradition has roots in the Victorian period. Two major differences between the nineteenth and twentieth century manifestations of the tradition indicate a significant shift of consciousness over the last century. Almost without exception, the earlier works are told by an omniscient narrator, who freely comments on the moral significance and probable consequences of the characters' actions and thoughts. Such narration rests on the assumptions that actions have clearly discernable moral significance and far-reaching, almost inevitable, consequences. Most modern manifestations of the form are, in effect, if not in fact, presented from the viewpoint of the young protagonist. From this limited perspective life is less continuous, and not at all like the rigorously sequential lives of Jo March and Tom Brown. Any given incident is altogether less significant as a causal factor in a person's life. Meaning is to be found in the immediate consequences of an action rather than in its far-reaching effects. No moral value is assigned to actions; at best, the character subjectively evaluates the situation, and the reader is left with that. Generally, the shift is from an outer to an inner view, the consequences of which are a personalization and fragmentation of experience that characterizes the modern age and the modern novel of crisis. In this respect, the adolescent novel parallels in its development the mainstream novel.

The novel of crisis has, appropriately, utopian and dystopian extremes. In the former a single experience, apparent in every aspect of life, or, at least, the protagonist's consciousness, informs the fiction. In the latter, the main character is involved in a number of crises simultaneously, or is involved in them sequentially, like Hercules undergoing his twelve labors. In both, the fiction begins with the inception or perception of the crisis, climaxes at its culmination, and ends with its resolution or passing away. In the utopian visions, far and away the majority, the character manages to live through the crisis; in the dystopian vision, the character succumbs. The character need not learn anything from the experience, but need only survive it. (A comparison of *Tom Brown's School Days* and *Eric, or Little by Little* shows these two extremes in the Victorian forerunners of the modern form.) Given these dominant characteristics, individual examples of the genre can be distinguished against a common background.

One of the simplest examples of the novel of crisis to be found in the fiction published in the past few years is Judy Blume's *Forever*. The book focuses on a young woman's first intimate sexual relationship. The plot climaxes (literally and figuratively) at the consummation of the sexual relationship, after which the relationship and the plot dissolve. Incident serves either to facilitate or interfere with the consummation. The story is related through the eyes and mind of Katherine, the main character, who is idiosyncratic enough to be the roundest of a host of flat characters, yet innocuous enough to permit vicarious identification. Several typical characters and current crises embellish the main event of the book, including an attempted suicide by a token homosexual, the birth of an illegitimate and unwanted child to a girl who had the baby just for the experience, the death of a favorite grandparent, and an inconvenient bout with the flu.

Convenient is an appropriate way to describe the world in which the characters posture. Katherine's parents are mindlessly liberal, her house is a veritable pleasure dome, her circumstances are comfortable to the nth degree. Michael, the *object* of her desires, is similarly well-situated. Katherine, fixated on genital intercourse, is virtually oblivious to anything else, and the presentation of sexuality is, at best, partial. The book, finally, is analogous to a television "dramatization" in which viewers, or, in this case, readers, realize that the actors are insignificant and that the message, the information conveyed, is all important. From the heavy-handed subtlety of the title to the equally crude suggestion that life goes on in the final brief sentence, the book is written to tell the reader about sex and "love." *Forever* is not literature and cannot be evaluated by literary standards. It is an information book and stands, or falls, finally, on the accuracy of the information it attempts to present. It has the form of the novel of crisis, but lacks the substance.

A less crude treatment of sexuality and its relation to aspects of identity is Norma Klein's *Hiding*. Again we see the action through the eyes of a young woman experiencing her first intimate relationship with a man. In this book, however, sex is not an obsession. It is, rather, one of several aspects of the character's identity that seem to be dissociated and the cause of confusion. Eighteen-year old Krii travels to England, ostensibly to attend ballet school, but, actually, to seek anonymity. There, to her dismay, several crises are precipitated in rapid succession. She becomes involved in a relationship with a young man who tries, using methods that inflict varying degrees of pain, to draw her out of her shell. At the same time she discovers that her parents' unconventional marriage arrangements have served to mask her father's extramarital relationships, which she, following this accidental discovery, is expected to accept, understand and keep to herself. Her discomfort with her own sexuality and the dissolution of her relationship with Jonathan coincide with the discovery of her father's infidelity and cause her to withdraw from the social world into herself. Succumbing to the confusion, she hides in the attic of her parents' home for several days. In the limbo of mental and emotional exhaustion, she gradually heals, and on re-entering the world is able to begin to sort out her life and to act again. No answers are offered; no information is relayed. Krii decides to return to the States, giving up dancing as a career in favor of going to college. Although seen from the outside, Jonathan moves through the story as a complex, albeit unknown, personality struggling in his own way with his own problems. The story ends with the two characters, as survivors, beginning a new relationship on the rubble of the old.

Penelope Farmer's *Year King* shares with *Hiding* a common treatment of identity and the relation of sexuality to identity. It is substantially more complex in its treatment, however, and it lends itself to (that is, will sustain and reward) critical attention. Working from the unlikely situation of a young man's intermittent and unexpected transfer of consciousness into his twin brother's body, the novel deals with problems of identity in psychological and, finally, archetypal terms. Through the eyes of Lan, the West Somerset countryside takes on human characteristics; the landscape reflects his emotional condition. In the midst of his struggle to free himself from the domination of his mother, and to sever his self-negating attachment to his popular and successful brother, Lew, Lan meets an American girl, Novanna, who introduces him to an entirely different vision, symbolized by strangely alluring pictures and tales of the American deserts and their inhabitants. Novanna teaches him about his sexuality, and he finds in it mindless release from his struggles. The culmination of his conflict with his brother is presented in a way that is comparable to certain scenes in the novels of D. H. Lawrence. Everything comes across as larger than life; emotions are world-transforming. Sexuality is the prevailing metaphor of the novel, and it is dealt with both evocatively and explicitly. *Year King* tries to present universal human conflicts and errs, perhaps, in being too self-conscious an attempt to do so. The author is constantly pointing out what she is doing. The book is overwritten, yet it does succeed in translating the novel of crisis into mythological terms.

Isabelle Holland's *Hitchhike* departs from the model of the novel of crisis presented above by harking back to a much different and older form, the exemplum or cautionary tale, yet its concerns are those common to the contemporary fiction already discussed. A sixteen-year-old who is miffed at her father for allowing a business deal to interfere with a long-anticipated camping trip decides to buy a coat with the money sent for her plane fare and to hitchhike home instead. She picks up a stray dog along the way and so complicates things. (Not since Toto got Dorothy caught in a tornado has a dog caused a heroine so much trouble.) Forcibly detained by a man seeking answers from her about why his daughter ran away and never contacted him, Pud escapes only to be kidnapped and very nearly raped by a group of teenage hoodlums. She manages to escape (with the dog) and so survives the crisis relatively unscathed. Her escapades may have left her a little less certain that she has life figured out, but for the most part they are just an adventurous interlude. At the end of the story she is awaiting the inevitable quarrel with her father with something akin to eagerness. The incident is realistically and convincingly portrayed. Its only apparent significance is to verify the warning, "don't hitchhike."

The first person point of view that characterizes the adolescent novel of crisis is discarded for an omniscient narrator in Paul Zindel's *Pardon Me, You're Stepping on My Eyeball,* in order to present the perspectives of two characters, "Marsh" Mellow and Edna Shinglebox. (In his earlier novel, *The Pigman,* Zindel retained the first person narration even though he dealt with two characters, by the simple device of alternating chapters in a chronicle they are jointly writing describing the events.) Each is struggling with his/her own identity against the backdrop of parental relationships. Marsh is trying to deal with the fact of his father's death and an alcoholic mother. Edna must exorcise the negative self-image that her misguided parents have foisted on her. These two meet in a special therapy class for disturbed students at their high school and discover that they are drawn to each other. As they come to know each other better, a bond grows between them that enables them to escape for a while from their problems at home. With Edna's active companionship Marsh is finally able to admit to himself and to her that his father is dead, and Edna, in committing herself to help her friend, is able to initiate an action on her own and accept the responsibility for that action.

The story is set in the almost surrealistic world of adolescence. It is a nightmare world, an exaggerated world. It is the world seen through the eyes of adolescence. The language is that of the hip underground, alien to child and adult alike, which serves to mark the alienation of the adolescents who speak it. The climax of the novel is cataclysmic, involving the destruction of a glass mansion by a fire caused by the orgy of the followers of a cult hero. Running from this, Marsh and Edna embark on a journey to find Marsh's dead father which ends when their car crashes. Seeking refuge in a cemetery, the two set off a rocket that marks their ritual and symbolic liberation. *Pardon Me, You're Stepping on My Eyeball* brings the novel of crisis as close to fantasy as it can go without sacrificing its basic form.

Perhaps the most dystopic of the novels of crisis under discussion is Robert Cormier's *I Am the Cheese.* (His very popular novel *The Chocolate War* is the best example of the continuity of the tradition of school stories mentioned above.) It is the story of a victim. Its informing crisis precedes the action of the novel. A young boy's parents are assassinated by underworld criminals against whom the boy's father, an investigative reporter, had testified. With the help of psychological therapy sessions, the boy attempts to remember that event which he witnessed. Transcripts of the sessions are counterpointed by the stages in an imagined bicycle trip the boy is making to see his father. The two stories converge when the odyssey ends on the grounds of the institution where Adam is being held, and all his adventures are seen to be the fantasy creations drawn from his surroundings and companions in the sanatorium. The boy's nagging fear that his psychiatrist is after information that he might have about his father's activities is realized at the end of the book which finishes with the sparse, codified memorandums to the effect that Adam is incurable, that he is withholding no information, and that he should be held until "termination procedures are approved" or until he "obliterates." *I Am the Cheese* shows the novel of crisis expanded to include a very contemporary political and cultural phenomenon, and its vision is bleak.

These examples suggest some of the variations of the form that is generally characterized at the beginning of this discussion. Coming to grips with crises of identity, be they social, familial or personal, informs each of the books. Adolescence is a time of rapid and confusing change in a person's life. What the novel of crisis has to offer, at its best, is the assurance that one can live through the changes, that they are shared by us all, even though they take on different forms. When poorly handled, the novel of crisis is a clumsy and patronizing medium for crudely constructed stories offering simplistic solutions or rendering misinformation. The best asserts the complexity and poignancy of the transitions that have to be lived through; the worst reduces life to categories of experience and treats them as if they can be dealt with separately. As long as cultures develop, the novel of crisis will assume new forms. Previously taboo subjects will serve as the focus of new stories. Presently "relevant" themes will become outdated and heretofore unimagined situations will replace them. The changes in treatment do not matter, as long as at the core of the vision is the realization of and concern with those crises that are typical to youth and that transcend all topical limitations.

A HARVEST OF SOUTHERN REALISM

William H. Green

Me Too, by Vera and Bill Cleaver. New York: J. B. Lippincott, 1973. $6.95.

The Whys and Wherefores of Littabelle Lee, by Vera and Bill Cleaver. New York: Atheneum, 1975. $6.95.

Doodle and the Go-Cart, by Robert Burch. New York: Viking Press, 1972. $4.75.

Hut School and the Wartime Home-Front Heroes, by Robert Burch. New York: Viking Press, 1974. $5.95.

Two That Were Tough, by Robert Burch. New York: Viking Press, 1976. $6.95.

A Taste of Blackberries, by Doris Buchanan Smith. New York: Thomas Y. Crowell, 1973. $3.95.

Kick a Stone Home, by Doris Buchanan Smith. New York: Thomas Y. Crowell, 1974. $6.95.

Kelly's Creek, by Doris Buchanan Smith. New York: Thomas Y. Crowell, 1975. $5.95.

The Integration of Mary-Larkin Thornhill, by Ann Waldron. New York: E. P. Dutton, 1975. $6.95.

The Golden Shores of Heaven, by Katie Letcher Lyle. New York: J. B. Lippincott, 1976. $6.95.

Quincy's Harvest, by Tom H. Forbes. New York: J. B. Lippincott, 1976. $6.95.

Return to South Town, by Lorenz Graham. New York: Thomas Y. Crowell, 1976. $6.50.

Johnny May, by Robbie Branscum. Garden City, N.Y.: Doubleday, 1973. $4.95.

Weakfoot, by Linda Cline. New York: Lothrop, Lee & Shepard, 1975. $4.95.

June the Tiger, by John Fort. Boston: Little, Brown and Company, 1975. $4.95.

Pinch, by Larry Callen. Boston: Little, Brown and Company, 1975. $5.95.

Cajun Night Before Christmas, by "Trosclair." Edited by Howard Jacobs. Illustrated by James Rice. Gretna, La.: Pelican, 1973. $4.95.

Gaston the Green-Nosed Alligator, written and illustrated by James
Rice. Gretna, La.: Pelican, 1974. $4.95.
Cajun Columbus, by Alice Durio. Illustrated by James Rice. Gretna,
La.: Pelican, 1975.

Into the 1970's Vera and Bill Cleaver, Robert Burch, and
(most recently) Doris Buchanan Smith have established themselves
in several books as practitioners of the realistic novel with a
Southern exposure. And efforts by other children's authors—ranging
widely in quality—reflect no pause in literary exploration of Southeastern subjects.

After the success of *Ellen Grae* in 1967, the Cleavers produced a
rapid sequence of well-written novels about children, usually set in
Florida towns or rural mountains. The style of their earlier books,
such as *Where the Lilies Bloom* and *I Would Rather Be a Turnip,* is
brightly lucid, alive with local color and comic details that spring
like traps. *Me Too* and *The Whys and Wherefores of Littabelle Lee*
reflect a shift in style with mixed results, a drift from Salinger (with
a dash of Saki) into almost turgidly evoked grotesques which at
their best recall Welty. But *Me Too* is not their best. The story of a
lonely girl's failure to communicate with her retarded twin, *Me Too,*
like its protagonist, fails nobly—ruined by its arid subject and in-
decisive ending. The climax, when a Florida sinkhole yawns under
her feet, is a creaking *deus ex machina,* timed as exactly as a Jules
Verne volcano, and as implausibly. With its grandiose style and
narrowly focused point of view, *Me Too* is character-starved and
loaded with tissues of allegory which come unstuck from realism.
Littabelle Lee is much better. The family of Ozarks grotesques
agrees with the erratic plot and lyrical style. With a resourceful
teenage heroine leading her family through a winter, maturing
under stress, and accepting the reality of adult sexual needs, the
book is a rococo redaction of *Where the Lilies Bloom,* a vindication
of the later Cleaver style. But its artistic density may overwhelm
young readers. Word magic is here, but are the children listening?

Robert Burch is more reliable. Writing from his childhood home
in Fayette County, just south of Atlanta, he is a master of the
regional "problem" novel. The problems are perennial: sickness,
death, poverty, disgrace, old age, and war, reflected in credible
characters without morbidity, escapism, or preaching. And under
Burch's hand problems evolve toward unexpected but satisfying

conclusions. In *Doodle and the Go-Cart,* the son of a marginal farmer dreams of buying a go-cart. With and without his mule's help, Doodle undertakes money-making projects and, despite pneumonia and bad timing, saves nearly enough money. In the end we expect Doodle either to give up or to buy the machine, but Burch is shrewder. Offered a chance to sell the mule, Doodle postpones the go-cart another year. Delicately and unexpectedly, we are left with the moral that material dreams are good but friends (even mule-friends) take precedence. Similarly, in *Hut School and the Wartime Home-Front Heroes,* set during World War II, expectation is oddly fulfilled. A popular young teacher seems marked for departure almost from the beginning. Not only do her methods cause trouble, but she is mysteriously absent for a medical examination, and the book is pervaded with a sense that good and bad times both pass. But neither teaching nor illness dispatches Miss Jordan; she joins the WAVES and the young protagonist's father is suddenly drafted. So *Hut School* ends in suspension, appreciation for the past and apprehension for the future. *Two That Were Tough,* Burch's most recent book, explores old age, a heavy subject for a children's book. It tells of a stubborn old grist-mill owner and a wild chicken, both faced with obsolescence. Dwindling business, influenza, an ice storm, and a daughter in Atlanta gradually force Mr. Hilton to abandon his mill. Fearing the chicken will perish without him, he traps it to take to Atlanta. Then suddenly he releases it, and the bird returns to the woods, a living symbol of the old man's unsubdued spirit. Even strong men must retire, but wild birds die free. Like *Queenie Peavy* and Burch's other novels, these three unfold in clear, almost faultless style with close attention to regional and historical detail. He has deep and solid roots.

In her first three books, Doris Buchanan Smith has emerged as an accomplished "problem" novelist, though perhaps not a mature stylist. The books each deal with one problem: *A Taste of Blackberries* with the sudden death of a boy's playmate; *Kelly's Creek* with the frustrations of a nine-year-old with a learning disability; and *Kick a Stone Home* with a tomboy (daughter of a divorcee) discovering her sexual identity. Each book is tightly unified around a relevant problem and its correct solution. As a result, the books are somewhat predictable and, moreover, suffer from occasional flatness of style. *Blackberries* portrays bereavement with effective symbolism and shrewd psychology, a treatment not only of a child's reactions, but of human universals. The simple dialogue and austere style achieve poignancy in some passages, but others are leveled to dullness by their puerile diction. This is the book's main weakness, a weakness shared by *Kelly's Creek*. Set in Brunswick, Georgia, *Kelly's Creek* is further hampered by an isolated narrator and an inconclusive conclusion—necessary because learning disabilities seldom vanish overnight. And such conclusion as Smith does force is, however salutary, still predictable and unconvincing. Where a sympathetic story about learning disability is needed, *Kelly's Creek* will do, but it is disappointing. More successful is *Kick a Stone Home,* set around an Atlanta apartment complex. Here an adolescent tomboy finds herself despite problems with boy friends, estranged parents, and a love for football. Probably because of the older target audience, Smith allows herself greater complexity of style and situation, producing a superb adolescent-identity novel with insights more plentiful and less contrived than in her other novels. The universality of adolescence, like the universality of bereavement, makes *Kick a Stone Home* her second important book.

Among recent realistic novels with Southern settings, three others are excellent. *The Integration of Mary-Larkin Thornhill,* set in a fictional analogue of Tallahassee, is the story of a junior-high girl's first four months in a nearly all-black school. Complex characterizations and a strong ethical tone recommend this simply mounted document of the "integration" of a middle-class Presbyterian minister's daughter, her achieving acceptance and accepting a non-racist view of those around her. Mary Larkin is an unwilling heroine but a genuine one, a plausible exponent of racial liberalism and the nobility of doing right even when it is unpopular.

The Golden Shores of Heaven is a well-written book about a nineteen-year-old girl's attempt to become a recording star in Nashville, an excellent book for anyone interested—if only imaginatively—in making it in the arts. The book is persuasive, even as a document, and projects a sane attitude toward the world and toward questing for large goals in it. Strong characters, vivid description, and gentle suspense drive the book to its semi-happy ending. Sex is handled delicately but with much emotional force. If this is a children's book, only the childishness of the protagonist makes it so, as she narrowly avoids sexual exploitation and learns to distinguish true friends from false in her first steps toward stardom and belated maturity.

Quincy's Harvest is an account of spring, summer, and fall in the life of a North Carolina sharecropper's son, his initiation into the rhythms that move animals, plants, and men. A father whose hunting seems cruel, a one-legged black man on the brink of death, a red-bone hound, and an accidentally trapped blue heron—these are the figures in Quincy's initiation. The story develops slowly, almost sluggishly, with local color spread so thick that folklore prospers at the expense of drama. Nevertheless, *Quincy's Harvest* builds finally to a strong epiphany.

Of the next three books, *Return to South Town* is by far the most effective. Its weakness—a severe one though practically its only weakness—is its flat made-for-television style, its typical new-South setting and two-dimensional characters, each representing a hue in the spectrum of 1970's race relations. Real situations were never so clear, so complete, so balanced, and so happily resolved—in a word, so plastic. The protagonist's girl friend, a junior college teacher, speaks her intention to do "a study of the changing attitudes among black and white people in the South" (p. 185). *Return to South Town* is such a study disguised as fiction, an optimistic but clear-sighted account of changing racial attitudes. The book is good fare for non-Southerners interested in the South, a fair sketch of residual racism overcome; and young blacks may well emulate Graham's protagonist, as the character named Junior does in the story. Graham's generalizations are healthy.

More seriously flawed is *Johnny May*. This local-color "problem" novel about puberty climaxes when its Ozarks heroine has a period, discovers boys, and accepts her sister's marriage. So far, so good; but the commendable sortie into sore breasts and other early-teen realities is hindered by a contrived plot and shoddy writing. The dialect was apparently proofread while asleep: butter is "yellow" on page 31, "yaller" on page 41, and "yeller" on page 48; "get" and "git" appear four lines apart in Johnny May's dialogue (p. 92); and other inconsistencies riddle this first-person narrative, symptoms of slipshod craftsmanship. Local color is heaped on with a selectivity which betrays an author trying to countrify her story, not a character actually ignorant of urban norms. And through the words of Johnny May an adult voice intrudes, contriving cuteness: lightning bugs, for instance, with "rear end lights" that "flash off and on like tiny fairy lanterns." Huck Finn this character is not.

Weakfoot is worse, a watered-down ecological version of *The Bear*, with the bear played by a sentimentalized mother panther, Sam Fathers by an implausible swamplands Crusoe. Add to this a gratuitous dash of romance and a Happy Farm Family (the laconic father, the doting Aunt Louise). Stew with obligatory cliffhangers, inconsistent point of view, and stale description, and there is *Weakfoot.* The swamplands descriptions suggest a cliche-artist loose in a botanical museum. On page 45 alone, for example, a pond is "mirror-smooth," a spider web is "laden with pearls of dew," a spider is "dancing," and a fox squirrel hugs a pine bough. A rustic character views the Okefenokee, and the result suggests a neo-classical pastoral. When it spawned a Walt Disney script, *Weakfoot* found its level. May it rest in peace.

Regional tall tales and humor, perhaps not strictly realistic, but deeply rooted in local culture, comprise the last group of books. John Fort's *June the Tiger* is a fast-moving piece in the folk-tale tradition, the story of an old woman's feisty dog and a bear who rules the edge of the Coolewahee Swamp. The characters warm, the style vigorous, the suspense taut, the book almost reads itself. And Larry Callen's *Pinch,* a droll tale set near Blind River in the bayou country, describes a boy's efforts to win the annual hunting pig championship. Tension lapses occasionally, but the book is unique: a sage and comic dissertation on training pigs to hunt. And the illustrations are as good as the text.

Also a delightful piece of Louisiana humor is *Cajun Night Before Christmas,* which translates the Christmas classic line for line. Santa, dressed in muskrat, arrives in a skiff pulled by 'gators, and the book is a masterpiece of dialect humor:

> An I hear him shout loud
> As a splashin' he go
> "Merry Christmas to all
> 'Til I saw you some mo'!"

James Rice, the illustrator, weds humor and folklore in detailed drawings. *Gaston the Green-Nosed Alligator,* a spin-off written and illustrated by Rice, suggests that he had better leave typewriters alone. Written in standard English, this "Rudolph" rehash is hobbled with forced rhymes and inane diction, the illustrations its only redeeming feature. But in *Cajun Columbus* Rice again finda a worthy subject for his illustrations. In this Cajun-chauvinist account of the discovery of America, the archetypal Pierre Lastrapes is shown receiving explorers from across "de big h'Atlantic Bayou." For instance, "Wit' dem Viking, Pierre, him, would make music on his windbox an' damonstrate dat Cajun twice-step." Children will enjoy this better if read aloud, but so will adults. Here, as in *Cajun Night Before Christmas,* bayou culture glows with good-natured *joie de vivre.*

Varia

DISSERTATIONS OF NOTE

Compiled by Rachel Fordyce

Abrahamson, Richard Frank. *"Nowhere Runner:* A Study in the Creation of a Novel for Adolescents." Ph.D. diss. University of Iowa, 1977. 38: 2026-A. 204 pp.
Following the author's original novel for teenagers is a journal which contains observations on writing for children.

Barr, Janet Louise Cook. "The Immigrant in Children's Fictional Books Recommended for American Libraries, 1883-1938." Ph.D. diss. Indiana University, 1976. 37: 1852-A. 185 pp.
Barr determines "the extent to which immigrants were depicted in children's fiction . . . The increases and decreases in number of books recommended," the demographic distribution of immigrants in relation to fictional characters, and the attitudes towards immigrants in the literature.

Bennett, Fordyce Richard. "Bronson Alcott: The Transcendental Reformer as Educator." Ph.D. diss. University of Illinois at Urbana-Champaign, 1976. 37: 2867-A. 440 pp.
Of particular note is Bennett's discussion of Alcott's *Conversations with Children on the Gospels* and the *Outline of Reading,* 1833.

Birchfield, James deMaris. "Swinburne's Views of Childhood." Ph.D. diss. Florida State University, 1976. 37: 6492-A. 349 pp.
Birchfield, among other things, is concerned with the Swinburne who was "an ardent reader of Victorian juvenile publications and at the same time the author of an epic poem on 'The Flogging Block.'"

Bland, Robert Lamar. "The Role of Folklore in Hawthorne's Literary Nationalism." Ph.D. diss. The University of North Carolina at Greensboro, 1976. 37: 2868-A. 226 pp.
Bland analyzes Hawthorne's use of "legends, marchen, oral tradition, folkloric characters, folklore motif, folkloric themes, and witchcraft and the supernatural" in the short fiction and *Twice-Told Tales.*

Cata, Juanita Opal. "The Portrait of American Indians in Children's Fictional Literature." Ph.D. diss. University of New Mexico, 1977. 38: 3266-A. 220 pp.
"Five hundred and four American Indian characters for 401 children's fictional stories published between the years 1900 and 1972" are analyzed for content. The author concludes that the fictional treatment of Indians in children's literature is just that, and there is a need for more accurate and honest portrayal.

Ferguson, Anne M. "Children's Self-Selection of Trade Books: Measured by the Cloze Procedure." Ph.D. diss. University of Arkansas, 1977. 38: 2543-A. 95 pp.
Ferguson concludes that, in a sixth grade level, Matt Christopher, Laura Ingalls Wilder, and Lois Lenski are the most popular trade book authors.

Frankel, Gusti Wiesenfeld. "Between Parent and Child in Colonial New England: An Analysis of the Religions Child-Oriented Literature and Selected Children's Works." Ph.D. diss. University of Minnesota, 1976. 38: 1572-A. 280 pp.

Frankel analyzes the concept of "duty" in relationship to love, obedience, honor, and recompense as it is exhibited in seventeenth century literature. He shows that "By the eighteenth century, duty was reduced to concrete behavioral terms and defined by such virtues as "respectful carriage to parents, kindness to friends and neighbors, diligence at work and school, clean language, and control of temper." Chapter IV is significant because of his treatment of dying child narratives.

Gamble, Michael Wesley. "Clare Tree Major: Children's Theatre, 1923-1954." Ph.D. diss. New York University, 1976. 37: 5441-A. 375 pp.

Gamble is concerned with artists, plays, productions and Major's direction in what was the first nationally known theatre for children. Of particular note is Chapter III, in which he critically analyzes existing scripts for *Alice in Wonderland, King Midas, Little Women, Captive Maid of Old Carlisle,* and *Robin Hood.*

Goldberg, Patricia Davis. "Development of a Category System for the Analysis of the Response of the Young Theatre Audience." Ph.D. diss. Florida State University, 1977. 38: 4452-A. 133 pp.

Of particular interest is Goldberg's analysis of audience response to *Wind in the Willows* and Gennadi Mamlin's *Hey there-Hello!*

Grover, Robert John. "The Relationship of Readability, Content, Illustrations, and other Formal Elements to the Library Book Preferences of Second Grade Children." Ph.D. diss. Indiana University, 1976. 37: 4672-A. 182 pp.

Grover analyzes the above categories to determine second graders' preferences, and also shows differences in preference by sex.

Kiah, Rosalie Black. "A Content Analysis of Children's Contemporary Realistic Fiction about Black People in the United States to Determine If and How a Sampling of These Stories Portray Selected Salient Shared Experiences of Black People." Ph.D. diss. Michigan State University, 1976. 37: 7381-A. 274 pp.

Kiah concludes that most children's stories about Black people address themselves to universal issues, rather than common experiences shared by Blacks. She further concludes that "many authors, both Black and White, are introducing social problems in their stories as a means of highlighting the salient shared experiences of Black people, but they are not developing the stories to the extent that the child will be able to gain from the experience."

Koppes, Phyllis Bixler. "The Child in Pastoral Myth: A Study in Rousseau and Wordsworth, Children's Literature and Literary Fantasy." Ph.D. diss. University of Kansas, 1977. 38: 4141-A. 386 pp.

Koppes' dissertation is an extensive critical evaluation of "the myth of the child as a pastoral figure" and she "seeks to determine whether this myth sheds light on the establishment and nature of children's literature as well as on the portrayal of the child in that literature." Attention is given to Rousseau's *New Eloise* and *Emile,* Wordsworth's *Prelude,* Grahame's *Wind in the Willows,* Tolkien's *Hobbit* and Ring Triology, as well as the work of Carroll, Burnett, MacDonald, Twain, Barrie, Milne, and others.

Lowe, Elizabeth Cochran. "Kenneth Grahame and the Beast Tale." Ph.D. diss. New York University, 1976. 37: 5817-A. 230 pp.
Lowe illustrates how Grahame's works "reveal a belief in man's mystical and anthropological kinship with animals." He is particularly concerned with the epistomological ramifications of Beast Tales in an age that exposed Romanticism, Darwinism, Industrialism, and Freudianism.

Mc Curry, Niki Alpert. "Concepts of Childrearing and Schooling in the March Novels of Louisa May Alcott." Ph.D. diss. Northwestern University, 1976. 37: 4356-A. 114 pp.
McCurry gives particular attention to *Little Women, Little Men,* and *Jo's Boys.* She analyzes the autobiographical nature of the works, the affect of Bronson and Abba Alcott on their daughter's writing, and then explores the theories of childrearing in the works themselves. She concludes that "Despite the fact that Louisa draws upon her father's favorite transcendental images of education as a spiritual pilgrimage and the process of natural growth, her ideas about education and the role of women become increasingly her own as the series develops."

Mac Donald, Ruth K. "Literature for Children in England, 1659-1774." Ph.D. diss. Rutgers University (New Brunswick), 1977. 38: 6744-A. 167 pp.
Taking the publication of Comenius' *Orbis Sensualium Pictus* (1659) as a starting place, MacDonald critically analyzes children's literature in six categories: "school books and other educational literature; religious works; courtesy literature; fables; works of fantasy such as fairy tales, nursery rhymes, and oriental tales, and works by booksellers." Her study continues through 1774, ending with the publication of Chesterfield's letters to his son. She discusses sectarian and ecumenistic interests in children's literature during the seventeenth and eighteenth centuries, and thoroughly digests the didactic nature of the literature.

Mauer, Ruth Apt. "Young Children's Affective Responses to a Physically Disabled Story Book Hero." Ph.D. diss. Columbia University Teachers College, 1976. 37: 918-A. 155 pp.
"The purpose of this study was to determine whether identification with a story book hero is a function of physical status of hero and reader, and whether friendship preference is also a function of physical status."

Meegan, Mary Ellen. "Bibliotherapeutic Facets in Literature for Children." Ph.D. diss. Boston College, 1976. 37: 786-A.
Meegan's study covers literature from 1959 to 1975, for children five through eight. She is concerned primarily with realistic fiction.

Nist, Joan Irene Stidham. "The Mildred L. Batchelder Award Books, 1968-1977: A Decade of Honored Children's Literature in Translation." Ph.D. diss. Auburn University, 1977. 38: 4633-A. 156 pp.
Nist examines both the award winning books and the nominees to determine trends and patterns in published translated work for children. She notes the wide range of publishers, subject matter, and locale in the works.

Olson, Joan Blodgett Petterson. "An Interpretive History of the *Horn Book Magazine,* 1924-1973." Ph.D. diss. Stanford Univeristy, 1976. 37:2875-A. 299 pp.
Olson's work is both a history and a criticism of fifty years of *Horn Book*

production: She covers book reviews, literary criticism, and changes in
American educational practices and philosophies.

Olson, Miken Rae. "Exposure to Fantasy Literature, Related Activities, and
Creativity in Kindergarten." Ph.D. diss. Arizona State University, 1977.
38: 4570-A. 127 pp.
Olson tried to determine if exposure to fantasy fostered creativity in young
children. For reasons unspecified, pretest scores tended to be higher than post
test scores.

Paris, Janelle Avenell. "A Comparative Analysis of Occupations Presented in
Children's Realistic Fiction, 1950-54 and 1970-74." Ph.D. diss. Texas Woman's
University, 1977. 38: 5105-A. 240 pp.
To test the hypothesis that there is "a discernible trend toward increasing
honesty and realism relating to career content in children's fiction" the author
sampled 150 children's realistic fiction books in terms of "diversity of occupations, characteristics of the employed," attitudes toward work and "evidence
of bias or stereotyping." Her conclusions are multiple and depressing:
children's fiction gives an "extremely limited view of the world work," especially in terms of female careers; "it places negative evaluations on . . . manual
labor"; "it perpetrates the division of labor by sex"; and it neither has kept
"pace with economic and social realities" or with changing life styles.

Parish, Margaret Holt. "Women at Work: Housewives and Paid Workers as Mothers
in Contemporary Realistic Fiction for Children." Ph.D. diss. Michigan State
University, 1976. 37: 7730-A. 221 pp.
Parish sees a "cultural lag" in the children's books which she studies. "While
the books do reflect the dissatisfaction with housewifery . . . they do not reflect the constraints of today's job market upon women. Young readers would
find in these books relatively little information that would alert them to the
challenges that face women who seek to find satisfying employment today."

Pattison, Robert Bruce. "The Little Victims: The Child Figure and Original Sin in
English Literature." Ph.D. diss. Columbia University, 1974. 37: 3647-A. 234 pp.
The study covers a wide range of examples, including Marvell, Gray, Blake,
Dickens, Henry James, Christina Rosetti, and Lewis Carroll, and is particularly
concerned with the religious and social role of the child in English literature.

Pettus, Eloise Spencer. "A Study of The Treatment of Ecology, Air Pollution, and
Water Pollution in Selected Recommended Books for Elementary Grades
Published in The United States, 1960-1975." Ph.D. diss. Florida State Univer-
sity, 1977. 38: 5106-A. 235 pp.
The author studies ninety-six children's books to determine their approach to
ecology and to analyze the interdisciplinary content of the works.

Poston, Tereas Gayle. "Preadolescent Needs and Problems as seen in Family Life
Fiction Published between the Years 1965 and 1975: A Content Analysis."
Ph.D. diss. Florida State University, 1976. 38: 1717-A. 242 pp.
Poston concludes that "the overall home environment and family relationships
described for the fictional preadolescent were not typical as compared to that
of the contemporary preadolescent living in the United States. The settings,
types of residences, size and composition of families, and relationships within

families present a false view of the majority of preadolescent's homes in this country." She does not discount the possibility, however, that the fictional books fulfill the need for which they were intended.

Rausch, Helen Martha. "The Debate over Fairy Tales." Ph.D. diss. Columbia University Teachers College, 1977. 38: 3918-A. 266 pp.
Rouch is concerned about the controversy centered on the "suitability" of fairy tales for preadolescent readers and listeners, as well as the critical points of view of educators and professionals in the field of children's literature. Rouch thoroughly analyzes the historical and contemporary aspects of the debate and concludes that "the weight of general opinion points to sustained support for fairy tales." The dissertation also treats aspects of realistic fiction as they differ from fairy stories.

Roggenbuck, Mary Jane. "*St. Nicholas* Magazine: A Study of the Impact and Historical Influence of the Editorship of Mary Mapes Dodge." Ph.D. diss. University of Michigan, 1976. 37: 6122-A. 434 pp.
Roggenbuck's thesis is a thorough break-down of the literary dimensions of *St. Nicholas* magazine during the thirty-two years Mary Mapes Dodge was editor, although, in a summary chapter, she does extend the discussion of the magazine to its demise.

Saleski, Rosemary Ann. "Alcohol Consumption in Literature for Children and Adolescents: A Content Analysis of Contemporary Realistic Fiction." Ph.D. diss. University of Georgia, 1977. 38: 4572-A. 186 pp.
Saleski's study deals with thirty-five books published from 1974-1976. She notes that there are frequent reference to alcohol and drinking in realistic books for children and adolescents, and that "a broad spectrum of drinking behaviors is revealed."

Steinfirst, Susan. "The Origins and Development of the ABC Book in English from the Middle Ages through the Nineteenth Century." Ph.D. diss. University of Pittsburgh, 1976. 37: 3973-A. 385 pp.
The dissertation shows how ABC books reflect "the historical, educational, cultural, social, religious, and literary trends" of the periods covered. "The form of the ABC book is traced from the fifteenth-century primer, hornbook, and ABC tract, to the seventeenth-century rhyming alphabets, to the textbook appendages of the eighteenth century, to alphabets which appeared in proliferating periodicals for children in the nineteenth century, and, finally, to the independent alphabet book of the late nineteenth century."

Weiger, Myra L. "Moral Judgment in Children: Their Responses to Children's Literature Examined Against Piaget's Stages of Moral Development." Ph.D. diss. Rutgers University (New Brunswick), 1977. 38: 4065-A. 222 pp.
The author of this dissertation "suggests that the field of English is an excellent avenue for values education, using language as the tool for communication and literature as a source of moral experience." [!]

Weller, Anna Elizabeth. "The Portrayal of the Female Character in the Newbery Award Books." Ph.D. diss. Indiana University, 1977. 38: 1718-A. 183 pp.
Weller concludes that there is less sexual stereotyping of central female fictional characters in recent Newbery award books than in earlier ones.

Yates, Twila Virginia. "Maria Edgeworth and the Art of Education." Ph.D. diss.
Purdue University, 1976. 37: 5150-A. 262 pp.
Yates shows that pedagogy was Edgeworth's concern, more than literary
artistry. She traces theories of knowledge through her writings, particularly
Belinda, Harrington, Patronage, and *Practical Education.*

CONTRIBUTORS AND EDITORS

PETER S. ANDERSON'S special interest is the Renaissance. He is also interested in children's literature.

JAN BAKKER is Assistant Professor of English at Utah State University, Logan.

JANE MISSNER BARSTOW is Assistant Professor of English at the University of Hartford, Connecticut. She has published articles on Dostoevsky, Henry James, and "The Use of Myth in Literature." She teaches courses in Modern European Literature and "The Cult of the Child."

FRANCELIA BUTLER is the author of *Sharing Literature with Children* and other books on children's literature and on the Renaissance.

CHARITY CHANG is Head of the Serials Department, Prescott Memorial Library, Louisiana Technical University, Ruston.

FEDERICA DOMINGUEZ COLAVITA is currently Associate Professor of Children's Literature at the Universidad Nacional de San Luis (San Luis, Argentina), where she directs a research project on literature for pre-school children.

KEN DONELSON is Professor of English at Arizona State University, Tempe. He has published numerous articles on censorship, adolescent literature, short films, and on the professional concerns of English teachers.

MARGARET P. ESMONDE is an Assistant Professor of English at Villanova University. She is the current president of the Children's Literature Association and editor of the *Newsletter of the Children's Literature Association*.

EDWARD G. FISHER has published four volumes of *Children's Literature*. He also has made a study of children's literature and the Bible.

T. C. FODOR is a Montreal writer, currently working on a novel.

RACHEL FORDYCE is Associate Professor of English and Assistant Dean of the College of Arts and Sciences, Virginia Polytechnic Institute and State University, Blacksburg, Virginia. She is Executive Secretary of the Children's Literature Association and on the Board of Directors of *Children's Literature An International Journal, Inc.*

WILLIAM H. GREEN is an Assistant Professor of English at Clayton Junior College, Atlanta, Georgia. The subject of his dissertation was *The Hobbit* (Louisiana State University, 1969), and he has published articles on children's literature for various periodicals. He is also the author of numerous poems and stories for children.

CAROLE HANKS teaches English at Baylor University, Texas.

D. T. HANKS, JR. is Assistant Professor of English at Baylor University.

ALETHEA HELBIG teaches English at Eastern Michigan State University, where she has helped develop a minor in children's literature and an interdepartmental major in drama and children's literature for the young. She has co-edited an anthology of poetry for children entitled *Straight on Till Morning*. She is a board member of the ChLA.

M. C. HODGE, JR. has taught English at Piedmont College, Demorest, Georgia. He has published poems in small magazines and is presently working on books about Joyce Carol Oates and James Dickey.

JACQUELINE JACKSON is Associate Professor of Literature at Sangamon State University, and co-teaches History of Children's Literature with Phillip Kendall. She is the author of nine children's books, and, for all ages, *Turn Not Pale, Beloved Snail,* and *A Book About Writing Among Other Things.*

MARILYN KAYE is a doctoral student in children's literature in the Graduate Library School, University of Chicago. She is an editorial assistant for *The Library Quarterly;* is on the editorial committee of *Top of the News,* and is on the advisory board of the *Bulletin of the Center for Children's Books.*

PHILLIP W. KENDALL is Dean of Public Affairs and Associate Professor of History at Sangamon State University, Springfield, Illinois.

PHYLLIS BIXLER KOPPES teaches children's literature at Kansas State University, Manhattan, Kansas, and is currently working on a book about the pastoral tradition in children's classics.

K. NARAYAN KUTTY who teaches children's literature at Eastern Connecticut State College, obtained his Ph.D. in English from the University of Connecticut with a dissertation on Samuel Beckett. He has published articles on Lewis Carroll, Andersen, and V. S. Naipaul.

LOIS R. KUZNETS teaches in the English Department of Herbert Lehman College, CUNY.

REBECCA LUKENS is the author of *A Critical Handbook of Children's Literature.* She teaches English at Miami University, Oxford, Ohio.

JAMES MARSHALL is an eminent writer and illustrator of children's books, including the George and Martha books.

MERADITH TILBURY MCMUNN has written and lectured extensively on medieval children's literature. She headed the first seminar on medieval children in literature at the Modern Language Association meetings, New York, 1976. She is also a contributor to the forthcoming Penguin *Companion to Children's Literature* and the author, with William Robert McMunn, of a forthcoming book on children and literature in the Middle Ages, to be published by Stonehill Publications.

LEONARD R. MENDELSOHN teaches English at Concordia University, Montreal. He is currently working on a book about the Shakers.

ROSA ANN MOORE is Assistant Professor of English at the University of Tennessee at Chattanooga. She has contributed critical biographies to the *Penguin Companion to Children's Literature* and is currently working on a book about the Laura Ingalls Wilder/Rose Wilder collaboration.

PRISCILLA A. ORD is a doctoral candidate in linguistics at the University of Pennsylvania who has completed three summers' research on the language and myths, legends, and folktales of the Jicarilla Apache Indians of northwestern New Mexico. She is currently a member of the English Department of Villanova University.

BERNARD QUEENAN is Director of the Audio-Visual Department at Concordia University, Montreal.

STEPHEN ROXBURGH is a doctoral student in English at the State University of

New York at Stony Brook where he has taught courses in children's literature. He is currently writing a dissertation on children's literature and is a member of the Children's Book Department of Farrar, Straus and Giroux, Inc.

JAMES SUCHAN is Instructor in Cinema, Literature and Humanities at the University of Arizona. He has written about E. B. White and is currently preparing articles on Jerzy Kosinski, and on the ambivalent attitude toward the orphan in the early Victorian novel.

WILLIAM SYLVESTER is Professor of Comparative Literature at the State University of New York at Buffalo. He has written on such diverse subjects as Horace, electronic poetry, and disjunctive principles in verse. He has translated the *Agamemnon.*

MAIA WOJCIECHOWSKA is a prolific, award winning author of children's books.

THOMAS A. ZANIELLO is Associate Professor of English at Northern Kentucky University. He has published articles on traditional literary figures, children's literature, popular culture, and folklore.

JACK D. ZIPES is an Associate Professor of German at the University of Wisconsin at Milwaukee. He has written and translated books on German literature and is an editor of *New German Critique: An Interdisciplinary Journal of German Studies.*